DEBATING AFFIRMATIVE ACTION

RACE, GENDER, ETHNICITY, AND THE POLITICS OF INCLUSION

EDITED AND WITH
AN INTRODUCTION BY

Nicolaus Mills

Delta
Trade
Paperbacks

A Delta Book
Published by
Dell Publishing
a division of
Bantam Doubleday Dell Publishing Group, Inc.
1540 Broadway
New York, New York 10036

Library of Congress Cataloging in Publication Data

Debating affirmative action : race, gender, ethnicity, and the politics of inclusion / edited and with an introduction by Nicolaus Mills.
    p.   cm.
  Includes bibliographical references.
  ISBN 0-385-31221-0
  1. Affirmative action programs—United States. 2. Affirmative action programs—Law and legislation—United States. 3. Minorities—Employment—United States. I. Mills, Nicolaus.
HF5549.5.A34D42 1994
331.13′3′0973—dc20   93-23253
                          CIP

Manufactured in the United States of America

Published simultaneously in Canada

April 1994

10 9 8 7 6 5 4 3 2 1

nedy. Reprinted from the *Harvard Law Review*, April 1986, by permission of the author and The Harvard Law Review Association. Copyright © 1986 by the Harvard Law Review Association.

3. "Feminism and Affirmative Action" by Alice Kessler-Harris. Printed by permission of the author.

4. "Equality and Identity" by Cornel West. Reprinted from *The American Prospect*, Spring 1992, by permission of the author and *The American Prospect*.

5. "Affirmative Action Goals and Timetables: Too Tough? Not Tough Enough!" by Clarence Thomas. Reprinted from *Yale Law and Policy Review*, Spring-Summer 1987, by permission of *Yale Law and Policy Review*.

6. "Opening the Work Door for Women" by Ellen Goodman. The Washington Post Writers Group. © 1987, The Boston Globe Newspaper Company. Reprinted with permission.

7. "Title VII of the Civil Rights Act of 1964: From Prohibiting to Requiring Racial Discrimination in Employment" by Lino A. Graglia. Reprinted from the *Harvard Journal of Law and Public Policy*, Winter 1991, by permission of the *Harvard Journal of Law and Public Policy*.

8. "The Death of the Profane" by Patricia J. Williams. Reprinted from *The Alchemy of Race and Rights*, 1991, by permission of Harvard University Press.

9. "The Civil Rights Act: White Men's Hope" by Julian Bond. Reprinted from *The New York Times*, June 26, 1990. Copyright © 1990–92 by the New York Times Company. Reprinted by permission.

10. "If You Hadn't Been Mexican" by Ruben Navarrette, Jr. Reprinted from the *Los Angeles Times*, May 12, 1991, by permission of the author.

11. "Beneath the Glass Ceiling" by Julie Hessler. Printed by permission of the author.

12. "The Candidate: Inside One Affirmative Action Search" by G. Kindrow. Reprinted from *Lingua Franca*, April 1991, by permission of *Lingua Franca*.

13. "Racial Preferences? So What?" by Stephen L. Carter. Excerpt from *Reflections of an Affirmative Action Baby*. First published in *The Wall Street Journal*. Copyright © 1991 by Stephen L. Carter. Reprinted by permission of Basic Books, a division of HarperCollins*Publishers* Inc.

14. "Race-Neutral Programs and the Democratic Coalition" by William Julius Wilson. Reprinted from *The American Prospect*, Spring 1990, by permission of *The American Prospect*.

15. "Just Say Latino" by Linda Chavez. Reprinted from *The New Republic*, March 22, 1993, by permission of *The New Republic*, © 1993, The New Republic Inc.

16. "The Politics of Diversion: Blame It on the Blacks" by William Greider. Reprinted from *Rolling Stone*, September 5, 1991. Straight Arrow Publishers, Inc. 1991. All rights reserved. Reprinted by permission.

17. "Affirmative Racism" by Charles Murray. Reprinted from *The New Republic*, December 31, 1984, by permission of *The New Republic*, © 1984, The New Republic Inc.

18. "The Great White Myth" by Anna Quindlen. Reprinted from *The New York Times*, January 15, 1992. Copyright © 1990–92 by The New York Times Company. Reprinted by permission.

19. "Education: Ethnicity and Achievement" by Andrew Hacker. Reprinted with

FOR
MIRANDA BLAŽEVIĆ
AND
ELINOR HORNER

Contents

PART THREE

PERSONAL PERSPECTIVES

PART FOUR

THE POLITICAL ARENA

PART FIVE

IVORY TOWERS UNDER SIEGE

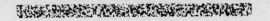

Acknowledgments

I am greatly indebted to my two researchers on this book, Samantha Fenrow and Dina Pancoast, and to the librarians of Sarah Lawrence College, especially Janet Alexander and Judy Kicinski, who continually found material in archives that seemed designed to thwart the curious.

DEBATING AFFIRMATIVE ACTION

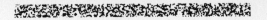

INTRODUCTION: TO LOOK LIKE AMERICA

Nicolaus Mills

It came as no surprise that when the Senate confirmation process was finally completed and Janet Reno was sworn in as attorney general the new Clinton cabinet contained more minorities and women than any previous cabinet in American history. In the third and final presidential debate of the 1992 campaign, Clinton had defined the criteria he intended to use in making his appointments. "I don't think we've got a person to waste," he declared. "I owe the American people a White House staff, a cabinet, and appointments that look like America but that meet high standards of excellence, and that's what I'll do."

In speaking of his future cabinet, candidate Clinton never mentioned affirmative action. But there was no mistaking the degree to which he was implicitly embracing affirmative action principles. He was not simply pledging that he would refuse to discriminate—would be color blind and gender blind in his choices. Rather he was saying that race and gender would be crucial to his selection process. By Inauguration Day 1993 it would not just be white men running his administration. The demographics of a Clinton cabinet might not precisely be the demographics of the nation, but taken as a whole, they would reflect America's diversity.

In their coverage of the final presidential debate, the media paid little attention to Clinton's remarks on how he would choose his cabinet. He had not talked about quotas or used the kinds of buzzwords that incite controversy. Indeed, in the campaign book *Putting People First* that Clinton and Al Gore issued during 1992, candidate Clinton seemed to go out of his way to distance himself from affirmative action. "Oppose racial quotas" is the closest he and Gore come to mentioning affirmative action.

A month after the election when, as President-Elect, Clinton began announcing who would fill his cabinet, his choices quickly became controversial, however. The attacks came from the right and the left. Evan Kemp, the outgoing chairman of the Equal Employment Opportunity Commission, accused Clinton of retreating from his opposition to quotas and group preferences. And from women's political groups, criticism of the President-Elect's cabinet choices was so intense that at a December news conference he lashed back at them, calling them "bean counters" intent on "playing quota games."

The President was right to conclude that in trying to appoint a cabinet that looked like America he was never going to satisfy his critics. Few issues so divide America in the 1990s as affirmative action. Once primarily a black-white issue, affirmative action has expanded far beyond its original base and in the process become increasingly controversial and costly—$17 to $20 billion annually for regulation and compliance alone, according to a 1993 *Forbes* study. Today it is not only African Americans who qualify for affirmative action but women and a broad spectrum of groups that includes Hispanics, Native Americans, Asian Americans, and Alaskan Natives.

Harvard law professor Randall Kennedy describes affirmative action as "policies that provide preferences based explicitly on membership in a designated group." Affirmative action is certainly that, but in practice it raises a series of additional issues, whether it is "soft" affirmative action that limits itself to special recruitment efforts or the kind of "hard" affirmative action that sets hiring goals. By insisting on the need for more than equality of opportunity for the victims of racism and discrimination, affirmative action calls into account both the historic wrongs that gave rise to it as well as our ideas of what constitutes a just society. In the 1990s it is not simply the damage—psychological, social, economic—done by past discrimination that affirmative action seeks to remedy. It also seeks to remedy practices that even if they do not intentionally discriminate have a disparate or adverse impact—that is, result in minorities or women being underrepresented.

There is hardly an area of our public life that affirmative action touches without bringing with it conflict. In the workplace, where federal affirmative action hiring programs alone cover thousands of companies, affirmative action can mean the difference between having a job or being unemployed.

In politics, where the courts and the Justice Department have regularly ruled that districts may be drawn so as to enhance minority representation and pave the way for the election of minority candidates, affirmative action can mean the difference between a safe seat or defeat.

In higher education, where a commitment to diversity has sanctioned the downplaying of grades and test scores for minority students, affirmative action can mean the difference between acceptance or rejection by an elite university.

The result is that affirmative action has become one of the most explosive issues in American life at a time when the federal government, saddled with a $4 trillion debt, is

cutting back on social programs and the nation's population, as a result of massive immigration over the last twenty
years, is increasingly diverse. Just how explosive an issue
affirmative action can be was epitomized in 1990 by a
television ad North Carolina's conservative Republican senator Jesse Helms used in his reelection campaign against
Harvey Gantt, a black Democrat and the former mayor of
Charlotte. The ad, which became known as the "White
Hands" spot, showed a pair of white hands crumpling a job
rejection letter while an announcer's voice intoned, "You
needed that job. And you were the best qualified. But they
had to give it to a minority because of a racial quota. Is that
really fair?"

Helms was playing the race card in an uphill campaign,
but the raw emotions that he was appealing to were easy to
exploit. In a tight job market those raw emotions exist for
countless workers who see themselves affected by affirmative action. One can, moreover, find similar reactions in
other areas where affirmative action has played a key role.
In the traditionally quiet world of higher education, affirmative action has provided the backdrop for unprece-
dented racial tensions. At the University of California at
Berkeley those tensions have, a university report noted,
split the campus into separate racial enclaves. At Yale
University they resulted in a swastika and the words *white
power* being painted on the African-American cultural center.

Unlike the debate over political correctness or multicul-
turalism, the debate over affirmative action is one in which
a broad cross section of the population believes it has a
personal stake in the outcome. For middle-class and working-class whites, who see themselves facing downward
mobility in the 1990s, the great fear is that affirmative
action will hasten their slide into poverty by closing off
opportunities they would have had a generation earlier. For

these whites, affirmative action, despite its emphasis on inclusion rather than exclusion, often seems tantamount to reverse discrimination. Women and minorities, especially minorities from the inner city, worry, on the other hand, that without affirmative action their chances for improving their situation will be lost. They fear that if affirmative action law isn't strictly enforced the nation will quickly forget that real equality of opportunity means making up for the damage done by past discrimination.

II

Our current battles over affirmative action did not suddenly arise with the hard times brought about by the 1980s. The roots of our affirmative action crisis lie in the 1960s, when affirmative action was still an uncontroversial term.

The link between affirmative action and civil rights was first made by John Kennedy in 1961, just months after taking office. On March 6 Kennedy signed Executive Order 10925, establishing the President's Commission on Equal Employment Opportunity and spelling out the obligations of contractors doing business with the government. "The contractor will take affirmative action to ensure that applicants are employed, and employees are treated during their employment, without regard to their race, creed, color, or national origin," Executive Order 10925 declared. By comparison with Franklin Roosevelt's tepid Executive Order 8802 of 1941, banning discrimination in war industries and the armed services, or Dwight Eisenhower's executive orders on federal contract compliance, Kennedy's declaration was clearly a step forward.

But nothing in Kennedy's 4,500-word decree linked affirmative action (he used the phrase only once) to anything more than the traditional goal of nondiscrimination. The executive order came because Kennedy did not believe he had the power to get civil rights legislation through Congress. Those the order was intended to impress with a new White House attitude on civil rights were Southern politicians from states where segregation still prevailed.

Two years later, when Kennedy proposed the legislation that finally became the Civil Rights Act of 1964, his target was still the South, and the meaning of affirmative action as spelled out in Title VII of his bill was the same as in Executive Order 10925. Kennedy and the leading liberals of the 1960s assumed that by banning discrimination government could create a level playing field on which equal opportunity was the norm. It was an assumption borrowed from baseball, where Jackie Robinson and other black players had eventually thrived once racial barriers were removed, and from Southern school desegregation cases, where success arose from dismantling dual educational systems.

The language of the Civil Rights Act of 1964 makes clear its traditional interpretation of affirmative action. Title VII not only prohibits an employer from discriminating because of an "individual's race, color, religion, sex, or national origin," it specifically declares that nothing in the act is designed "to grant preferential treatment to any group because of race, color, religion, sex, or national origin." The cautious language of the act is deliberate. In order to get it passed over a Southern filibuster that consumed a record eighty-two working days, its Senate sponsors had to promise that the bill would not legalize preferences.

"The title does not provide that any preferential treatment shall be given to Negroes or to any group or persons," Senator Hubert Humphrey, the Civil Rights Act's chief sponsor, declared during the Senate debate. The bill, he went on to say, "would prohibit preferential treatment for any particular group." In an Interpretative Memorandum of Title VII, published in the *Congressional Quarterly* in April 1964, Senators Joseph Clark and Clifford Case, the bill's floor managers, were equally emphatic in denying any "hidden meanings" in the act's most controversial section. "There is no requirement in Title VII that an employer maintain a racial balance in his work force," they argued. "On the contrary, any deliberate attempt to maintain a racial balance, whatever such a balance may be, would involve a violation of Title VII, because maintaining such a balance would require an employer to hire or to refuse to hire on the basis of race."

It was the last time affirmative action would have such a clear and circumscribed meaning. A year later the Johnson administration began to redefine affirmative action. Like Kennedy before him, Johnson used executive orders— in his case Executive Orders 11246 in 1965 and 11375 in 1967—to implement affirmative action policy. But the key Johnson declaration on affirmative action came in a speech, "To Fulfill These Rights," delivered at the Howard University commencement in June 1965.

Knowing that the Voting Rights Act of 1965 would soon become law, Johnson began his speech by celebrating the degree to which racial barriers were being knocked down. Quickly, however, the President changed his tone. "But freedom is not enough," he told his Howard audience. "You do not take a person who, for years, has been hobbled by chains and liberate him, bring him to the starting line of a race and then say, 'You are free to compete with all others' and still justly believe you have been completely fair." Johnson's figure of speech combined sports competition and America's slave past, but what distinguished it from previous playing-field analogies on civil rights was that it held that equalizing the rules of competition was insufficient. Special help was also needed. "Equality as a result" and "not just legal equity," the President insisted, had to be provided for those previously excluded from competing on fair terms.

It would be a while before women (feminist historian Alice Kessler-Harris insists that serious affirmative action on their behalf did not begin until the early 1970s) and nonblack minorities drew the kind of concern that Johnson expressed in his Howard University speech, but the President had, nonetheless, reshaped the affirmative action debate. In addition to the Great Society programs of the 1960s, what followed was a crucial change in the definition of affirmative action. As Edward Sylvester, Jr., the first director of the Office of Federal Contract Compliance, later observed in Senate hearings on equal employment opportunity, "simple nondiscrimination as a passive activity" no longer met the requirements of the federal government after 1965. By the time the Johnson administration ended, government contractors with fifty or more employees and $50,000 or more in government business were expected to come up with affirmative action hiring plans that *resulted* in minority employees being added to their work force in order to win Labor Department approval of their contracts.

To bring about this transformation, the Department of Labor, which under Executive Order 11246 now bore primary responsibility for enforcing affirmative action, began to change its methods of operation dramatically. In 1966, reversing a policy that under pressure from civil rights groups had been implemented by Dwight Eisenhower in 1955 and John Kennedy in 1962, Labor started keeping personnel records by race and using them to evaluate hiring practices. At the same time the Labor Department's newly created Office of Federal Contract Compliance (OFCC) began a preaward program for the construction industry.

Under Title VII of the 1964 Civil Rights Act judicial relief in employment could not be provided without a finding of unlawful discrimination. The preaward program avoided the need for such a finding by taking advantage of the government's economic leverage. With the preaward program contractors were required to show "bid responsiveness"—that is, demonstrate that they were actually prepared to meet affirmative action obligations. Without such a demonstration no contract would be awarded. With it low bidders received quick approval.

Two years later in 1968, the Office of Federal Contract Compliance tightened its affirmative action requirements further. Contractors doing government work were now required to present a "written affirmative action compliance program" plus "an evaluation of opportunities for the utilization of minority group personnel." The new regulations declared, "The contractor's program shall provide in detail for specific steps to guarantee equal employment opportunity keyed to the problems and needs of minority groups, including, when there are deficiencies, the development of specific goals and timetables for the prompt achievement of full and equal employment opportunity." What exactly constituted a satisfactory goal or timetable remained unspecified, but a corner had been turned in the legal evolution of affirmative action.

When the Johnson administration ended and the Nixon administration took office in 1969, support for affirmative action still rested on shaky ground, however. Nixon had made his opposition to the liberalism of Johnson's Great Society programs part of his campaign, and his administration was in a position to halt, if not reverse, the new version of affirmative action that the Johnson Labor Department had brought about. Opposition to the Johnson administration's view of affirmative action came not only from such traditional Democratic party supporters as the nation's then powerful labor unions but from key Republican and Democratic senators.

The Nixon administration chose, however, not to alter the course affirmative action had begun to take in the Johnson years. It sought instead to make sure that the urban unrest of the late 1960s, exacerbated in no small measure by joblessness among young blacks, did not become one of its problems. The change from a Johnson Labor Department headed by liberal Willard Wirtz, to one headed by George Shultz, the former dean of the University of Chicago Business School—who years later would become secretary of state under Ronald Reagan—gave new momentum to affirmative action.

When the Johnson administration left office, it had been struggling to put in place its Philadelphia Plan, an affirmative action program designed to force Philadelphia's highly segregated construction companies to hire more minority workers. The plan, originally conceived during the tense period following the Detroit riots of 1967, had drawn fierce opposition, not only from the construction industry and its unions, but from Controller General Elmer Staats, who insisted it was illegal. By the time the Nixon administration took office, the Philadelphia Plan appeared to be dead. But rather than let the plan be buried under the weight of the political and legal opposition it had aroused, George Shultz revived it in 1969.

Shultz's Philadelphia Plan was, moreover, no watered-down version of its predecessor. Shultz's plan made tough demands on the Philadelphia construction industry, calling for minority hiring in terms of percentages that gave contractors a specific target range to aim for. The percentages were not, as critics charged, rigid quotas, but they were an indication of the no-nonsense route the Nixon administration was prepared to follow in pursuing affirmative action.

A year later the Nixon administration made clear that its Philadelphia Plan was not just a symbolic gesture, designed to score easy civil rights points against an industry notorious for its lily-white work force. In February 1970 the Labor Department issued a new set of affirmative action plans, Order No. 4, that included all government contractors with fifty or more employees and at least $50,000 in government business. Order No. 4 redefined affirmative action in such a way that at the federal level it could only be talked about in terms of results that led to a proportional representation of minorities in the work force.

Order No. 4's definition of affirmative action as "a set of specific and result-oriented procedures" made clear how far behind it had left the old notion of discriminatory intent. Even more important, Order No. 4 redefined the concept of "underutilization," which had been terribly vague in the Johnson administration's 1968 affirmative action guidelines. Underutilization now meant "having fewer minorities in a particular job class than would reasonably be expected by their availability." The order required contractors to take into consideration "the percentage of the minority work force as compared with the total work force in the immediate labor areas," and on the basis of that ratio design "specific goals and timetables" to correct any hiring problems. The contractor then had 120 days to present the OFCC with an affirmative action plan or else cease doing business with the government.

The question now became whether the new affirmative action could withstand scrutiny in the courts. In March 1970 a federal district judge in Philadelphia in the case of *Contractors Association of Eastern Pennsylvania v. Secretary of Labor* granted the Justice Department's motion to dismiss a suit that declared the Philadelphia Plan illegal. But the big breakthrough in affirmative action rulings came in March 1971 in an 8-to-0 Supreme Court decision in the case of *Griggs v. Duke Power Company*. In *Griggs* the black petitioners argued that their rights under Title VII had been violated because in order to get hired or promoted by Duke Power they needed either a high school diploma or a passing score on a standardized intelligence test. In a ruling that would shape affirmative action thinking for the next two decades, the Court agreed with the petitioners' claims.

Duke Power's requirements, the Court declared, could not be shown to have "a manifest relationship to the employment in question." But they could be shown to act as "built-in headwinds" against minorities, and that was enough to make them illegal. "The [1964 Civil Rights] Act proscribes not only overt discrimination but also processes that are fair in form, but discriminatory in operation," the Court declared. "Congress directed the thrust of the Act to the *consequences* of employment practices, not simply their motivation." Nowhere in the Court's opinion do the words *affirmative action* appear, but in its focus on the disparate impact of Duke Power's job requirements, there is no mistaking the parallel between the Court's emphasis on "consequences" and Order No. 4's emphasis on "result-oriented procedures."

The way was now open for affirmative action to expand still further, and in December 1971, when the Labor Department made permanent a Revised Order No. 4, it seemed to be reflecting the changing times. Revised Order No. 4 specifically included women in the "affected class" it was designed to protect.

Within academic circles as well as within the federal government, the new affirmative action was not without its critics. In a book provocatively entitled *Affirmative Discrimination*, Harvard sociologist Nathan Glazer decried the shift that in his judgment had changed the focus of civil rights from equality of opportunity to racial statistical parity, and after leaving office, Laurence Silberman, Nixon undersecretary of labor from 1970 to 1973, observed in a *Wall Street Journal* op ed, "Our use of numerical standards in pursuit of equal opportunity has ineluctably led to the very quotas guaranteeing equal results that we initially wished to avoid."

During the Nixon years such criticism was not, however, voiced with enough power or frequency to deter the evolution of affirmative action. The Nixon administration not only went on to strengthen affirmative action requirements, instituting compliance reviews in 1974, it also did not hesitate to back them up with legal muscle. In the wake of the *Griggs* decision, the Labor Department took on Bethlehem Steel, winning a major settlement from it for a seniority system that discriminated against black workers. Then Labor, along with an Equal Employment Opportunity Commission (EEOC) strengthened by changes Congress made in its structure in 1972, took on the nation's largest private employer, AT & T. A consent decree was won that in 1973 awarded $15 million in back pay to 13,000 women and 2,000 minority men and established new affirmative action goals in hiring and promotion. Universities also did not escape affirmative action scrutiny during the Nixon years. The office of Civil Rights, under the direction of Nixon appointee J. Stanley Pottinger, made Columbia University submit three different affirmative action plans before finally restoring $13 million in funding that it had suspended on the basis of its disapproval of Columbia's hiring policies with regard to women and minorities.

Affirmative action had shown that it could thrive under both Democrats and Republicans, and when in 1977 Jimmy Carter brought the Democrats back into power, the only question was whether affirmative action would continue to expand as dramatically as it had from the late 1960s to the middle 1970s. The answer came in September 1978 when the Carter administration introduced the Uniform Guidelines on Employee Selection Procedures. As

tight as it had been, Revised Order No. 4 had still left a key
question unsettled. At what point does an affirmative action
plan succeed in "utilizing" the minority and female labor
population it is expected to hire from? Revised Order No. 4
used the words *reasonably to be expected* to formulate the
kind of result it was after, but that was still a vague concept.
The 1978 Uniform Guideliness ended the vagueness.

Adverse impact and the *four-fifths rule* now became
the cornerstones of affirmative action policy at the federal
level. The Guidelines held that any employer practice that
had an adverse impact on any race, sex, or ethnic group
was illegal unless justified by business necessity. The
Guidelines went on to assert that adverse impact was a job
selection rate for any race, sex, or ethnic group that fell
below four fifths that of the group with the highest selection rate. Employers now had a clear standard to fulfill
when they signed a government contract. What is more, as
a supplement to the Guidelines spelled out, employers
could be "justifiably race, sex, or ethnic conscious" in
undoing past practices that caused adverse impact.

By the close of the 1970s, it was not, however, only the
federal government's view of affirmative action that was
evolving. So, too, was the Supreme Court's. Between 1978
and 1980 the Court rendered three decisions—one in education and two in employment—that changed the judicial
and political climate surrounding affirmative action.

In its 1978 case, *Regents of the University of California
v. Bakke,* a divided Court gave its first indication of the
degree to which it was now prepared to allow racial preferences. Allan Bakke, a white medical school applicant,
charged that he had been discriminated against by the
University of California at Davis's admission program,
which set aside sixteen places out of one hundred for
disadvantaged students. Bakke, whose test scores were
significantly higher than those of the admitted minority

students, based his claim on the Civil Rights Act of 1964 and the Equal Protection Clause of the Fourteenth Amendment. Davis in turn cross-claimed for a declaration that its special admissions program was lawful. Four of the justices agreed with Bakke. Four others disagreed and sided with Davis. The decisive fifth vote was cast by Justice Lewis Powell, who took a position that combined the thinking of both groups. Powell held that Bakke should be admitted to Davis because the sixteen places reserved for disadvantaged students constituted an impermissible quota, but he also went on to say that in the future there was no reason why race or ethnic background could not be treated by Davis as a "plus" in an applicant's file. Davis had, Powell reasoned, a "compelling state interest" in achieving diversity among its student body.

The *Bakke* decision was a delicate balancing act that left neither side satisfied. A year later, however, in the 1979 case of *United Steelworkers of America v. Weber,* the Court was not nearly so tentative in upholding preferences. By a 5-to-2 decision the Court gave its approval to an agreement between the Steelworkers' union and Kaiser Aluminum and Chemical Corporation to carry out a training program in which 50 percent of the trainees would be black until the percentage of black skilled workers at fifteen Kaiser plants approximated the percentage of blacks in the local labor force. The Court held that because the Kaiser plan was "voluntarily adopted by private parties to eliminate traditional patterns of racial segregation" it was not forbidden by Title VII of the Civil Rights Act. The plan, the Court's majority went on to say, would not unduly harm whites because it was "a temporary measure," designed only to eliminate "manifest racial imbalance."

The Court's view that Kaiser and the Steelworkers had acted voluntarily (both had notorious segregation records and had seemed on a collision course with the government) was a stretch, but it did signal the direction in whicn ute justices were moving. A year later in the 1980 case of *Fullilove v. Klutznick,* the Court sanctioned an affirmative action decision that allowed Congress to go farther than it ever had in establishing preferences. The case arose as a result of the minority business enterprise provisions of the Public Works Employment Act of 1977, which set aside 10 percent of $4 billion in funding for businesses owned by minority groups. The 10 percent set-aside seemed exactly the kind of provision the Court had ruled illegal in *Bakke.* But by a 6-to-3 margin the justices held that there was enough flexibility in the conditions surrounding the set-aside for it to avoid being a quota. Most important, the Court held that Congress, as an independent branch of the government, had far-reaching powers under the Constitution to employ racial or ethnic remedies for past discrimination. It did not have to offer precise findings for its actions. It could legislate on the basis of the broad historical record before it.

The Court's affirmative action decisions came with a price, however. Looking back on them a decade later from his perspective as a Yale law professor, current Solicitor General Drew Days III, who as assistant attorney general for civil rights in the Carter administration represented the government in *Fullilove,* observed in the *Yale Law Journal* that in the key affirmative action cases decided by the Supreme Court during the Carter years the grounds for affirmative action were never established as solidly as they should have been. In an article published in 1979 in the *Washington University Law Quarterly,* future Supreme Court Justice Antonin Scalia, at the time a University of Chicago law professor, was even more critical. "I have grave doubts about the wisdom of where we are going in affirmative action, and in equal protection generally," Scalia wrote. "It is increasingly difficult to pretend to one's students that the decisions of the Supreme Court are tied together by threads of logic and analysis—as opposed to what seems to be the fact that the decisions of the justices on the Court are tied together by threads of social preference and predisposition."

By the start of the 1980s what was disturbing to Days and Scalia—the one a judicial liberal, the other a conservative—was, however, even more disturbing to the public. The distinctions the Court had drawn between a goal and a quota, between a voluntary and required affirmative action plan, between what the Civil Rights Act of 1964 allowed and prohibited, often seemed like legal double-talk. The contrast with the 1950s, when the Court had been unified and clear in the principles it used to end school desegregation, was striking, and the contrast was made all the more vivid because those now on the defensive were people, such as future doctor Allan Bakke or Louisiana factory worker Brian Weber, who had played by the rules all their lives. By the close of the Carter administration, the seeds had been sown for the Reagan counterrevolution of the 1980s and an increasingly conservative Supreme Court that would dramatically narrow the scope of affirmative action.

III

In 1980 candidate Ronald Reagan promised to halt affirmative action on taking office. "We must not allow," Reagan declared, "the noble concept of equal opportunity to be distorted into federal guidelines or quotas which require race, ethnicity, or sex—rather than ability and qualifications—to be the principal factor in hiring or education." On assuming the presidency, Reagan made sure that his key civil rights appointees shared his opposition to affirmative action.

To head the Civil Rights Division of the Justice Department, Reagan appointed William Bradford Reynolds, a corporate lawyer, who in a law review article, "The Reagan Administration and Civil Rights," summed up his thinking on affirmative action by declaring, "I regard government tolerance of favoring or disfavoring individuals because of their skin color, sex, religious affiliation, or ethnicity to be fundamentally at odds with the country's civil rights policies." As chairman of the Civil Rights Commission, Reagan chose Clarence Pendleton, Jr., a highly vocal opponent of "quotas, proportional representation, or the setting aside of government contracts for minority businesses," and to run the Equal Employment Opportunity Commission, Reagan selected future Supreme Court Justice Clarence Thomas, a conservative who did not hesitate to describe himself as "unalterably opposed to programs that force or even cajole people to hire a certain percentage of minorities."

Reagan's anti–affirmative action appointments reflected his determination to slow the course of civil rights as much as possible. During the 1960s Reagan had opposed the Civil Rights Act of 1964, the Voting Rights Act of 1965, and the Open Housing Act of 1968, and in the 1980s he was willing to take similar stands. One year after taking office, he reversed an eleven-year-old federal policy of denying tax-exempt status to schools and nonprofit institutions that practice racial discrimination. The following year he fired three Democratic members of the Civil Rights Commission, charging that they favored racial quotas, and in 1988 he vetoed the Civil Rights Restoration Act, designed to overturn a Supreme Court decision that said federal subsidies to colleges that practice discrimination could only be cut for the program in question, not the whole college.

By an 8-to-1 vote the Supreme Court in the 1983 case of *Bob Jones University v. United States* declared the Reagan administration had violated the law in granting tax-exempt status to schools and nonprofit institutions that engage in discrimination, and in 1988 Congress overrode the President's veto to pass the Civil Rights Restoration Act. Most of the time, however, the Reagan administration was highly effective in its anti–affirmative action stands.

Between 1981 and 1983 the budgets of the Equal Employment Opportunity Commission and the Office of Federal Contract Compliance were cut by 10 and 24 percent, their staffs by 12 and 34 percent, thus crippling the ability of both agencies to pursue affirmative action cases. "The federal policy of affirmative action effectively passed away with the inauguration of the Reagan administration," University of California Business School Professor Jonathan Leonard later concluded in a 1990 essay for the *Journal of Economic Perspectives*. "Affirmative action under the contract compliance program virtually ceased to exist in all but name after 1980."

By his personal stance and his administration's actions, Ronald Reagan was able to give new respectability to the opponents of affirmative action. They could now see themselves as centrists rather than reactionaries. Most important, before the decade was over, the Supreme Court, headed by a Reagan-appointed Chief Justice, William Rehnquist, and realigned with two conservative Reagan Justices, Antonin Scalia and Anthony Kennedy, was ready to abandon the expansive view of affirmative action that it had taken in the 1970s.

The Court's rightward shift on affirmative action was not immediately apparent. In the 1986 case *Local 28 of the Sheet Metal Workers v. the Equal Employment Opportunity Commission*, the Court did not hesitate to impose "race-conscious affirmative relief" that involved "long-standing or egregious discrimination." A year later, in the 1987 case *Johnson v. Transportation Agency of Santa Clara*, the

Court approved a voluntary affirmative action plan that benefited women by making gender a plus in hiring decisions, and three years later in the 1990 case *Metro Broadcasting v. Federal Communications Commission*, the Court approved a Congressionally mandated affirmative action plan designed to correct "underrepresentation of minorities in the media."

But during the period it was making these decisions, the Court was also showing signs of its desire to limit affirmative action. In the 1984 case *Firefighters Local Union No. 1784 v. Stotts,* the Court refused to apply affirmative action requirements to a layoff plan, arguing that the seniority system that determined the order of the layoffs was valid. And in 1986 in the case of *Wygant v. Jackson Board of Education,* the Court made a similar ruling, this time noting that affirmative action with regard to layoffs imposed an unfair burden on innocent parties.

The turning point for the Rehnquist Court came in the 1988 case *Watson v. Fort Worth Bank and Trust.* There the Court said it was appropriate for it to extend its authority to disparate-impact cases involving subjective job criteria. But at the same time it extended its reach, the Court dramatically undermined the power it had given workers in previous affirmative action rulings. Contradicting its 1971 *Griggs v. Duke Power Company* decision, which made employers ultimately responsible for showing the "business necessity" of any employment practice that had discriminatory impact, the Court declared in *Watson* that "the ultimate burden of proving that discrimination against a protected group has been caused by a specific employment practice rests with the plaintiff at all times."

A year later the full implications of this dramatic shift in affirmative action law became apparent in the landmark case *Wards Cove Packing Company v. Atonio.* The case arose when minority workers charged that the company, which hired predominantly white workers for its skilled positions and nonwhites, Filipinos, and Alaska Natives for its unskilled positions, was guilty of disparate-impact violations. The Court ruled for the company, declaring that a plaintiff does not make out a case of disparate impact simply by showing that there is a racial imbalance in the work force. "As a general matter," the Court held, "a plaintiff must demonstrate that it is the application of a specific or particular employment practice that has created the disparate impact under attack. Such a showing is an integral part of the plaintiff's prima facie case in a disparate-impact suit under Title VII." Disparate impact, as it had been understood for eighteen years, was now over. And gone, too, were the chances for most plaintiffs—unless they could afford a detailed study of a company's specific employment practices—to win affirmative action suits.

Wards Cove v. Atonio did not, however, stand alone in 1989. It was part of an overall rollback. In *City of Richmond v. J. A. Croson* the Court held illegal a Richmond affirmative action plan, modeled on the one the Court had approved in *Fullilove v. Klutznick*. The Court ruled that city governments could not be granted the same judicial leeway as Congress. In *Martin v. Wilks* the Court said white firefighters could challenge an affirmative action consent decree to which they had not been a party, despite the lapse in time their suit involved. But in *Lorance v. AT & T Technologies* the Court restricted the time in which a group of women employees could file a bias suit, and in *Patterson v. McLean Credit Union,* the Court ruled that the Civil Rights Act of 1866 applied to racial discrimination in hiring but not to harassment and other forms of racial discrimination on the job.

A year after his departure from the White House, the Court had given Ronald Reagan the victory over affirmative action that he had been seeking since 1980. Twenty-five years after the Civil Rights Act of 1964, it had also brought the civil rights movement to a new crossroads. As the 1990s began, both friends and foes of affirmative action knew that the only way to blunt the impact of the Court's 1989 decisions was with the kind of civil rights legislation that had not been passed since the 1960s.

Civil rights groups, no longer as influential as they had been in the 1960s, but still powerful, began pressuring Congress for overriding legislation soon after the Supreme Court decisions were in. By the spring of 1990, the result was a civil rights bill that not only sought to reverse the Court's new reading of disparate impact but undo its narrow interpretation of the Civil Rights Act of 1866 and allow minorities and women who were the victims of employment discrimination on the job to collect damages as well as back pay.

The Bush administration's initial response to the proposed Civil Rights Act of 1990 was hostile, and in an April 3 letter to Senator Kennedy, the bill's chief sponsor, Attorney General Richard Thornburgh spelled out the President's objections. The administration rejected, Thornburgh wrote, the idea that *Wards Cove* was "a radical change in law." It wanted to keep "the burden of persuasion" with the plaintiff in disparate-impact cases, and it wanted an employer charged with practices that result in disparate impact only to have to show that the practices served legitimate employment goals rather than that they were essential to business. The administration was, Thornburgh conceded, willing to give victims of discrimination a longer period to file claims than the Court said they had, and it was also willing to see the protections of civil rights law extended to cover what occurred on the job as well as what occurred in seeking a job. But these, Thornburgh warned, were the only concessions the administration was prepared to make, and he closed his letter to Senator

Kennedy by threatening an administration veto of the Civil Rights Act of 1990 if it passed Congress without revision.

A month later the administration softened its public opposition to the Kennedy-Hawkins civil rights bill. In middle May the President declared he had only "minimal" differences with the pending legislation and "would like to sign a civil rights bill." But a series of meetings with civil rights leaders produced little change in the White House position, and by early August, after the House of Representatives joined the Senate in passing the Civil Rights Act of 1990, the battle lines that continued for the rest of the year were drawn.

By fall the administration was on the offensive again, and on October 22, when the President finally vetoed the Civil Rights Act of 1990, he went out of his way to distinguish his political views from those of the bill's sponsors. The proposed legislation, the President announced in his veto message, "employs a maze of highly legalistic language to introduce the destructive force of quotas into our Nation's employment system." Employers, the President declared, "will be driven to adopt quotas in order to avoid liability," and the country will be pushed into "years—perhaps decades—of uncertainty and expensive litigation."

Given the large majorities by which the Civil Rights Act of 1990 had been passed by both the House and the Senate—the latter fell only one vote short of overriding the President's veto—the President's tough words were a shock to many. But in the fall of 1990, it seemed as if he had accurately gauged the mood of the country. Jesse Helms's ability to use his "White Hands" television commercial to achieve a come-from-behind victory in his bellwether North Carolina Senate race only added strength to the notion that at the grassroots level the political opposition to affirmative action was intense.

A year later, as liberals in the Democratic party, aided

by a handful of Republicans, geared up for a second try at a civil rights bill, the obstacles before them appeared greater than before. The battle for public approval of affirmative action seemed to be swinging to the right rather than to the left. In the spring of 1991, the Department of Labor's then little-known practice of race norming—ranking minority test scores only with regard to the test scores of other minorities in the same group—began drawing heavy fire, and, inspired by a controversy at Georgetown Law School that revealed that the grades and Law School Admission Tests of blacks were significantly lower than those of whites, preferential admissions in higher education came in for new criticism. Worse still for those hoping to enact a civil rights legislation, a poll by the Leadership Conference on Civil Rights, designed to develop a strategy to win approval for the Civil Rights Act of 1991, showed that among the white electorate there was now a widespread belief that civil rights leaders were more interested in special preferences than equal opportunity.

It looked as if the President would have no trouble vetoing the Civil Rights Act of 1991 and that his strategy of describing it as a "quota bill" would work again. Then in the fall of 1991, events suddenly took an unexpected turn. On October 6 the President's plan to replace outgoing Supreme Court Justice Thurgood Marshall with conservative Clarence Thomas received a major setback when law professor Anita Hill testified that she had been sexually harassed by Thomas when she worked for him. By a narrow 52-to-48 Senate vote Thomas was finally confirmed on October 15, in no small measure because of the efforts of his chief sponsor, liberal Republican John Danforth. But the confirmation victory, which ended a 107-day debate, cost the President enormous political capital, and on October 20, when former grand wizard of the Ku Klux Klan David Duke, running as a Republican in the Louisiana gubernatorial primary, beat out the official Republican candidate to finish a close second, the President and his party were again put on the defensive with regard to civil rights.

By late November, when he faced the choice of signing or vetoing the Civil Rights Act of 1991 (favored by Senator John Danforth, among others), the President's options were limited to a degree they had not been in 1990 if he wanted to preserve his image as a conservative who wasn't a racist. On November 21 the President gave in, signing the legislation that until the eleventh hour he had consistently labeled a quota bill.

The Supreme Court's cluster of 1989 civil rights decisions was no longer the law. The new Civil Rights Act shifted the burden of proof in disparate-impact cases back to the employer and required a company with an employment practice that resulted in disparate impact to demonstrate that the practice was both "job related" and "consistent with business necessity." The Act also provided remedies for intentional discrimination and unlawful harassment in the workplace, allowing women and minorities who were the victims of intentional discrimination to collect up to $300,000 in compensatory damages.

The signing of the Civil Rights Act of 1991 would, however, provide no relief from the battles that led up to it. The bitterness surrounding the bill was epitomized by two op eds that appeared in *The Washington Post* the week before the bill became law. In the first op ed, "Civil Rights: We Won, They Capitulated," C. Boyden Gray, the White House Counsel, wrote that the new bill, despite its specific references to changing *Wards Cove,* was consistent with the disparate-impact ruling in that case. Gray then went on to say that, with the exception of some minor compromises, the Bush administration made no concessions to get the bill it wanted. Four days later in an op ed entitled, "How the

Civil Rights Bill Was *Really* Passed," Vernon Jordan, past president of the National Urban League, and William Coleman, Jr., chairman of the NAACP Legal Defense and Educational Fund and a former Republican secretary of transportation, responded with a history of the bill that branded Gray's claims "patently false." Not only did the new bill reverse *Wards Cove* in every major respect, they noted, it also amounted to the White House belatedly agreeing to the changes civil rights leaders had been seeking for the last two years.

At the White House signing ceremony the same rancor prevailed. Nothing was more apparent than President Bush's sense that he had signed the Civil Rights Act of 1991 because he had no choice. The day before the signing, the White House had circulated, then hastily withdrawn, a proposed presidential order ending the use of affirmative action and hiring guidelines for federal jobs. And in the signing statement he issued along with the bill, the President again took a hostile stance, describing the authoritative guide to the Civil Rights Act of 1991 as the analysis (a virtual duplicate of Boyden Gray's) that conservative Republican Senator Robert Dole had placed in the *Congressional Record* on October 30. The result was a Rose Garden ceremony in which civil rights leaders and sponsors of the Civil Rights Act kept their distance from the President and his staff.

IV

Today the differences that could not be smoothed over at the White House signing ceremony for the Civil Rights Act of 1991 are still with us. In making sure that his initial cabinet—with three women, four African Americans, and two Hispanics—was diverse, President Clinton was signaling the country that on matters of race and gender he was going to be very different from his predecessors. But the president's cabinet appointments, as the Lani Guinier controversy of June 1993 showed, have not shielded him from racial criticism nor made affirmative action less divisive than it was in the 1980s.

Among those excluded from its benefits, affirmative action continues to be a backlash issue, fueling a politics of resentment. For the 95,000 companies employing the twenty-seven million workers that, according to the Labor Department, federal affirmative action programs cover, the Civil Rights Act of 1991 clarifies the law, but it does not lessen the massive paperwork affirmative action compliance requires if those companies are to retain the $184 billion in business they do with the government. Similar tensions hold true in higher education, whether the students are the thousands trying to find their way through the racially proportioned admissions procedures of a large state university like Berkeley or the elite handful trying to make *Harvard Law Review,* which since 1981 has reserved slots for groups "historically underrepresented on the review." Even those who vote on affirmative action law cannot escape its consequences, as nine-term liberal New York Congressman Stephen Solarz discovered in 1992 when his heavily Jewish district was eliminated and he lost the Democratic primary election running in a new, predominantly Hispanic district, created in order to comply with the affirmative action goals of the 1982 amendments to the Voting Rights Act.

Most disturbing, three decades after the first affirmative action programs, we lack basic agreement on the justification for them. The contrast with the desegregation battles of the 1950s and 1960s is striking. When in its 1954 *Brown* decision the Supreme Court said that the concept of "separate but equal" as articulated in the 1896 *Plessy v. Ferguson* decision had no place in American law anymore, it was possible, despite the bitterness the ruling produced, to begin moving to a new consensus about racial justice. A decade later, introducing the legislation that became the Civil Rights Act of 1964, John Kennedy could count on a sympathetic response when in a national television address he asked, "If an American because his skin is dark cannot eat in a restaurant, cannot send his children to the best public school available, cannot vote for the elected officials who represent him, then who among us would be content to have the color of his skin changed and stand in his place?"

By the early 1960s it was possible to be both for ending discrimination and for maintaining traditional values. Support for civil rights laws that promised a level playing field for all rested on belief in a society in which people were judged by their deeds, and the passage of such laws seemed to justify the optimism Martin Luther King, Jr., voiced in his "I Have a Dream" speech at the 1963 March on Washington, when he envisioned an America in which his children would be judged by "the content of their character."

But affirmative action has produced no such optimism or consensus about the future; nor have its demands lessened with time. In the South of the 1960s eliminating a whites-only drinking fountain or desegregating a dual school system provided a clear remedy for a wrong. Such action produced visible results and brought immediate relief to the victims or the children of the victims of discrimination. But increasingly affirmative action cases have resisted neat cause-and-effect solutions or a sense of being confined to a limited period of time. If the remedy involves a hiring program that has as its goal a racial proportionalism in the work force, it may take years before the plan is completed, and if the affirmative action involves a college seeking a diverse class by giving preferences based on race, the issue may be even more complex. The problems—poor preparation and low test scores—that the college is trying to overcome usually originate in the secondary schools from which the college draws its student body, and those hurt by the college's affirmative action policies are typically students too young to bear responsibility for the racial injustices of the past. The result in the 1990s is an affirmative action debate in which all sides can point to the burdens imposed on them and simultaneously claim the moral high ground.

The advocates of affirmative action admit that its costs can be high in terms of the resentments it causes among those who are hurt by group preferences for which they don't qualify. But far worse, they argue, is a system that allows the inequities of the past to continue into the present. It is naive, they argue, to think that after centuries of racism America can just adopt color-blind standards and expect the vestiges of racism to disappear. As Justice Harry Blackmun observed in the *Bakke* case, "In order to get beyond racism, we must first take account of race. There is no other way."

Affirmative action, its defenders contend, is our only significant counterweight to the institutional racism that makes it natural for our largest corporations and elite universities to draw on the groups they have always turned to. Without affirmative action a company such as AT & T would not have made the kind of back-pay and hiring agreements it did in the 1970s. Nor would the number of new black officers entering the police force between 1970 and 1990 have been 41 percent of the total. Nor would there be 1.3 million blacks currently working in government service.

Color-blind social policy at this stage is too little, too late, affirmative action proponents insist. It puts too much reliance on the goodwill of institutions in which women and minorities are still underrepresented at the highest levels. As Roderic Park, the vice-chancellor of Berkeley from 1980 to 1990, observed in defense of his university's affirmative action admissions policy, "Without including race we could not get either black or Chicano students above two percent of the freshman class. Race has to be a factor."

To call preferences, such as those mandated by Berkeley's admissions policy, reverse discrimination is, moreover, affirmative action advocates argue, to decontextualize history. Traditional discrimination, whether based on race or gender, was invidious. It assumed the inferiority of those it excluded. By contrast the benign preferences of affirmative action carry with them no stigma. Their aim is inclusionary rather than exclusionary, and in a society in which preferences—whether by the government for veterans or colleges for the children of alums—are commonplace, it makes no sense for affirmative action to be so resented. What affirmative action is doing, especially when its beneficiaries are inner-city blacks, is making up for government policies—from slavery to Jim Crow laws to restrictive housing covenants—that were intentionally racist.

There is, affirmative action proponents insist, no way America can finally be a just society without providing the remedies affirmative action requires. Affirmative action has become essential to our future. Its defenders argue that, in a society in which by the year 2000 two out of three new workers will be either a woman or a member of a minority group, the racial and gender balancing that affirmative action mandates is itself a merit. Affirmative action benefits all. We are better off as a nation when those who run our schools, our businesses, our police departments, reflect our population as a whole. A Balkanized America that ignores the need for such representativeness is a nation asking for social turmoil.

For the opponents of affirmative action, social turmoil is also a critical issue. But they see the turmoil resulting from, instead of being eased by, affirmative action. They do not deny the impact that past and present discrimination has had on American life. Their point is rather that under affirmative action the best and fairest remedy for discrimination—equality of opportunity—has been replaced by a demand for equality of results.

Affirmative action, as authorized by the Civil Rights Act of 1964 was, affirmative action critics contend, inspired by conditions in the South and intended to provide relief to those who (individually or as a class) directly experienced discrimination. But what has happened since 1964, they argue, is that the remedial focus of affirmative action has disappeared. Affirmative action is now essentially prospective in nature and has been redefined in terms of disparate-impact theory, which holds that equity only exists in society when groups are proportionately represented in government and all key institutions.

What this distortion of equality of opportunity has meant, affirmative action opponents argue, is a new victims class. The price for affirmative action is not paid, like a tax that benefits welfare recipients, by the population as a whole. Instead the price for affirmative action falls disproportionately on innocent third parties, often themselves at the margins of society, who bear no responsibility for the vestiges of discrimination under attack. The white college student hurt by an affirmative action admissions policy is someone too young to be held responsible for educational racism. The blue-collar worker, especially if from a family that immigrated to America in the late nineteenth century, is someone whose ancestors themselves were the victims of discrimination and who has typically not benefited from racism in such a way as to justify losing out on a job simply because of not being a minority.

Equally important, affirmative action critics point out, affirmative action has brought benefits to those who have no right to claim them. The point of Lyndon Johnson's affirmative action metaphor about the runner who has been hobbled by chains is that once the runner is made equal with the other runners he is expected to compete on his own. But affirmative action makes no such distinction. The black high school student who has middle-class parents and who was educated in the suburbs is recruited by colleges seeking diversity as if he were disadvantaged. The Hispanic immigrant who recently arrived in America—and cannot claim to have been hobbled by America's racial chains—is treated as if he were the victim of an historic wrong and owed a social debt.

Finally, affirmative action opponents argue, with its emphasis on group rights over individual rights, affirmative action resists closure. We are now caught up in a cycle of racial and gender balancing in which differences will always be a justification for compensatory preferences. For businesses this prospect means, as Justice Sandra Day O'Connor noted in *Watson v. Fort Worth Bank & Trust,* "If quotas and preferential treatment become the only cost-effective means of avoiding expensive litigation and potentially catastrophic liability, such measures will be widely adopted." But such cynicism is not, affirmative action critics point up, limited to those in power. The beneficiaries of affirmative action have a stake in clinging to their victimhood. As long as they retain their victim status, they guarantee themselves a measure of public sympathy as well as preferences in every area of American life in which they are underrepresented.

V

What will it take to bring the affirmative action controversy to an end? An improved economy is the most obvious answer. So long as jobs are scarce, so long as there are limited scholarships and limited places for the college students who need them, affirmative action will remain a battleground. It is hardly surprising, as a recent *New York Times*-CBS poll found, that 71 percent of blacks, as compared to just 17 percent of whites, favor affirmative action. Affirmative action has become a bread-and-butter issue in which how people feel about it is inseparable from how they see themselves benefiting from it.

Three decades ago Bayard Rustin, the principal organizer of the 1963 March on Washington, saw a similar economic problem confronting the civil rights movement. In his 1965 essay "From Protest to Politics: The Future of the Civil Rights Movement," Rustin wrote that the next step for the civil rights movement and its allies had to be one in which they made their focus the creation of an expanded economy built around new jobs, housing, and schools. Without such a focus, Rustin argued, the civil rights movement would never draw the support it needed or make the transition from breaking down barriers of opportunity to achieving the fact of equality.

Today Rustin's thinking, his appeal for what amounts to a Third Reconstruction, has been voiced most persuasively by University of Chicago sociologist William Julius Wilson. In his essays, as well as in his book *The Truly Disadvantaged*, Wilson emphasizes the need for coalition politics and "race-neutral" social programs that feature full employment, job retraining, and health care. Like Rustin before him, Wilson is convinced that so long as racial politics is played as a zero-sum game in which one side's gain is the other side's loss, genuine progress, especially for those minorities who constitute the underclass, is doomed.

The question for the 1990s is whether our ongoing affirmative action debate will stand in the way of or bring

us closer to the kind of expanded economy Rustin and
Wilson have called for. The long-term answer to that question is unclear. The short-term one is not. It depends on
those who have become opponents in the affirmative action
debate realizing the anger they bring with them need not
be a permanent weapon. It can also be a reason to listen to
each other more compassionately, to view one another as
future allies. For what lies behind that anger is not irrational. It is the shared perception that in the current
American economy temporary exclusion is all too often the
first step toward permanent exclusion.

VI

The essays of *Debating Affirmative Action* reflect the fears
as well as the search for common ground that have characterized the affirmative action controversy in America.
The essays are arranged so that different views of affirmative action—from its origins to its political future—may be
set in opposition. Without such conflict a collection like
this would lose its purpose. But no effort has been made to
have the essays follow each other in a one-for-one, pro-con
order. Affirmative action is too complicated a subject for
such an arrangement, and so are the writers it has engaged. Like affirmative action itself, they resist easy definition.

PART ONE

OVERVIEWS

A NEGATIVE VOTE ON AFFIRMATIVE ACTION

Shelby Steele

Shelby Steele is the author of *The Content of Our Character*. "A Negative Vote on Affirmative Action" first appeared in *The New York Times Magazine*, May 13, 1990.

In a few short years, when my two children will be applying to college, the affirmative-action policies by which most universities offer black students some form of preferential treatment will present me with a dilemma. I am a middle-class black, a college professor, far from wealthy, but also well removed from the kind of deprivation that would qualify my children for the label "disadvantaged." Both of them have endured racial insensitivity from whites. They have been called names, have suffered slights, and have experienced firsthand the peculiar malevolence that racism brings out of people. Yet they have never experienced racial discrimination, have never been stopped by their race on any path they have chosen to follow. Still, their society now tells them that if they will only designate themselves as black on their college applications, they will probably do better in the college lottery than if they conceal this fact. I think there is something of a Faustian bargain in this.

Of course many blacks and a considerable number of whites would say that I was sanctimoniously making affirmative action into a test of character. They would say that this small preference is the meagerest recompense for centuries of unrelieved oppression. And to these arguments other very obvious facts must be added. In America, many marginally competent or flatly incompetent whites are hired every day—some because their white skin suits the conscious or unconscious racial preference of their employers. The white children of alumni are often grandfathered into elite universities in what can only be seen as a residual benefit of historic white privilege. Worse, white incompetence is always an individual matter, but for blacks it is often confirmation of ugly stereotypes. Given that unfairness cuts both ways, doesn't it only balance the scales of history, doesn't this repay, in a small way, the systematic denial under which my children's grandfather lived out his days?

In theory, affirmative action certainly has all the moral symmetry that fairness requires. It is reformist and corrective, even repentant and redemptive. And I would never sneer at these good intentions. Born in the late 1940s in Chicago, I started my education (a charitable term, in this case) in a segregated school, and suffered all the indignities that come to blacks in a segregated society. My father, born in the South, made it only to the third grade before the white man's fields took permanent priority over his formal education. And though he educated himself into an advanced reader with an almost professorial authority, he could only drive a truck for a living, and never earned more than $90 a week in his entire life. So yes, it is crucial to my sense of citizenship, to my ability to identify with the spirit and the interests of America, to know that this country, however imperfectly, recognizes its past sins and wishes to correct them.

Yet good intentions can blind us to the effects they generate when implemented. In our society affirmative action is, among other things, a testament to white goodwill and to black power, and in the midst of these heavy investments its effects can be hard to see. But after twenty years of implementation I think that affirmative action has shown itself to be more bad than good and that blacks— whom I will focus on in this essay—now stand to lose more from it than they gain.

In talking with affirmative-action administrators and with blacks and whites in general, I found that supporters of affirmative action focus on its good intentions and detractors emphasize its negative effects. It was virtually impossible to find people outside either camp. The closest I came was a white male manager at a large computer company who said, "I think it amounts to reverse discrimination, but I'll put up with a little of that for a little more diversity." But this only makes him a halfhearted supporter of affirmative action. I think many people who don't really like affirmative action support it to one degree or another anyway.

I believe they do this because of what happened to white and black Americans in the crucible of the 1960s, when whites were confronted with their racial guilt and blacks tasted their first real power. In that stormy time white absolution and black power coalesced into virtual mandates for society. Affirmative action became a meeting ground for those mandates in the law. At first, this meant insuring equal opportunity. The 1964 civil-rights bill was passed on the understanding that equal opportunity would not mean racial preference. But in the late sixties and early seventies, affirmative action underwent a remarkable escalation of its mission from simple antidiscrimination enforcement to social engineering by means of quotas, goals, timetables, set-asides, and other forms of preferential treatment.

Legally, this was achieved through a series of executive orders and Equal Employment Opportunity Commission guidelines that allowed racial imbalances in the workplace to stand as proof of racial discrimination. Once it could be assumed that discrimination explained racial imbalance, it became easy to justify group remedies to presumed discrimination rather than the normal case-by-case redress.

Even though blacks had made great advances during the sixties without quotas, the white mandate to achieve a new racial innocence and the black mandate to gain power, which came to a head in the very late sixties, could no longer be satisfied by anything less than racial preferences. I don't think these mandates, in themselves, were wrong, because whites clearly needed to do better by blacks and blacks needed more real power in society. But as they came together in affirmative action, their effect was to distort our understanding of racial discrimination. By making black the color of preference, these mandates have reburdened society with the very marriage of color and preference (in reverse) that we set out to eradicate.

When affirmative action grew into social engineering, *diversity* became a golden word. *Diversity* is a term that applies democratic principles to races and cultures rather than to citizens, despite the fact that there is nothing to indicate that real diversity is the same thing as proportionate representation. Too often the result of this, on campuses for example, has been a democracy of colors rather than of people, an artificial diversity that gives the appearance of an educational parity between black and white students that has not yet been achieved in reality. Here again, racial preferences allow society to leapfrog over the difficult problem of developing blacks to parity with whites and into a cosmetic diversity that covers the blemish of disparity—a full six years after admission, only 26 to 28 percent of blacks graduate from college.

Racial representation is not the same thing as racial development. Representation can be manufactured; development is always hard earned. But it is the music of innocence and power that we hear in affirmative action that causes us to cling to it and to its distracting emphasis on representation. The fact is that after twenty years of racial preferences the gap between median incomes of black and white families is greater than it was in the 1970s. None of this is to say that blacks don't need policies that insure our right to equal opportunity, but what we need more of is the development that will let us take advantage of society's efforts to include us.

I think one of the most troubling effects of racial preferences for blacks is a kind of demoralization. Under affirmative action, the quality that earns us preferential treatment is an implied inferiority. However this inferiority is explained—and it is easily enough explained by the myriad deprivations that grew out of our oppression—it is still inferiority. There are explanations and then there is the fact. And the fact must be borne by the individual as a condition apart from the explanation, apart even from the fact that others like himself also bear this condition. In integrated situations in which blacks must compete with whites who may be better prepared, these explanations may quickly wear thin and expose the individual to racial as well as personal self-doubt. (Of course whites also feel doubt, but only personally, not racially.)

What this means in practical terms is that when blacks deliver themselves into integrated situations they encounter a nasty little reflex in whites, a mindless, atavistic reflex that responds to the color black with negative stereotypes, such as intellectual ineptness. I think this reflex embarrasses most whites today and thus it is usually quickly repressed. On an equally atavistic level, the black will be aware of the reflex his color triggers and will feel a stab of horror at seeing himself reflected in this way. He, too, will do a quick repression, but a lifetime of such stabbings is what constitutes his inner realm of racial doubt. Even when the black sees no implication of inferiority in racial preferences, he knows that whites do, so that—consciously or unconsciously—the result is virtually the same. The effect of preferential treatment—the lowering of normal standards to increase black representation—puts blacks at war with an expanded realm of debilitating doubt, so that the doubt itself becomes an unrecognized preoccupation that undermines their ability to perform, especially in integrated situations.

I believe another liability of affirmative action comes from the fact that it indirectly encourages blacks to exploit their own past victimization. Like implied inferiority, victimization is what justifies preference, so that to receive the benefits of preferential treatment one must, to some extent, become invested in the view of oneself as a victim. In this way, affirmative action nurtures a victim-focused identity in blacks and sends us the message that there is more power in our past suffering than in our present achievements.

When power itself grows out of suffering, blacks are encouraged to expand the boundaries of what qualifies as racial oppression, a situation that can lead us to paint our victimization in vivid colors even as we receive the benefits of preference. The same corporations and institutions that give us preference are also seen as our oppressors. At Stanford University, minority-group students—who receive at least the same financial aid as whites with the same need—recently took over the president's office demanding, among other things, more financial aid.

But I think one of the worst prices that blacks pay for

preference has to do with an illusion. I saw this illusion at work recently in the mother of a middle-class black student who was going off to his first semester of college: "They owe us this, so don't think for a minute that you don't belong there." This is the logic by which many blacks, and some whites, justify affirmative action—it is something "owed," a form of reparation. But this logic overlooks a much harder and less digestible reality, that it is impossible to repay blacks living today for the historic suffering of the race. If all blacks were given a million dollars tomorrow it would not amount to a dime on the dollar for three centuries of oppression, nor would it dissolve the residues of that oppression that we still carry today. The concept of historic reparation grows out of man's need to impose on the world a degree of justice that simply does not exist. Suffering can be endured and overcome, it cannot be repaid. To think otherwise is to prolong the suffering.

Several blacks I spoke with said they were still in favor of affirmative action because of the "subtle" discrimination blacks were subject to once they were on the job. One photojournalist said, "They have ways of ignoring you." A black female television producer said: "You can't file a lawsuit when your boss doesn't invite you to the insider meetings without ruining your career. So we still need affirmative action." Others mentioned the infamous "glass ceiling" through which blacks can see the top positions of authority but never reach them. But I don't think racial preferences are a protection against this subtle discrimination; I think they contribute to it.

In any workplace, racial preferences will always create two-tiered populations composed of preferreds and unpreferreds. In the case of blacks and whites, for instance, racial preferences imply that whites are superior just as they imply that blacks are inferior. They not only reinforce

America's oldest racial myth but, for blacks, they have the effect of stigmatizing the already stigmatized.

I think that much of the "subtle" discrimination that blacks talk about is often (not always) discrimination against the stigma of questionable competence that affirmative action marks blacks with. In this sense, preferences make scapegoats of the very people they seek to help. And it may be that at a certain level employers impose a glass ceiling, but this may not be against the race so much as against the race's reputation for having advanced by color as much as by competence. This ceiling is the point at which corporations shift the emphasis from color to competency and stop playing the affirmative-action game. Here preference backfires for blacks and becomes a taint that holds them back. Of course one could argue that this taint, which is after all in the minds of whites, becomes nothing more than an excuse to discriminate against blacks. And certainly the result is the same in either case—blacks don't get past the glass ceiling. But this argument does not get around the fact that racial preferences now taint this color with a new theme of suspicion that makes blacks even more vulnerable to discrimination. In this crucial yet gray area of perceived competence, preferences make whites look better than they are and blacks worse, while doing nothing whatever to stop the very real discrimination that blacks may encounter. I don't wish to justify the glass ceiling here, but only suggest the very subtle ways that affirmative action revives rather than extinguishes the old rationalizations for racial discrimination.

I believe affirmative action is problematic in our society because we have demanded that it create parity between the races rather than insure equal opportunity. Preferential treatment does not teach skills, or educate, or instill motivation. It only passes out entitlement by color, a situation that in my profession has created an unrealistically high demand for black professors. The social engineer's assumption is that this high demand will inspire more blacks to earn Ph.D.'s and join the profession. In fact, the number of blacks earning Ph.D.'s has declined in recent years. Ph.D.'s must be developed from preschool on. They require family and community support. They must acquire an entire system of values that enables them to work hard while delaying gratification.

It now seems clear that the Supreme Court, in a series of recent decisions, is moving away from racial preferences. It has disallowed preferences except in instances of "identified discrimination," eroded the precedent that statistical racial imbalances are prima facie evidence of discrimination, and, in effect, granted white males the right to challenge consent degrees that use preference to achieve racial balances in the workplace. Referring to this and other Supreme Court decisions, one civil-rights leader said, "Night has fallen . . . as far as civil rights are concerned." But I am not so sure. The effect of these decisions is to protect the constitutional rights of everyone, rather than to take rights away from blacks. Night has fallen on racial preferences, not on the fundamental rights of black Americans. The reason for this shift, I believe, is that the white mandate for absolution from past racial sins has weakened considerably in the 1980s. Whites are now less willing to endure unfairness to themselves in order to grant special entitlements to blacks, even when those entitlements are justified in the name of past suffering. Yet the black mandate for more power in society has remained unchanged. And I think part of the anxiety many blacks feel over these decisions has to do with the loss of black power that they may signal.

But the power we've lost by these decisions is really only the power that grows out of our victimization. This is not a very substantial or reliable power, and it is important that we know this so we can focus more exclusively on the kind of development that will bring enduring power. There is talk now that Congress may pass new legislation to compensate for these new limits on affirmative action. If this happens, I hope the focus will be on development and antidiscrimination, rather than entitlement, on achieving racial parity rather than jerry-building racial diversity.

But if not preferences, what? The impulse to discriminate *is* subtle and cannot be ferreted out unless its many guises are made clear to people. I think we need social policies that are committed to two goals: the educational and economic development of disadvantaged people regardless of race and the eradication from our society—through close monitoring and severe sanctions—of racial, ethnic, or gender discrimination. Preferences will not get us to either of these goals, because they tend to benefit those who are not disadvantaged—middle-class white women and middle-class blacks—and attack one form of discrimination with another. Preferences are inexpensive and carry the glamour of good intentions—change the numbers and the good deed is done. To be against them is to be unkind. But I think the unkindest cut is to bestow on children like my own an undeserved advantage while neglecting the development of those disadvantaged children in the poorer sections of my city who will most likely never be in a position to benefit from a preference. Give my children fairness; give disadvantaged children a better shot at development—better elementary and secondary schools, job training, safer neighborhoods, better financial assistance for college, and so on. A smaller percentage of black high school graduates go to college today than fifteen years ago; more black males are in prison, jail, or in some other way under the control of the criminal-justice system than in college. This despite racial preferences.

The mandates of black power and white absolution out

of which preferences emerged were not wrong in themselves. What was wrong was that both races focused more on the goals of those mandates than on the means to the goals. Blacks can have no real power without taking responsibility for their own educational and economic development. Whites can have no racial innocence without earning it by eradicating discrimination and helping the disadvantaged to develop. Because we ignored the means, the goals have not been reached and the real work remains to be done.

PERSUASION AND DISTRUST:
THE AFFIRMATIVE ACTION DEBATE

Randall Kennedy

Randall Kennedy is professor of law at Harvard University
Law School and the editor of *Reconstruction*. He was law
clerk for Supreme Court Justice Thurgood Marshall in
1983–84. "Persuasion and Distrust: The Affirmative Action
Debate" first appeared in *Harvard Law Review*, April 1986.

The controversy over affirmative action constitutes the
most salient current battlefront in the ongoing conflict over
the status of blacks in American life. No domestic struggle
has been more protracted or more riddled with ironic
complication. One frequently noted irony is that the affirmative action controversy has contributed significantly
to splintering the coalition principally responsible for the
civil rights revolution. That coalition was comprised of a
broad array of groups—liberal Democrats, moderate Republicans, the national organizations of the black and
Jewish communities, organized labor, and others—that
succeeded in invalidating de jure segregation and passing
far-reaching legislation in support of the rights of blacks,
including the Civil Rights Act of 1964 and the Voting
Rights Act of 1965.

For over a decade this coalition has been riven by bitter disagreement over the means by which American society should attempt to overcome its racist past. Opponents of affirmative action maintain that commitment to a nonracist social environment requires strict color-blindness in decision-making as both a strategy and a goal. In their view, "one gets beyond racism by getting beyond it now: by a complete, resolute, and credible commitment *never* to tolerate in one's own life—or in the life or practices of one's government—the differential treatment of other human beings by race." Proponents of affirmative action insist that only *malign* racial distinctions should be prohibited; they favor *benign* distinctions that favor blacks. Their view is that "[i]n order to get beyond racism, we must first take race into account" and that "in order to treat some persons equally, we must treat them differently."

Part I of this Commentary considers aspects of two principal objections to affirmative action: that it harms rather than helps blacks in American society, and that it violates the Constitution. My discussion does not attempt to analyze this large and complicated subject comprehensively but rather seeks to focus upon certain vexing areas of the public debate. I conclude that affirmative action should generally be retained as a tool of public policy because, on balance, it is useful in overcoming entrenched racial hierarchy.

Part II explores an issue widely ignored by academic commentators: whether covert motivations play a role in the political, judicial, and intellectual reaction against affirmative action. I defend the utility of the question and suggest an answer to it. I argue that division within the civil rights coalition is not the *only* conflict permeating the affirmative action controversy. Also involved is a much older conflict involving sectors of our society that have never authentically repudiated the "old style religion" of white supremacy. The most important of these sectors is the Reagan administration. I contend that a tenacious and covert resistance to further erosion of racial hierarchy explains much of the Reagan administration's racial policy, especially its attacks on affirmative action.

I focus on both overt and covert discourse, because the affirmative action debate cannot be understood without acknowledging simultaneously the force of the openly stated arguments for and against preferential treatment and the submerged intuitions that disguise themselves with these arguments. To disregard either of these features of the debate is to ignore an essential aspect of the controversy. To appreciate both is to recognize the frustrating complexity of our racial situation.

I. The Efficacy and Lawfulness of Affirmative Action

The Case for Affirmative Action

Affirmative action has strikingly benefited blacks as a group and the nation as a whole. It has enabled blacks to attain occupational and educational advancement in numbers and at a pace that would otherwise have been impossible. These breakthroughs engender self-perpetuating benefits: the accumulation of valuable experience, the expansion of a professional class able to pass its material advantages and elevated aspirations to subsequent generations, the eradication of debilitating stereotypes, and the inclusion of black participants in the making of consequential decisions affecting black interests. Without affirmative action, continued access for black applicants to college and professional education would be drastically narrowed. To insist, for example, upon the total exclusion of racial factors in admission decisions, especially at elite institutions, would mean classes of college, professional, and graduate students that are virtually devoid of African-American representation.

Furthermore, the benefits of affirmative action redound not only to blacks but to the nation as a whole. For example, the virtual absence of black police even in overwhelmingly black areas helped spark the ghetto rebellions of the 1960s. The integration of police forces through strong affirmative action measures has often led to better relations between minority communities and the police, a result that improves public safety for all. Positive externalities have accompanied affirmative action programs in other contexts as well, most importantly by teaching whites that blacks, too, are capable of handling responsibility, dispensing knowledge, and applying valued skills.

The Claim That Affirmative Action Harms Blacks

In the face of arguments in favor of affirmative action, opponents of the policy frequently reply that it actually harms its ostensible beneficiaries. Various interrelated claims undergird the argument that affirmative action is detrimental to blacks. The most weighty claim is that preferential treatment exacerbates racial resentments, entrenches racial divisiveness, and thereby undermines the consensus necessary for effective reform. The problem with this view is that intense white resentment has accompanied every effort to undo racial subordination no matter how careful the attempt to anticipate and mollify the reaction. The Supreme Court, for example, tried mightily to preempt white resistance to school desegregation by directing that it be implemented with "all deliberate speed." This attempt, however, to defuse white resistance may well have caused the opposite effect and, in any event, doomed from the outset the constitutional rights of a generation of black schoolchildren. Given the apparent inevitability of white resistance and the uncertain efficacy of containment, proponents of racial justice should be wary of allowing fear of white backlash to limit the range of reforms pursued. This admonition is particularly appropriate with respect to affirmative action insofar as it creates vital opportunities the value of which likely outweigh their cost in social friction. A second part of the argument that affirmative action hurts blacks is the claim that it stigmatizes them by implying that they simply cannot compete on an equal basis with whites. Moreover, the pall cast by preferential treatment is feared to be pervasive, hovering over blacks who have attained positions without the aid of affirmative action as well as over those who have been accorded preferential treatment. I do not doubt that affirmative action causes some stigmatizing effect. It is unrealistic to think, however, that affirmative action causes most white disparagement of the abilities of blacks. Such disparagement, buttressed for decades by the rigid exclusion of blacks from educational and employment opportunities, is precisely what engendered the explosive crisis to which affirmative action is a response. Although it is widely assumed that "qualified" blacks are now in great demand, with virtually unlimited possibilities for recognition, blacks continue to encounter prejudice that ignores or minimizes their talent. In the end, the uncertain extent to which affirmative action diminishes the accomplishments of blacks must be balanced against the stigmatization that occurs when blacks are virtually absent from important institutions in the society. The presence of blacks across the broad spectrum of institutional settings upsets conventional stereotypes about the place of blacks and acculturates the public to the idea that blacks can and must participate in all areas of our national life. This positive result of affirmative action outweighs any stigma that the policy causes.

A third part of the argument against affirmative action

is the claim that it saps the internal morale of blacks. It renders them vulnerable to a dispiriting anxiety that they have not truly earned whatever positions or honors they have attained. Moreover, it causes some blacks to lower their own expectations of themselves. Having grown accustomed to the extra boost provided by preferential treatment, some blacks simply do not try as hard as they otherwise would. There is considerable power to this claim; unaided accomplishment does give rise to a special pride felt by both the individual achiever and her community. But the suggestion that affirmative action plays a major role in undermining the internal morale of the black community is erroneous.

Although I am unaware of any systematic evidence on the self-image of beneficiaries of affirmative action, my own strong impression is that black beneficiaries do not see their attainments as tainted or undeserved—and for good reason. First, they correctly view affirmative action as rather modest compensation for the long period of racial subordination suffered by blacks as a group. Thus they do not feel that they have been merely *given* a preference; rather, they see affirmative discrimination as a form of social justice. Second, and more importantly, many black beneficiaries of affirmative action view claims of meritocracy with skepticism. They recognize that in many instances the objection that affirmative action represents a deviation from meritocratic standards is little more than disappointed nostalgia for a golden age that never really existed. Overt exclusion of blacks from public and private institutions of education and employment was one massive affront to meritocratic pretensions. Moreover, a longstanding and pervasive feature of our society is the importance of a wide range of nonobjective, nonmeritocratic factors influencing the distribution of opportunity. The significance of personal associations and informal networks is what gives durability and resonance to the adage: It's not *what* you know, it's *who* you know. As Professor Wasserstrom wryly observes, "Would anyone claim that Henry Ford II [was] head of the Ford Motor Company because he [was] the most qualified person for the job?"

Finally, and most importantly, many beneficiaries of affirmative action recognize the thoroughly political— which is to say contestable—nature of "merit"; they realize that it is a malleable concept, determined not by immanent, preexisting standards but rather by the perceived needs of society. Inasmuch as the elevation of blacks addresses pressing social needs, they rightly insist that considering a black's race as part of the bundle of traits that constitute "merit" is entirely appropriate.

A final and related objection to affirmative action is that it frequently aids those blacks who need it least and who can least plausibly claim to suffer the vestiges of past discrimination—the offspring of black middle-class parents seeking preferential treatment in admission to elite universities and black entrepreneurs seeking guaranteed set-asides for minority contractors on projects supported by the federal government. This objection, too, is unpersuasive. First, it ignores the large extent to which affirmative action has pried open opportunities for blue-collar black workers. Second, it assumes that affirmative action should be provided only to the most deprived strata of the black community or to those who can best document their victimization. In many circumstances, however, affirmative action has developed from the premise that special aid should be given to strategically important sectors of the black community—for example, those with the threshold ability to integrate the professions. Third, although affirmative action has primarily benefited the black middle class, that is no reason to condemn preferential treatment. All that fact indicates is the necessity for additional social intervention to address unmet needs in those sectors of the black community left untouched by affirmative action. One thing that proponents of affirmative action have neglected to emphasize strongly enough is that affirmative discrimination is but part—indeed a rather small part—of the needed response to the appalling crisis besetting black communities. What is so remarkable—and ominous— about the affirmative action debate is that so modest a reform calls forth such powerful resistance.

Does Affirmative Action Violate the Constitution?

The constitutional argument against affirmative action proceeds as follows: *All* governmental distinctions based on race are presumed to be illegal and can only escape that presumption by meeting the exacting requirements of "strict scrutiny." Because the typical affirmative action program cannot meet these requirements, most such programs are unconstitutional. Behind this theory lies a conviction that has attained its most passionate and oft-quoted articulation in Alexander Bickel's statement:

> The lesson of the great decisions of the Supreme Court and the lesson of contemporary history have been the same for at least a generation: discrimination on the basis of race is illegal, immoral, unconstitutional, inherently wrong, and destructive of democratic society. Now this is to be unlearned and we are told that this is not a matter of fundamental principle but only a matter of whose ox is gored.

Among the attractions of this theory are its symmetry and simplicity. It commands that the government be color blind in its treatment of persons, that it accord benefits and burdens to black and white individuals according to precisely the *same* criteria—no matter whose ox is gored. According to its proponents, this theory dispenses with manipulable sociological investigations and provides a clear *rule* that compels consistent judicial application.

In response, I would first note that the color-blind theory of the Constitution is precisely that—a "theory," one of any number of competing theories that seek to interpret the Fourteenth Amendment's Delphic proscription of state action that denies any person "the equal protection of the laws." Implicitly recognizing that neither a theory of original intent nor a theory of textual construction provides suitable guidance, Professor Bickel suggests that a proper resolution of the affirmative action dispute can be derived from "the great decisions of the Supreme Court." Certainly what Bickel had in mind were *Brown v. Board of Education* and its immediate progeny, the cases that established the foundation of our postsegregation Constitution. To opponents of affirmative action, the lesson of these cases is that, except in the narrowest, most exigent circumstances, race can play no legitimate role in governmental decision-making.

This view, however, is too abstract and ahistorical. In the forties, fifties, and early sixties, against the backdrop of laws that used racial distinctions to exclude blacks from opportunities available to white citizens, it seemed that racial subjugation could be overcome by mandating the application of race-blind law. In retrospect, however, it appears that the concept of race-blindness was simply a proxy for the fundamental demand that racial subjugation be eradicated. This demand, which matured over time in the face of myriad sorts of opposition, focused upon the *condition* of racial subjugation; its target was not only procedures that overtly excluded blacks on the basis of race, but also the self-perpetuating dynamics of subordination that had survived the demise of American apartheid. The opponents of affirmative action have stripped the historical context from the demand for race-blind law. They have fashioned this demand into a new totem and insist on deference to it no matter what its effects upon the very group the Fourteenth Amendment was created to protect. *Brown* and its progeny do not stand for the abstract principle that governmental distinctions based on race are unconstitutional. Rather, those great cases, forged by the gritty particularities of the struggle against white racism, stand for the proposition that the Constitution prohibits any arrangements imposing racial subjugation—whether such arrangements are ostensibly race neutral or even ostensibly race blind.

This interpretation, which articulates a principle of antisubjugation rather than antidiscrimination, typically encounters two closely related objections. The first objection is the claim that the constitutional injury done to a white whose chances for obtaining some scarce opportunity are diminished because of race-based allocation schemes is legally indistinguishable from that suffered by a black victim of racial exclusion. Second, others argue that affirmative discrimination based on racial distinctions cannot be satisfactorily differentiated from racial subjugation absent controversial sociological judgments that are inappropriate to the judicial role.

As to the first objection, the injury suffered by white "victims" of affirmative action does not properly give rise to a constitutional claim, because the damage does not derive from a scheme animated by racial prejudice. Whites with certain credentials may be excluded from particular opportunities they would receive if they were black. But this diminished opportunity is simply an incidental consequence of addressing a compelling societal need: undoing the subjugation of African Americans. Whites who would be admitted to professional schools in the absence of affirmative action policies are not excluded merely because of prejudice, as were countless numbers of blacks until fairly recently. Rather, whites are excluded "because of a rational calculation about the socially most beneficial use of limited resources for [professional] education."

As to the second objection, I concede that distinctions between affirmative and malign discrimination cannot be made in the absence of controversial sociological judgments. I reject the proposition, however, that drawing these distinctions is inappropriate to the judicial role. Such a proposition rests upon the assumption that there exists a judicial method wholly independent of sociological judgment. That assumption is false; to some extent, whether explicitly or implicitly, *every* judicial decision rests upon certain premises regarding the irreducibly controversial nature of social reality. The question, therefore, is not whether a court will make sociological judgments, but the content of the sociological judgments it must inevitably make.

Prior to *Brown*, the Supreme Court's validation of segregation statutes rested upon the premise that they did not unequally burden the black. A perceived difficulty in invalidating segregation statutes was that, as written, such laws were race neutral; they excluded white children from black schools just as they excluded black children from white schools. The Court finally recognized in *Brown* that racial subjugation constituted the social meaning of segregation laws. To determine that social meaning, the Court had to look past form into substance and judge the legitimacy of segregation laws given their intended and actual effects. Just as the "neutrality" of the segregation laws obfuscated racial subjugation, so, too, may the formal neutrality of race-blind policies also obfuscate the perpetuation of racial subjugation. That issue can only be explored by an inquiry into the context of the race-blind policy at issue, an inquiry that necessarily entails judicial sociology.

II. The Question of Racism

The Need for Motive Analysis

Much has been written about the issues discussed in Part I of this Comment. However, there remains a disturbing lacuna in the scholarly debate. Whether racism is partly responsible for the growing opposition to affirmative action is a question that is virtually absent from many of the leading articles on the subject. These articles typically portray the conflict over affirmative action as occurring in the context of an overriding commitment to racial fairness and equality shared by *all* the important participants in the debate. For example, a recent article by Professors Richard Fallon and Paul Weiler depicts the conflict in terms of "contending models of racial justice"—a depiction suggesting that, despite its bitterness, the affirmative action debate is at least bounded by common abhorrence of explicit racial hierarchy. This portrait, however, of conflict-within-consensus is all too genial. It conjures up the absurd image of Benjamin Hooks and William Bradford Reynolds embracing one another as ideological brethren, differing on the discrete issue of affirmative action but united on the fundamentals of racial fairness. It obscures the emotions that color the affirmative action debate and underestimates the alienation that separates antagonists. It ignores those who believe that much of the campaign against affirmative action is merely the latest in a long series of white reactions against efforts to elevate the status of blacks in American society. These observers perceive critics of affirmative action not merely as *opponents* but as *enemies*. They perceive ostensibly nonracist objections to affirmative action as rationalizations of white supremacy. They fear that the campaign against affirmative action is simply the opening wedge of a broader effort to recapture territory "lost" in the

Civil Rights Revolution of the 1960s. And it is precisely this apprehension that explains the bitterness and desperation with which they wage the affirmative action struggle— emotions that are simply inexplicable in terms of the picture of race relations portrayed by conventional analyses.

The conventional portrait also implicitly excludes from consideration those whose opposition to affirmative action stems from racism. It concedes the presence of prejudice "out there" in the workaday world of ordinary citizens. But it assumes that "in here"—in the realm of scholarly discourse and the creation of public policy—prejudice plays no role. In other words, conventional scholarship leaves largely unexamined the possibility that the campaigns against affirmative action now being waged by political, judicial, and intellectual elites reflect racially selective indifference, antipathy born of prejudice, or strategies that seek to capitalize on widespread racial resentments.

Why have scholars consistently avoided scrutinizing the motives of policymakers and fellow commentators? The explanations offered for the absence of such inquiry resemble those advanced to explain the futility or inappropriateness of inquiry into legislative motive. One objection centers on the evidentiary difficulties involved in ascertaining someone's motives. If the devil himself knoweth not the mind of man, how can mortal commentators know the motivation of officials and fellow analysts? A second objection is that the cost of the inquiry, including the inevitable possibility of error, outweighs any gains. A third objection is that, whatever the propriety of motive review in adjudication, it is an improper mode of analysis within intellectual discourse because it strongly tends toward ad hominem attacks on honesty that are impossible to disprove. Moreover, scrutiny of motive is a mode of analysis easily susceptible to reductionism: by focusing on the proponent of an idea and his suspected aims, one tends to reduce the idea itself to the status of a mere instrument. A fourth objection is that motive-centered inquiries are irrelevant: after all, a policy stemming from bad motives can nevertheless turn out to be a positive contribution to the public good, fully justifiable on the basis of sound reasons unrelated to covert and evil motives.

These objections serve a useful cautionary function. They fail, however, to show that motive analysis is misplaced in intellectual discussion and policy analysis. First, awkward problems in assembling evidence regarding the suspected objectives of a scholar or public official need not justify a wholesale rejection of the inquiry. Such problems merely indicate that a motive-centered analysis is difficult—not that it is improper or unfruitful. Second, although motive analysis does entail the possibility that a person or institution may be wrongly accused of harboring racist sentiments, forgoing such inquiry also imposes a high cost: loss of information regarding the nature of our society. Conclusions as to motive are admittedly uncertain, but so are the conclusions that result from many of the most important inquiries we are forced to make in our intellectual as well as personal and political lives. Furthermore, while charging someone with either consciously or unconsciously falsifying his motives is undeniably an insult, it is equally undeniable that the search for truth often causes pain—and that the deliberate hiding of motive constitutes an affront to all of those to whom the lie is addressed.

Third, the danger that concern with motive will overshadow attentiveness to ideas is simply another of the many dangers of excess that adhere to *any* methodology. The proper reaction is not wholesale rejection, but rather a disciplined use of the methodology that is informed by the limits of any one particular line of inquiry. Finally, to suggest that a policy is completely distinct from the motive from which it arises simply distorts reality. The animating motive is an integral aspect of the context in which a policy emerges, and there is no such thing as a policy without a context. A policy is "not a crystal, transparent and unchanged, it is the skin of a living thought and may vary greatly in color and content according to the circumstances and the time in which it is used."* In other words, no unchanging essence exists within any policy, including a policy rejecting affirmative action. Such a policy could have a wide variety of meanings, depending upon, among other things, the motive behind the policy. Rejecting affirmative action for nonracist reasons is simply not the same policy as rejecting affirmative action for reasons infected with racism. The two policies share obvious traits: they both reject preferential treatment. But they also differ fundamentally—the former may constitute an error, the latter is certainly an insult.

Motivation, then, always matters in determining the meaning of a policy, although it is not all that matters. But attentiveness to motive should be an important aspect of ongoing analysis of the affirmative action controversy for other reasons as well. The simple but basic desire to document accurately the history of our era is justification enough for inquiring into the motives animating political action. That inquiry is essential to answering the most difficult of the questions that beset historians—the question of *why* particular actions are taken, given decisions made. Furthermore, baleful consequences attend dependence upon false records of social reality. After all, blindness to contemporary social realities helped spawn the montrous lie, propagated by the Supreme Court in *Plessy v. Ferguson*, that the segregation of African Americans had

---

*Towne v. Eisner, 245 U.S. 418, 425 (1918) (Holmes, J.) (referring to the interpretation of a word rather than a policy).

nothing to do with racial oppression. Bitter experience should remind us, then, that in matters touching race relations there is an especially pressing need to keep the record straight.

The Importance of Motive Inquiry: The Case of the Reagan Administration

A good way to begin setting the record straight is by assessing the motives of those in high public office. Suspicion characterizes the disposition with which I begin that assessment. My suspicion stems from the recognition that racism in America is an enormously powerful ideological institution, considerably older than the political institutions of our republic, and has often influenced the actions of the executive branch and indeed all levels of government. My preexisting distrust is heightened, however, by the particular background of the Reagan administration and, more specifically, by the political biography of Ronald Reagan himself.

As President, Ronald Reagan declared himself "heart and soul in favor of the things that have been done in the name of civil rights and desegregation." This commitment, he maintained, accounted for his opposition to affirmative discrimination. What justifies skepticism toward the President's account is his long history of suspect views on racial issues. His active opposition to racial distinctions *benefiting* African Americans is not matched by analogous opposition to racial distinctions *harming* African Americans. Indeed, a strikingly consistent feature of President Reagan's long political career has been his resistance to practically every major political effort to eradicate racism or to contain its effects. During the height of the civil rights revolution, he opposed the Civil Rights Act of 1964, the Voting Rights Act of 1965, and the Open Housing Act of 1968, legislation that his own assistant attorney general rightly described as "designed to make equal opportunity a reality."

Of course, although opposition to this landmark legislation is itself tremendously revealing, limits exist to the inferences that one can properly draw from positions adopted over twenty years ago. But President Reagan provided additional reasons for distrusting his explanation of his racial policies. Repeatedly his administration showed callous disregard for the particular interests of blacks and resisted measures designed to erode racial hierarchy. These actions included the administration's opposition (1) to the amendments that strengthened and extended the Voting Rights Act, (2) to anything more than the most cramped reading of the Civil Rights Act of 1964, (3) to creating a national holiday honoring Dr. Martin Luther King, Jr., (4) to maintaining the integrity of agencies involved in federal enforcement of civil rights, and (5) to imposing sanctions on South Africa for its policy of apartheid.

Perhaps the most instructive episode was the position the Reagan Administration took in the now infamous *Bob Jones University* case on the issue of tax exemption for private schools that discriminate against blacks. The platform of the Republican party in 1980 promised that its leaders would "halt the unconstitutional regulatory vendetta launched . . . against independent schools." President Reagan fulfilled that pledge by reversing the policy of the Internal Revenue Service (IRS) denying exempt status to discriminatory private schools. The administration stated that it had acted out of a desire to end the IRS's usurpation of powers beyond those authorized by Congress. Subsequent revelations called the honesty of this explanation into doubt. That apparent dishonesty—coupled with the administration's overwhelming defeat in the Supreme Court—turned the tax exemption imbroglio into one of the administration's most politically embarrassing moments. For present purposes, however, the significance of the episode lies in the stark illustration it provides of the underlying impulse behind the Reagan administration's racial policy—an impulse to protect the prerogatives of whites at the least hint of encroachment by claims of racial justice.

There are, of course, alternative explanations to the one advanced above. One could disaggregate the record of Ronald Reagan and his administration and rationalize each position on a case-by-case basis, by reference to concerns having nothing to do with racist sentiments or strategies. Concerns about freedom of association might have prompted Reagan's opposition to the Civil Rights Act of 1964. Concerns about federalism might account for his opposition to the Voting Rights Act of 1965. Concerns about the proper allocation of responsibility between the executive and legislative branches might explain the administration's stance in the tax exemption controversy. And authentic regard for the philosophical premises of individualism might theoretically explain the administration's opposition to affirmative action.

The problem with this mode of defense is that it ignores the strong *systematic* tilt of the administration's actions. It disregards as well the political milieu in which debate over affirmative action and other racial policies has been waged over the past decade—a period during which there has been a discernible attenuation of public commitment to racial justice and, even more troubling, a startling reemergence of overt racial animosity. The Reagan administration's policies reflect, reinforce, and capitalize on widespread feelings that blacks have received an undeserved amount of the nation's attention. Unburdened by the inhibitions imposed by public office, ordinary white citizens have expressed quite openly the feelings that color their analysis of the affirmative action issue. The Reagan administration expertly tapped these feelings for political gain by dint of arguments for race-blindness that were, in fact, exquisitely attuned to the racial sensitivities of the dominant white majority. Those who have ignored racism as an important element of the affirmative action controversy should consider SPONGE (The Society for the Prevention of Niggers Getting Everything), an organization of disaffected whites in the Canarsie section of Brooklyn, New York, whose arresting title is more revealing of at least part of the opposition to affirmative action than many commentators seem willing to acknowledge.

III. Conclusion

In the end, perhaps the most striking feature of the affirmative action debate is the extent to which it highlights the crisis of trust besetting American race relations. Proponents of affirmative action view their opponents with suspicion for good reason. They know that not all of their opponents are racist; they also know that many of them are. Such suspicions corrode reasoned discourse. Contending claims to truth and justice are often reduced by opposing camps to disguised grasps for power and privilege. It would be a mistake, however, to suppose that the antidote to such corrosion is willful blindness to pretext. The only thing that will enable affirmative action—or any similarly controversial policy—to be debated in an atmosphere free of suspicion is for the surrounding social context to be decisively transformed. The essential element of this transformation is the creation of a sentiment of community strong enough to enable each group to entrust its fate to the good faith and decency of the other—the sort of feeling that in the 1960s impelled groups of black and white mothers to exchange their children during civil rights marches. Only the presence of such sentiment can enable the force of persuasion to supplant the force of distrust.

At this point, *even if* a demonstration of policy and fact decisively pointed toward eliminating affirmative action, many of its proponents might well refuse to recognize such a showing and continue to support preferential treatment. Their reaction would stem in large measure from their fears regarding the ulterior motives of their opponents. This is another reason why, as a practical matter, motive is so important. As long as suspect motivation justifiably remains a point of apprehension, inquiry into "the merits" of affirmative action will play a peripheral, instrumental role in the resolution of the controversy.

FEMINISM AND AFFIRMATIVE ACTION

Alice Kessler-Harris

Alice Kessler-Harris is professor of history and director of women's studies at Rutgers University in New Brunswick, New Jersey. She is author of *Out to Work: A History of Wage-Earning Women in the United States; Women Have Always Worked: A Historical Overview;* and *A Woman's Wage: Historical Meanings and Social Consequences.* "Feminism and Affirmative Action" was written for *Debating Affirmative Action.*

When on March 25, 1987, the Supreme Court ruled that in order to correct "a manifest imbalance in traditionally segregated job categories" Diane Joyce was entitled to a job dispatching road crews in California, it made legal history. Affirmative action plans that took into account the sex of underrepresented workers were, the Court signified, to be treated with the same seriousness as those that took race into account.

The decision aroused immediate controversy. Norman Podhoretz, editor of *Commentary,* described the Court's 6-to-3 decision as "a complete perversion" of Title VII of the 1964 Civil Rights Act. The normally conservative Chamber of Commerce of the United States hailed it as "very positive for business."

Among women there was also intense debate over the decision that gave Diane Joyce her job promotion over a male candidate whose ranking was actually two points above hers. Like many women's rights activists, Judith Lichtman of the Women's Legal Defense Fund described her group as "ecstatic." Others were more cautious. Linda Chavez, former executive director of the U.S. Commission on Civil Rights, called it "the worst affirmative action decision ever issued by the Supreme Court."

It is hardly surprising that the Court's 1987 decision over Diane Joyce's job aroused such bitter feelings. Since 1964, when Title VII of the Civil Rights Act provided the basis for legal action against employers who discriminated against particular groups of workers, women had generally been treated like other disadvantaged groups under the law. The Civil Rights Act was designed to meet the overwhelming needs of people of color, and as the Supreme Court addressed the act's implications, it did so with this history in mind. Women, who had fought to be included, were, so to speak, brought along for the ride. The decision to give Diane Joyce hiring preference over a comparably qualified man changed this pattern. Equally important, it stimulated the question that had been begging for an answer: Is there anything different about affirmative action when it speaks to issues of gender rather than to those of race?

The answer to this question is rooted in the historical treatment of women in the work force. In the early twentieth century, women social reformers and some trade union women fought for protective labor legislation that would provide shorter hours, rest periods, and proper sanitation and ventilation for women who worked in stores and factories. In a period when the courts rigidly denied such protections to male workers on the grounds that they were free to negotiate their own working conditions on an individual basis, special legislation for women workers seemed like the best way to protect their health and their capacity to care for their families. But the cost of this legislation was steep. The remedies placed all women into a legally protected "class." They required that women, even those well situated to compete freely, give up their right to be treated as individuals in the work force. All women were to be protected because the state had an interest in their capacity to function effectively as mothers.

For the most part the compromise continued into the 1940s and 1950s, when working conditions became the subject of regulation for both sexes. But among feminists and social reformers, legislative protections that applied only to women workers engendered a lasting debate over whether special treatment was a privilege that enabled wage-earning women to continue functioning as family members or whether it ultimately disadvantaged women who wished to compete with men for jobs.

When Title VII of the Civil Rights Act prohibited discrimination against women in the labor force, it also provided the basis for wiping out the remnants of the special-treatment legislation enacted two generations before. Title VII removed, after all, formal barriers to the entrance of women, leveling the playing field and allowing women to compete for the first time on an equal basis.

But the equal opportunity Title VII provided soon became problematic. Women fell uncomfortably within the framework of emerging civil rights law. They had been excluded from earlier executive orders barring discrimination issued by Presidents Roosevelt and Truman. Nor were they mentioned in President John Kennedy's Executive Order 10925 of 1961. That order, the first to require federal contractors to take affirmative action to ensure equity in their work forces, spoke only to issues of race and ethnicity. The 1964 Civil Rights Act incorporated sex as a protected category after Representatives Martha Griffiths and Katherine St. George encouraged Virginia's Howard Smith to include it. Though Smth probably hoped that adding sex would defeat the whole bill, the women who supported it on the House floor were always clear that they did not want to exclude women. Prohibiting discrimination on the grounds of sex provided women for the first time with federal legislative protection against intentional discrimination.

Before 1987, the law was unevenly developed, ambiguously interpreted, and indifferently enforced with regard to women. President Johnson's 1965 Executive Order 11246, issued less than a month after the 1964 bill went into effect, mandated that employers take action to correct statistical disparities between the pool of minority workers available for jobs and the numbers actually employed. It failed to include women. The Equal Employment Opportunities Commission, created by the 1964 Civil Rights Act to enforce its provisions, began its work by paying attention almost exclusively to race and ethnicity. And while President Johnson's 1967 Executive Order 11375 did mandate preferential action on behalf of women as well as minorities, most analysts concede that little regulatory muscle existed until 1972, when an Equal Employment Act was passed by Congress. This act gave the EEOC power to sue in court and required federal contractors with as few as fifteen employees to set "goals and timetables" for correcting underrepresentation. Its provisions explicitly covered women.

From that point on, women, once again placed in a protected category, began to use the law aggressively to confront discriminatory practices and effects. But unlike opponents of race discrimination, feminist advocates first had to deal with the meaning of discrimination itself. Did the term apply to behavior occasioned by long-standing cultural biases predicated on women's traditional roles in the family? Were employers who favored male breadwinners for the most lucrative jobs and training guilty of discrimination? What about those who balked at hiring women with small children? Was sexual harassment a form of discrimination? What about displaying "pinups" in the workplace?

Over the span of twenty years, state and federal courts slowly evolved a definition of discrimination that took account of biology and cultural roles. When the Supreme Court articulated this stance in its 1987 decision, it brought into focus fundamental tensions inherent in women's full participation in the labor force and propelled a reexamination of some basic assumptions around which Americans have tended to agree. These include the meritocratic paradigm that has traditionally legitimized workforce opportunity, the meanings and salience of gender difference, and the validity of firmly held notions of individual rights.

To most people, for most of the recent past, favoring men for many jobs did not seem inherently unfair. Employers' behavior merely confirmed deeply held social beliefs about women's roles in the family. As late as 1971, only 4 percent of the general public believed sex discrimination was a problem. Ten years later, not quite half of all men and just a little more than half of all women thought that discrimination barred women's access to good jobs. This transformation of belief may well have pushed the Court into including women. Still, its effects are complicated. Many white women did not suffer the cultural disadvantages imposed by racial stigmas. Compared with people of color, they tended to be far less educationally disadvantaged than men of their cohort. Some benefited from their family positions and wealth as well as from traditions of continuity. At the same time, even well-educated white women could be condemned to poverty by an unsympathetic job market, revealing a flaw in the notion that the market always rewarded merit.

Does the changing cultural climate offered by court protection account for the immediate improvement in the economic position of young, especially white, women? In the well-educated professional and managerial sectors women quickly increased their representation in formerly segregated jobs. Since 1970, the number earning advanced professional degrees has risen by more than 50 percent. As a result, women have become lawyers, architects, doctors, and managers in large numbers. Between 1975 and 1985, a period when the real income of most workers stagnated, that of young, college-educated women soared by 20 percent. For educated women in their twenties, income now approaches parity with that of men. But all of this might well be a result of class and race privilege rather than of affirmative action.

Less-educated and less-skilled women have not fared as well as those with cultural and social advantages. As jobs in the traditional blue-collar sectors have declined, fewer opportunities are available to women trained in these areas. Gains from affirmative action programs often succumbed to stringent seniority rules when layoffs occurred. In the skilled crafts, where affirmative action programs have been targeted, women made tiny, but measurable, gains between 1972 and the early 1980s, doubling their representation in the crafts from about 2 to 4 percent. A worsening economy and lack of enforcement created slippage by the mid-1980s. These job losses were compensated for by new jobs (often part time and contingent) in such traditional female areas as personal services and retail and wholesale trade. Poverty among women expanded in a decade of opportunity.

Where it is enforced and where economic opportunity permits, affirmative action has worked. It has had a positive impact for black women. Their representation in sales, clerical, laborer, and white-collar trainee positions has increased at double the rate of white women. But as hopeful as this seems at first glance, it compares unfavorably with the increases recorded for employment of black men. Though neither number is impressive, the modest gains among people of color of both sexes, as compared to white women, reveal the constraints on affirmative action programs when they address issues of gender. Their somewhat paradoxical result is more jobs at less pay for women of color.

If, however ineffectively, affirmative action has worked better for people of color than for women of any race, it remains vulnerable to challenge as a remedy for issues of sex discrimination. It was one thing to forbid, as Title VII had done, discrimination on the grounds of sex, among other categories. And it was unproblematic for the law to ask courts to remedy discrimination by providing victims with jobs and back pay. But when the law began to require employers to adopt preemptive strategies designed to correct underrepresentation of certain groups, it sharpened the differences between the treatment of people of color of both sexes and the treatment of women of any color. Preemptive strategies based on sex required employers and courts to decide not only what jobs women were trained to take, but what jobs, given family circumstances, they might be able and willing to do. An affirmative action program that addressed constraints in women's work would have to compensate not only for deficits in education and training but ensure as well that women were not disadvantaged by both their ability to bear children and their primary responsibility for rearing them.

In 1978 Congress agreed to reduce the negative job effects of childbearing by insisting that employers treat pregnant women comparably with others who had the same ability (or inability) to work. The Pregnancy Disability Act, passed in that year as an amendment to Title VII, gave women the right to demand institutional accommodations to their childbearing roles. The law seemed relatively uncontroversial at first, but it became the basis of several conflicts around more significant benefits granted by states.

California, for example, permitted women to take four months of unpaid leave around childbirth, requiring employers to give them back the same or comparable jobs. When Lillian Garland took a leave in 1982, the bank for which she worked declared that it could not give her an appropriate job and sued the state for forcing them to violate the provisions of Title VII and the Pregnancy Disability Act. Providing a benefit for women that was not offered to men forced the bank, its lawyers argued, to discriminate against men. Lawyers from a variety of women's groups split on the issue. Some agreed with the state that since pregnancy was a condition that affected only women, to grant them special privileges merely equalized the disadvantages they experienced in the workplace. Others, without siding with the bank, suggested that the appropriate remedy was to treat pregnancy like any other disability and to extend the benefits of the California law to men similarly disabled. In January 1987, the Supreme Court decided for the state, clearing the way for Lillian Garland to get her job back without forcing the state to extend its provisions to men. For women it was an ambiguous legal victory. Had they won special treatment? Or were vital gender differences simply being acknowledged?

Affirmative action provisions that speak less directly to pregnancy—the essential difference—can leave women vulnerable to retaliation. For example, legislation such as the 1993 Family and Medical Leave Act, which allows workers to fulfill family responsibilities, seems gender neutral on its face. But because the leaves the act permits are unpaid, women are expected to take advantage of them far oftener than men, leading some to believe that employers will favor male workers for a series of jobs.

This is an altogether reasonable fear. In constructing hypothetical pools of available workers against which they are asked to compare the number of women or minorities in their own work force, employers don't just look for workers who have the skills and education they need. They look for those who can blend into the social milieu of the factory or the office. If women are perceived as causing special problems, they are immediately put at a disadvantage.

The courts are still trying to measure the effects of employers' assessments. When the EEOC brought suit against Sears Roebuck and Company in 1979, for example, the company agreed that the proportion of women working in lucrative commission sales jobs was lower than that among lesser-paying retail clerks. But, it argued, women were simply not interested in the better-paying jobs. In the company's view, they had not been socialized for steady work. They lacked the competitive spirit, the verve of successful salespersons. The appeals court decided for Sears. But when the General Telephone Company of the Northwest defended itself against a similar suit two years later, another appeals court rejected the company's argument that men and women had different career interests and could not be expected to work at the same jobs.

Similar subjective qualifications provided the defense of a Fort Worth, Texas, bank against the allegations of Clara

Watson, a black bank teller. This time the Supreme Court ducked. Watson won her case, but not on the grounds of sex discrimination. In the current shift from an economy based on production to one that rotates around services, Eleanor Holmes Norton points out, employers increasingly rely on subjective judgments, dramatically increasing the possibilities for introducing cultural bias into employment decisions.

Finally, women face the problem that expanding opportunities for one group limits the opportunities of unprotected individuals. What justifies providing opportunities for women where none exist for men? This question is raised to counter the claims of all minority groups, but it takes on particular meaning with regard to women, partly because issues of fairness and of the primacy of women's family roles have not yet been resolved. Women are such a large group that preferential treatment for them seems to place an enormous burden on the rights of men to compete freely for jobs and to be treated equitably in the labor market. Since many women live with and rely on the support of men who see themselves as the victims of "reverse discrimination," preferences for women often make them targets for anger and raise questions as to whether the government is not promoting what one Supreme Court justice called proportional representation in the job market.

Counterbalancing this argument are the responsibilities borne by the large number of women who now support themselves and their families. One in four children currently lives in a household supported by a woman, and given the increase in poverty among children, the effort to provide more jobs for women has a practical as well as an ideological justification. The problem comes in trying to get approval of affirmative action legislation that acknowledges this situation. So long as our culture says female job holding is less valuable than that of men, politicians will tend to underfund legislation that provides new opportunities for women.

More subtly, but just as importantly, government requirements that private employers hire more women remain problematic because they appear to contravene long-standing cultural preferences for traditional family life. The government is put in the paradoxical position of supporting women's work even at the cost of the families it theoretically wants to preserve. The result is a situation in which women can't win. They are, on the one hand, held responsible for the breakdown of the family, and, on the other hand, they are put in a position where they cannot both meet family responsibilities and work.

In this context opposition to affirmative action for women becomes extraordinarily formidable. Its proponents are able to cite their support of such conservative principles as faith in traditional family values, belief in a competitive, nonpreferential job market, and limits on government intervention in the lives of ordinary people. In turn, women on both sides of the political spectrum find themselves occupying ambivalent positions.

Ambivalence toward affirmative action reflects the unsettled nature of attitudes toward women at large, especially over the relationship between wage work and family life. Justice Antonin Scalia caught this ambivalence in his scathing dissent to the Johnson decision. "There are of course those," he noted, "who believe that the social attitudes which cause women themselves to avoid certain jobs and to favor others are as nefarious as conscious, exclusionary discrimination. Whether or not that is so (and there is assuredly no consensus on the point equivalent to our national consensus against intentional discrimination), the two phenomena are certainly distinct."

There is the nub of the disagreement. While many

women believe that social attitudes embedded in our families, schools, religious institutions, and the media construct the subtle biases that restrain women's capacity to choose jobs, others disagree. The state misuses its power, they suggest, when it uses affirmative action to erode deeply rooted social traditions.

However desirable affirmative action seems in the abstract, its practical victories will wait upon shifts in the cultural context within which men and women live and work. That leaves us with two choices: We can support judicial and legislative discussion in order to accelerate the rate of change in the context; or we can work on the social issues that have led women to require affirmative action to begin with.

Perhaps we need to do both.

PART TWO

JOBS AND EQUITY

EQUALITY AND IDENTITY

Cornel West

Cornel West is professor of religion and director of Afro-
American Studies at Princeton. His books include
Prophetic Fragments and *Race Matters*. "Equality and Iden-
tity" first appeared in *The American Prospect*, Spring 1992.

The fundamental crisis in black America is twofold: too
much poverty and too little self-love. The urgent problem
of black poverty is primarily due to the distribution of
wealth, power, and income—a distribution influenced by
the racial caste system that denied opportunities to most
"qualified" black people until two decades ago.

The historic role of American progressives is to promote
redistributive measures that enhance the standard of living
and quality of life for the have-nots and have-too-littles.
Affirmative action was one such redistributive measure that
surfaced in the heat of battle in the 1960s among those
fighting for racial equality. Like earlier de facto affirmative
action measures in the American past—contracts, jobs,
and loans to select immigrants granted by political ma-
chines; subsidies to certain farmers; FHA mortgage loans
to specific home buyers; or GI Bill benefits to particular

courageous Americans—recent efforts to broaden access
to America's prosperity have been based upon preferential
policies. Unfortunately, these policies always benefit middle-class Americans disproportionately. The political power
of big business in big government circumscribes redistributive measures and thereby tilts these measures away from
the have-nots and have-too-littles.

Every redistributive measure is a compromise with and
concession from the caretakers of American prosperity—
that is, big business and big government. Affirmative action
was one such compromise and concession achieved after
the protracted struggle of American progressives and liberals in the courts and in the streets. Visionary progressives
always push for substantive redistributive measures that
make opportunities available to the have-nots and have-too-
littles, such as more federal support to small farmers, or
more FHA mortgage loans to urban dwellers as well as
suburban home buyers. Yet in the American political system, where the powers that be turn a skeptical eye toward
any program aimed at economic redistribution, progressives must secure whatever redistributive measures they
can, ensure their enforcement, then extend their benefits
if possible.

If I had been old enough to join the fight for racial
equality in the courts, the legislatures, and the boardrooms
in the 1960s (I *was* old enough to be in the streets), I
would have favored—as I do now—a class-based affirmative
action in principle. Yet in the heat of battle in American
politics, a redistributive measure in principle with no power
and pressure behind it means no redistributive measure at
all. The prevailing discriminatory practices during the sixties, whose targets were working people, women, and people of color, were atrocious. Thus, an *enforceable* race-
based—and later gender-based—affirmative action policy
was the best possible compromise and concession.

Progressives should view affirmative action as neither a major solution to poverty nor a sufficient means to equality. We should see it primarily playing a negative role—namely, to insure that discriminatory practices against women and people of color are abated. Given the history of this country, it is a virtual certainty that without affirmative action racial and sexual discrimination will return with a vengeance. Even if affirmative action fails significantly to reduce black poverty or contributes to the persistence of racism in the workplace, without affirmative action black access to America's prosperity would be even more difficult and racism in the workplace would persist anyway.

This claim is not based on any cynicism toward my white fellow citizens; rather, it rests upon America's historically weak will toward racial justice and substantive redistributive measures. This is why an attack on affirmative action is an attack on redistributive efforts by progressives unless there is a real possibility of enacting and enforcing a more wide-reaching affirmative action policy.

In American politics, progressives must not only cling to redistributive ideals, but also fight for those policies that—out of compromise and concession—imperfectly conform to those ideals. Liberals who give only lip service to these ideals, trash the policies in the name of realpolitik, or reject the policies as they perceive a shift in the racial bellwether, give up precious ground too easily. And they do so even as the sand is disappearing under our feet on such issues as regressive taxation, layoffs or take-backs from workers, and cutbacks in health and child care.

Affirmative action is not the most important issue for black progress in America, but it is part of a redistributive chain that must be strengthened if we are to confront and eliminate black poverty. If there were social democratic redistributive measures that wiped out black poverty, and if racial and sexual discrimination could be abated through the goodwill and meritorious judgments of those in power, affirmative action would be unnecessary. Although many of my liberal and progressive comrades view affirmative action as a redistributive measure whose time is over or whose life is no longer worth preserving, I question their view because of the persistence of black social misery, and the warranted suspicion that goodwill and fair judgment among the powerful does not loom as large toward women and people of color.

If the elimination of black poverty is a necessary condition of substantive black programs, then the affirmation of black humanity, especially among black people themselves, is a sufficient condition of such progress. Such affirmation speaks to the existential issues of what it means to be a degraded African (man, woman, gay, lesbian, child) in a racist society. How does one affirm oneself without reenacting negative black stereotypes or overreacting to white supremacist ideals?

The difficult and delicate quest for black identity is integral to any talk about racial equality. Yet it is not solely a political or economic matter. The quest for black identity involves self-respect and self-regard, realms inseparable from yet not identical to political power and economic status. The flagrant self-loathing among black middle-class professionals bears witness to this painful process. Unfortunately, black conservatives focus on the issue of self-respect as if it is the one key that opens all doors to black progress. They illustrate the fallacy of trying to open all doors with one key: They wind up closing their eyes to all doors except the one the key fits.

Progressives, for our part, must take seriously the quest for self-respect, even as we train our eye on the institutional causes of black social misery. The issues of black identity— both black self-love and self-contempt—sit alongside black poverty as realities to confront and transform. The uncritical acceptance of self-degrading ideals that call into question black intelligence, possibility, and beauty not only compounds black social misery; it also paralyzes black middle-class efforts to defend broad redistributive measures.

This paralysis takes two forms: black bourgeois preoccupation with white peer approval and black nationalist obsession with white racism.

The first form of paralysis tends to yield a navel-gazing posture that conflates the identity crisis of the black middle class with the state of siege raging in black working-poor and very poor communities. That unidimensional view obscures the need for redistributive measures that significantly affect the majority of blacks, who are working people on the edge of poverty.

The second form of paralysis precludes any meaningful coalition with white progressives because of an undeniable white racist legacy of the modern West. The anger this truth engenders impedes any effective way of responding to the crisis in black America. Broad redistributive measures require principled coalitions, including multiracial alliances. Without such measures, black America's sufferings deepen. White racism indeed contributes to this suffering. Yet an obsession with white racism often comes at the expense of more broadly based alliances to affect social change, and borders on a tribal mentality. The more xenophobic versions of this viewpoint simply mirror the white supremacist ideals we are opposing and preclude any movement toward redistributive goals.

How one defines oneself influences what analytical weight one gives to black poverty. Any progressive discussion about the future of racial equality must speak to black poverty and black identity. My views on the necessity and limits of affirmative action in the present moment are informed by how substantive redistributive measures and human affirmative efforts can be best defended and expanded.

AFFIRMATIVE ACTION GOALS AND TIMETABLES: TOO TOUGH? NOT TOUGH ENOUGH!

Clarence Thomas

Clarence Thomas was appointed to the Supreme Court by George Bush in 1991. He was assistant secretary for civil rights in the Education Department from 1981 to 1982 and chairman of the Equal Employment Opportunity Commission from 1982 to 1990. "Affirmative Action Goals and Timetables: Too Tough? Not Tough Enough!" first appeared in *Yale Law and Policy Review*, Spring-Summer 1987.

Given all the media hoopla over the Supreme Court's recent approval of racially and sexually defined employment goals and timetables, one would think that a weapon of awesome power and broad scope had been added to the enforcement arsenal of the Equal Employment Opportunity Commission [EEOC or the Commission]. I am sorry to disappoint you, but the availability of goals and timetables will not mean the end of employment discrimination. Goals and timetables, long a popular rallying cry among some who claim to be concerned with the right to equal employment opportunity, have become a sideshow in the war on discrimination. The vast majority of all charges of employment discrimination now filed with the EEOC involve violations for which goals and timetables are not appropriate as a form of relief. Even in those circumstances where goals are available as a remedy, there are generally tougher and more effective alternatives available. Despite my personal disagreement with the Court's approval of numerical remedies, as Chairman of the EEOC, I am nevertheless grateful that the legal debate over goals and timetables has been resolved so that attention can be focused on the facts and the real issues in the EEOC's battle against employment discrimination.

I. Past Uses of Goals and Timetables

To explain why I consider goals and timetables to be at best a relatively weak and limited weapon against existing forms of discrimination, I offer some background on the Commission's enforcement efforts. During the mid- and late-1970s the Commission concentrated its efforts to enforce Title VII on suits that would affect large numbers of people. The EEOC first obtained authority to litigate employment discrimination suits under a 1972 amendment to the Civil Rights Act of 1964. At that time blatant discrimination was still prevalent. Many employers openly maintained "No Blacks/Women Need Apply" policies, and many others had moved such practices underground. Minorities and women were not advancing into the work force in as great numbers as many had hoped.

The Commission, confronted with the enormity of the problem and limitations on its litigation resources, took a "bang for the buck" approach to fighting discrimination. Although Title VII guaranteed *individuals* the right to be free of discrimination in employment, the Commission did not attempt to right every wrong individually, a task for which its litigation machinery was not prepared. Instead, the Commission tried to make quick statistical progress by funneling resources into challenges against the hiring practices of some of the country's largest employers. During this period suits were brought against such companies as American Telephone and Telegraph, General Electric, Ford Motor, General Motors, and Sears Roebuck.

The use of remedies that included racially defined goals and timetables was a necessary consequence of the emphasis on this kind of litigation. Under then-prevailing judicial standards, many of these cases were based solely on statistical disparities. Frequently, all that was known was that members of one group were substantially underrepresented in the employer's work force. It was rarely possible to say which of the many rejected applicants would have been hired absent discrimination, since many of the jobs in question required only unskilled labor and records of unsuccessful job applicants were incomplete. In such cases, back pay for actual victims was not an available form of relief. Therefore, the Commission would agree to settlements or would seek relief under which other members of the victims' class were given positions as substitutes for those who would have been employed had nondiscriminatory selection criteria been used.

This emphasis on "systemic" suits led the Commission to overlook many of the individuals who came to our offices to file charges and seek assistance. If an individual's allegations did not involve a priority issue or apply to other members of a class, the Commission was unlikely to go to bat for the individual in court.

The Commission has now entered a new stage in its enforcement work. Although systemic litigation is still an area of emphasis for the Commission, it no longer need consume our resources to the exclusion of other types of cases. Many of the very large employers who once appeared to discriminate have been brought into compliance through lawsuits and Commissioner Charges. Other large and so-

phisticated employers, in response to the publicity surrounding the Commission's efforts, voluntarily changed
their discriminatory practices and sought to remedy the
continuing effects of those practices. Now, for the first
time, the Commission has the luxury and freedom to fight
to vindicate the Title VII rights of every individual victim
of discrimination. The Commission has committed itself to
a policy of seeking full relief for every victim of discrimination who files a charge. In addition, the Commission has
developed and implemented policies designed to make
itself more effective in obtaining necessary information
from uncooperative employers, thereby speeding along investigations. The new enforcement stance has already begun to have positive effects. In fiscal year 1986 the Commission filed over five hundred suits—more than ever
before—and this year we are ahead of last year's pace.

It is now more likely that the Commission will be able
to identify the discriminatees entitled to back pay or place-
ment after making a finding of discrimination in hiring or
promotion. Our emphasis on helping all individuals who
come to the Commission's offices with claims of discrimination means that in most cases we will know who the
victims are. Even many of our larger class action cases are
set in motion by complaints filed by individuals rather than
by the observation of a statistical disparity. Needless to say,
the Commission's ability to produce flesh-and-blood victims is very helpful when we go to court to prove discrimination.

In addition, most of our cases involve discrimination by
a particular manager or supervisor, rather than a "policy"
of discrimination. Many discriminating employers first responded to Title VII by turning from explicit policies
against hiring minorities and women to unstated ones.
Now even such veiled policies are uncommon; discrimination is left to individual bigots in positions of authority. As

a result, the discrimination that we find today more often has a narrow impact, perhaps influencing only a few hiring decisions, and does not warrant the use of a goal that will affect a great number of subsequent hires or promotions.

II. Weaknesses of Goals and Timetables

Even in those situations in which goals and timetables are available, one should not overlook other remedies in the rush to achieve statistical equality. This is not because goals and timetables are too "tough" a remedy. On the contrary, although group-defined numerical relief is a somewhat imaginative extension of Title VII principles, these remedies are fairly easy on *employers*. In many cases there are tougher and more effective remedies available.

One of the first things I noticed when I came to the Commission was that often it was the employer who pushed for the use of numerical goals in a settlement agreement. Employers seek such a resolution even before the Commission has shown that it can identify actual victims. The reason for this is obvious. In those cases where numerical relief is possible—that is, where there has been a pattern or practice of discrimination affecting a large class—every identified victim has a right to "make whole" relief. Giving back pay to each actual victim can be quite expensive, but the cost of agreeing to hire a certain number of blacks or women is generally *de minimis*. The employer's expense for "make whole" relief may also include extensive hearings to determine who among rejected applicants would have been hired. There is, in other words, an economic incentive for an employer to settle the case before it becomes necessary to identify actual victims. It should therefore come as no surprise that large firms such as E. I. Dupont de Nemours, Inc., and Potomac Electric Company and groups such as the National Association of

Manufacturers were falling over each other to applaud the Court's approval of affirmative action. The recent decisions will decrease the chances that employers will be forced to hire those persons actually discriminated against (who would be entitled to back pay) and will increase the probability that employers will escape fully addressing discrimination by merely hiring a certain number of blacks or women (who are not entitled to back pay). Moreover, the approval of goals and timetables allows yet-undetected discriminators to create a numerical smokescreen for their past or present violations. The use of affirmative action, rather than a victim-specific form of relief, effectively allows employers to shift the cost of the remedy from themselves to the actual victims of their past discrimination, who never receive the back pay and jobs to which they are entitled, and to the qualified persons who will be deprived of an employment opportunity because someone else was given a preference under the remedial plan.

Goals and timetables are sometimes defended, not as a way of making up for yesterday's discrimination, but as a way of monitoring a past discriminator to ensure that he or she is extending an equal opportunity to today's applicants and employees. However, once again, numerical goals are a relatively ineffective way to accomplish the stated ends. The use of goals to monitor a past discriminator is based on the assumption that, absent discrimination, members of various groups would reap the benefits of occupational opportunities in proportion to their representation in the relevant labor market. When the employer begins to hire members of the victimized group at levels that mirror their availability, it is presumed that discrimination has ceased.

Even granting the dubious assumption that, absent discrimination, work-force representation of all groups would precisely mirror their availability in the work force, this policy fails because it allows an employer to hide continuing discrimination behind good numbers. For example, in *Connecticut v. Teal,* the Supreme Court found that while an employer had a good "bottom line" number of black hires, one component of the selection process nevertheless impermissibly discriminated against minorities. A preference for minorities at some other point in the process produced hiring that mirrored availability, but a discriminatory written test had been used that unfairly excluded some blacks from consideration. *As a group,* blacks received their fair share of positions, but the Court recognized that numerical justice did not eviscerate the right of individual black applicants to receive nondiscriminatory consideration. This distinction is not merely abstract. Some better-qualified blacks were eliminated from consideration by the discriminatory test. Giving preference to another, less-qualified, black was little consolation to the qualified person who had been passed over. Moreover, because some of the better qualified blacks were excluded by the invalid test, one can expect that black members of the work force would be less likely to rise to positions of authority where they could help assure fair treatment and hiring of others.

In another case, the Commission found that a fire department that until 1978 had employed no blacks had adopted a policy of reserving a number of positions exclusively for black firefighters. The department held to this quota, and even went so far as to replace blacks who left with other blacks, and whites with other whites, presumably under the impression that this was what was meant by equal opportunity. However, lurking behind the numbers was continued discrimination. The blacks hired under the program were subjected to racial harassment and generally did not advance. One black firefighter, who resigned after four years with the department, said that blacks knew they were there "because they need a quota." The policy, far from eliminating consideration of race in the workplace, actually seems to have encouraged the treatment of blacks as fungible and fundamentally unlike nonblacks.

III. Alternative Enforcement Strategies

Reliance on numerical targets to determine whether a past discriminator has foresworn illegal practices will sometimes lead us to overlook continuing discrimination. One alternative monitoring technique would be to require that the employer submit detailed information on all hiring and promotion decisions. Of course compliance with this requirement is tougher on employers than simply reporting the number of group members hired, but it also provides the Commission with more of the information necessary to determine whether each individual is receiving fair consideration. Evaluating this data would also be more burdensome for the Commission than merely checking to see that a quota had been met. However, in my opinion, it is worth the additional effort to have as much information as possible about a discriminator's activities. At the very least, this approach would provide the statistical evidence that is obtained by using a numerical goal, without resort to an explicitly race-conscious remedy.

Goals are also sometimes extolled for their ability to force a recalcitrant discriminator into line. There are, however, tougher means of deterrence. One such approach would be for courts to impose heavy fines and even jail sentences on discriminators who defy court injunctions against further discrimination. I am not aware of any case where a court has resorted to such measures, and I must wonder why they are so reluctant. To those of us who consider employment discrimination not only unlawful but also a moral abomination, such measures are altogether fitting.

Another way to stop a recalcitrant discriminator would be for a court to hand over control of an employer's personnel operations to a special master. The special master would handle personnel decisions such as hiring and promotion, and we could be certain that discrimination would be discontinued immediately. The use of special masters is provided for by Rule 53 of the Federal Rules of Civil Procedure, and special masters have been used with great success in some school desegregation cases. Wresting personnel decisions from the employer would be tougher and more effective than using the quotas of which employers are so fond.

The courts have also occasionally looked to goals as a means of eliminating the continuing effects of past discrimination. By this is meant two things: first, an employer's reputation for discrimination may discourage members of the victimized group from applying, even after the employer stops discriminating; and second, the results of past discrimination may cause a facially neutral recruitment or selection procedure to adversely affect persons on the basis of race or sex. An example of the latter would occur where past discriminatory hiring practices had produced an all-white work force, which was then perpetuated both by the employer's facially neutral policy of giving hiring preferences to family members of current employees and by a recruitment program consisting largely of referrals from current employees.

Although hiring goals are offered as a solution to this problem, they do not directly address it. Numerical targets are expected to encourage the employer to adopt other facially neutral means of recruitment and hiring that will more rapidly lead to integration of the work force. However, the tougher and more direct approach would be for the Commission to seek specific changes in recruitment and hiring practices. In the example above, a court could require the employer to eliminate the family member preference and place "help wanted" ads in media outlets that reach members of the previously excluded group. Employers naturally prefer numerical goals that leave the particulars of how those goals are to be reached to their discretion. As in *Teal*, many employers will no doubt choose a quick fix that meets the target without actually purging discrimination from the process. By seeking specific changes in recruitment and hiring practices, however, the Commission could ensure the institution of a self-perpetuating fair process, not just the several years' worth of "equal" results that a quota would yield.

Proponents of affirmative action also argue that goals offer a way to compensate for socially created "headwinds" against achievement by certain groups. For example, many blacks attended schools that were denied the resources provided to schools that whites attended, and many women were shepherded away from analytic curricula. Hiring targets are said to be a way to make up for these disadvantages, or headwinds, created by prior discrimination. One problem with this approach, as Professor Drew Days has noted, is that concentrating on societal discrimination rather than the discrimination by a particular institution "discourages the search for evidence of past discriminatory practices and for remedies tailored to rectify that discrimination."

Moreover, there are more effective and direct ways of addressing the problem. To the extent that some have been unfairly deprived of education, training, and other advantages, the obvious solution is to provide training and education to those who have gone without. Rather than offer the individuals pity or handouts, we should provide them with the tools that may allow them to help themselves. The need for remedial education and training is especially urgent as widespread technological advances and the shift from a manufacturing to a services-based economy increasingly affect the employability of the unskilled. In the future, proper skills will be so important that employment preferences will not be able to compensate for their absence. Moreover, to whatever extent we do want to give preferences to compensate those who have been unfairly deprived of certain advantages, we should do so in a manner that is just. Any preferences given should be directly related to the obstacles that have been unfairly placed in those individuals' paths, rather than on the basis of race or gender, or on other characteristics that are often poor proxies for true disadvantage.

Conclusion

The legal debate over affirmative action, which has so long and so bitterly divided those who are concerned with civil rights, is behind us, and there is now an opportunity for cooperation and progress. As we begin, I would like to caution again that numerically based affirmative action is the easy, but rarely the best, solution. Goals and timetables are easy on employers who want to avoid back pay liability and easy on interest groups that are more concerned with advancing group interests than with the rights of particular individuals. They are especially easy on the Commission in that they offer a remedy that requires no lengthy investigation to identify actual victims, no task of crafting specific changes in an employer's practices, and no burden of evaluating reams of records. Unfortunately, the use of numerical goals is tough on those actual victims of discrimination who are never identified or compensated and on those victims down the line for whom filling a quota never quite adds up to a truly equal opportunity. The temptation to do things the easy way is always great, but before we succumb we should remember these victims, and then choose the tougher course that promises to yield genuine and lasting equal opportunities.

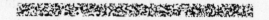

OPENING THE WORK DOOR
FOR WOMEN

Ellen Goodman

Ellen Goodman is associate editor of *The Boston Globe* and a nationally syndicated columnist. Her books include *Turning Points, Close to Home,* and *Making Sense.* "Opening the Work Door for Women" first appeared in her syndicated column, April 2, 1987.

By now I am not surprised at any reaction to affirmative action. The issue has been hanging around so long that attitudes have hardened into reflexes.

Indeed, last week when the Supreme Court made a definitive—at last, at last—decision upholding a voluntary plan in Santa Clara County, California, that takes gender into account in hiring and promoting, the comments sounded as if they were all pre-scripted.

The winner, Diane Joyce, cried out: "A giant victory for womanhood." The loser, Paul Johnson, growled: "Putting it mildly, I think it stinks."

From the left, Judith Lichtman of the Women's Legal Defense Fund volleyed: "Ecstatic."

From the Reagan right, Clarence Thomas of the Equal Employment Opportunity Commission thundered: "Social engineering."

So it wasn't the predictable public noises that struck me this past week. It was rather the undertone. I heard the low and lingering rumble of those who believe that affirmative action is a pole used by inferior candidates to jump over their superiors.

In the wake of this decision, almost all of those opposed to affirmative action, and even some who support it, talk as if the court had simply chosen gender over merit. As if it was allowing employers to favor random women or minorities over qualified men and whites.

These are the same perverse or reverse rumblings heard in a thousand offices when someone "new" gets a post from which "their kind" was excluded. At least one disgruntled co-worker is sure to suggest that "if Diane Joyce had been Don Joyce, she wouldn't have her promotion today."

With this widespread sort of sentiment, it is possible to win the advantages of affirmative action in the courts and lose them in the public consciousness.

But if this case can clear up the fuzzy legal status of plans such as the Santa Clara County one, it can also be used to clarify the whole peculiar matter of "qualifications."

Consider the protagonists, Diane Joyce and Paul Johnson. When the job of road dispatcher came open in 1979, Diane, a forty-two-year-old widow, and Paul, a fifty-four-year-old, were among twelve applicants. Nine of the twelve were considered "qualified." They went before a board and got ranked. Paul tied for second with a 75 and Diane came in right behind with a 73. This is how Paul got the public title of "more qualified."

These very objective, even scientific-sounding numbers were assigned by a very subjective oral interviewing process. In the real world, there is little pure and perfect ranking of qualifications.

Paul and Diane were then given a second interview by

three agency supervisors. Who were these arbiters of merit? The same men who had been selecting and promoting the candidates for skilled work at this agency throughout its recent history. Not one of their 238 skilled workers was female.

Diane, who was also the first woman to be a road-maintenance worker, had reportedly had some run-ins with two of the three men. Indeed, one is said to have called her "a rabble-rousing, skirt-wearing person," whatever that might mean.

As you might have predicted from this history, the board unanimously chose Paul. So it is not shocking that the county, instead, gave Diane the job. Its affirmative-action plan was made for the Diane Joyces, excellent candidates for jobs in a carefully kept male preserve.

The scales of tradition were balanced against her; the affirmative-action plan did just what it was intended to do, added weight to her side, to open up the door for women.

As the Brennan opinion makes clear, the plan didn't discharge a white male, it didn't set up quotas, and, most of all, it didn't give preference to women whose only credential was in their chromosomes. It said, in essence, that a subjective two-point difference between Diane and Paul wasn't as important as a 238-job difference between men and women.

I think this distinction is important, because there is something insidious about the "qualification" issue. For most of history, the men in power determined that women were intrinsically disqualified for "men's jobs." Eventually we labeled that attitude discrimination. But when we implement plans to open up the work world, many carry along the closed mind.

Women, such as Diane Joyce, who were once barred on account of their sex, are now told they were chosen only on account of their sex. Permit me a groan.

After this decision, Charles Murray, a conservative political scientist, commented that "affirmative action is just leaking a poison into the system." But the poison was already there. It's wearing the same old label: prejudice.

TITLE VII OF THE CIVIL RIGHTS ACT OF 1964: FROM PROHIBITING TO REQUIRING RACIAL DISCRIMINATION IN EMPLOYMENT

Lino A. Graglia

Lino A. Graglia is A. Dalton Cross Professor of Law, University of Texas Law School, and the author of *Disaster by Decree: The Supreme Court Decisions on Race and Schools.* "Title VII of the Civil Rights Act of 1964: From Prohibiting to Requiring Racial Discrimination in Employment" first appeared in *Harvard Journal of Law and Public Policy,* Winter 1991.

The modern law of racial discrimination began with the Supreme Court's decision in *Brown v. Board of Education of Topeka,* which prohibited compulsory racial segregation in public schools. It soon became clear that *Brown* stood for the principle that all racial discrimination by government is unconstitutional. The principle that government should not discriminate on the basis of race—a principle strengthened by the Hitler experience—proved so appealing as to be irresistible. It led, against all odds, to a civil rights revolution, and to the enactment of the Civil Rights Act of 1964, the greatest civil rights legislation in our history. In the 1964 Act, Congress adopted and ratified the

Brown nondiscrimination principle and extended it to almost all areas of public life, including discrimination by private persons in places of public accommodation and employment.

The history of the law of racial discrimination since the 1964 Act, however, is the history of a Supreme Court–led counterrevolution. The Court has converted the *Brown* nondiscrimination principle and the various provisions of the Act that embodied it into essentially their opposites: authorizations or even requirements of racial discrimination. The Court has never admitted (indeed, it has always denied) that it was making such a change, always insisting that it was merely continuing to enforce the *Brown* principle. The result is that a regime of permissible or compulsory racial discrimination has been established by the Court in the name of enforcing constitutional and statutory prohibitions against such discrimination, a judicial feat without parallel in the history of law.

Like the revolution itself, the civil rights counterrevolution began with the schools. With the 1964 Act, the era of "all deliberate speed" was over. Compulsory school segregation quickly came to an end throughout the South and compliance with *Brown* was finally achieved. The end of compulsory racial segregation in the schools did not result, however, in a high degree of racial integration in the schools. Residential racial concentration meant that racial separation in the schools would continue to exist in the South as it had always existed in the North—one-race neighborhoods necessarily produce one-race neighborhood schools. The triumph of *Brown*, therefore, was found dissatisfying, and the Supreme Court—widely perceived more as a moral leader than as a Court, as a result of *Brown*—succumbed to the urgings of many that it undertake a new crusade. The crucial move from prohibiting segregation to requiring integration—compulsory racial discrimination in the name of enforcing a prohibition against racial discrimination—was made in the 1968 case of *Green v. County School Board of New Kent County*. The Court held that the complete elimination of racial discrimination from the operation of a school system no longer constituted compliance with *Brown* when all-white and, more significantly, all-black schools continued to exist. *Brown*, it appeared, was now to be understood not as prohibiting, but as *requiring* racial discrimination by government when necessary to achieve a high (though undefined) degree of school racial integration or "balance."

The Court's new requirement was not identified and justified as a requirement of integration for its own sake, however, which would have been applicable everywhere, but as a requirement of "desegregation," which would presumably be applicable only in the South. This enabled the Court to avoid the politically impossible task of qualifying *Brown* as prohibiting official racial discrimination only when it is used to separate the races, not when used to mix them. It also enabled the Court to avoid having to justify a constitutional requirement of integration in terms of expected benefits; the Court's justification—inaccurate as a matter of fact and senseless as a matter of policy—was, instead, that it was merely "remedying" (undoing) the compulsory segregation that was prohibited by *Brown*.

Three years later, the Court carried *Green* to its logical conclusion in *Swann v. Charlotte-Mecklenburg Board of Education*. In *Swann*, the Court held, incredibly, that "desegregation" requires that public schoolchildren be excluded from their neighborhood schools because of their race and transported across large school districts to achieve a near-perfect racial balance. Title IV of the 1964 Act, however, defines "desegregation" as "the assignment of students to public schools . . . without regard to their race," and adds (just to be doubly sure) that desegregation "shall not mean the assignment of students to public schools in order to overcome racial imbalance." The Act goes on to insist, still again, that it does not authorize federal courts to order the transportation of students for racial balance. Despite these caveats, in *Swann,* a unanimous Supreme Court held that court-ordered assignment and transportation of children to schools by race to increase racial balance were not inconsistent with the Act. "Congress," the Court said, without citation and without the slightest basis in fact, "was concerned that the Act might be read as creating a right of action under the Fourteenth Amendment in the situation of so-called 'de facto segregation'. . . ." If this brazen defiance of congressional intent did not constitute an impeachable offense—as indicated by the fact that the protests of Senator Sam Ervin and other representatives of the South got nowhere in Congress—then the Court had nothing to fear as it turned its attention to the Act's other titles. On moral crusades, morality is often the first casualty.

The Court then did to Title VI of the 1964 Act what it had done to Title IV in *Green* and *Swann.* In *Regents of the University of California v. Bakke,* the Court held that Title VI's requirement that "no person" be discriminated against on grounds of race by institutions receiving federal funds did not apply to discrimination against whites. The Court similarly perverted Title VII in *Griggs v. Duke Power Company* and *United Steelworkers v. Weber.* In *Griggs,* the Court held that Title VII's prohibition of racial discrimination in employment does not mean that employers must ignore race in setting employment qualifications, but that they must take race into account, and that they may be required to eliminate standard employment criteria that blacks as a group find difficult to meet, even though sufficient numbers of whites meeting the criteria are available. In *Weber,* the Court carried this "affirmative action" approach to its logical conclusion by holding that Title VII does not prohibit racial discrimination against whites. In the tradition of *Swann* and *Bakke,* Justice Brennan explained for the Court that a ruling in direct conflict with the plain terms of the Act may nonetheless be required by its "spirit."

Griggs established the "adverse impact" or "effects" test for prohibited racial discrimination, disallowing the use of employment criteria that proportionately more blacks than whites cannot meet, unless the employer can prove to the satisfaction of various administrative agencies and the courts that the criteria are "job related." Opponents of *Griggs* contend that racial discrimination cannot properly be found on the basis of the use of nonracial criteria unless a finding of a "racially discriminatory intent" is made. The distinction between the effects test and the intent test is not, however, as clear as it might seem at first glance.

A racially discriminatory act is, quite simply, an action taken on the basis of race. Racial discrimination is, of course, most easily found when it is explicit, that is, when the challenged act is based on a rule or requirement that "on its face" classifies on the basis of race. It is not reasonable to insist, however, that racial discrimination can properly be found only where it is explicit. An employer could not, for example, without good reason, refuse to hire all applicants living in a defined residential area that happened to be all black, even though the explicit discrimination would be solely in terms of geography. In such a case, an effects theorist would find prohibited racial discrimination on the basis of unjustified disparate impact. An intent theorist would undoubtedly also find racial discrimination, but only after first finding a racially discriminatory intent. That intent, however, could and should be found on the basis that the geographic discrimination has a disparate racial impact and apparently cannot be justified as a criterion for employment. This is, of course, the same as the effects test.

Purporting to make the legal consequences of acts turn on the actor's purpose or intent is, in this area as elsewhere, highly problematic. The issue is not whether the actor meant to do what he did (the setting of employment qualifications is always deliberate), but rather why he did what he clearly meant to do. The search is for the "subjective intent" or state of mind. This search raises serious questions about exactly what is being looked for, how to go about looking, and what the purpose of the search is. Modern psychology teaches that it is often difficult to know one's own motives, much less those of another individual or, even worse, of a group. The fact that the "philosophy of mind" is a major branch of philosophical study may be taken as a sufficient indication that it is a mysterious subject involving a possibly nonexistent entity.

The law usually handles supposed issues of subjective intent by stating that rational adults are presumed to intend the natural and foreseeable consequences of their acts (indeed, in what sense can one be said not to intend consequences one knowingly brings about?). But this, of course, is to introduce the issue of intent only to eliminate it, to make legal consequences in fact turn only on conduct. *Personnel Administrator v. Feeney* illustrates this difficulty. In *Feeney,* the Court attempted to give meaning to a supposed requirement of "discriminatory purpose" by stating that it "implies more than intent as volition or intent as awareness of consequences. It implies that the decisionmaker . . . selected or reaffirmed a particular course of action at least in part 'because of,' and not merely 'in spite of,' its adverse effects upon an identifiable group." In other words, the issue is not whether the actor deliberately brought about a particular result, but whether he desired or deplored (though obviously not enough to refrain from the act) the result that he caused. But why should a state of mind, whatever that may be, be determinative? The law has enough to do in regulating conduct on the basis of its objective effects without also seeking to regulate on the basis of "mental states." Why should an employer's use of an educational qualification that works to upgrade the work force, but also to exclude blacks disproportionately, be legal if the employer is a member of the NAACP, but not if he is a member of the Ku Klux Klan?

The true difference between an effects test and an intent test is the different level of justification proponents of the tests typically demand for employment criteria having disparate racial impact. The effects theorist would require justification of such criteria by the employer, and make justification difficult or virtually impossible. The intent theorist would find standard employment criteria presumptively valid, requiring no justification. Those who seek to expand employer liability under Title VII by expanding the definition of racial discrimination to include "unjustified disparate impact" will necessarily adopt a very restrictive view of justification. It is an inherent drawback of civil rights legislation that those who will want to enforce it will also want to expand its coverage, with the virtually invariable result that a needed social reform becomes a socially destructive force.

The tragedy of the Civil Rights Act of 1964 is that it fell into the hands of bureaucrats and judges who saw the total abolition of racial discrimination by government and business as much too limited a goal, and saw proportional representation by race in all institutions and activities as a more desirable objective. One example of this attitude can be seen in the actions of the Equal Employment Opportunity Commission (EEOC), which is, among other government entities, responsible for administering Title VII. For some years, the EEOC was directed by Eleanor Holmes Norton, to whom attempts to justify employment criteria disparately impacting blacks were little more than devices by which employers sought to circumvent *Griggs* and deny blacks employment. Unfortunately, the continued objective of the civil rights bureaucracy, aided and abetted by judges equally eager to improve on the work of Congress, is to make justification so difficult and expensive as not to be feasible or worthwhile, and to give employers no realistic choice except to hire a minimum quota of blacks in all positions. The objective, in other words, is not to *prevent*, as authorized by law, but to *require* the practice of racial discrimination.

On the other hand, intent theorists who are genuinely interested in preventing racial discrimination would hold that standard employment criteria, such as literacy, verbal and arithmetical skills, educational qualifications, and absence of a record of criminal convictions, are ordinarily so obviously justified as to require no further justification. There can be no doubt that employers reasonably may and usually will prefer literate to illiterate employees, for example, regardless of the duties of a particular job, and totally apart from any consideration of race. Literate employees may reasonably be assumed to be better employees, regardless of their particular positions, because, for example, it may make them eligible for advancement to higher positions. Such employment criteria, therefore, can never properly be held to constitute racial discrimination. A judge who holds otherwise is simply usurping the employer's power to set employment qualifications, and making a policy judgment that the employer's interest in efficiency should be sacrificed in the interest of increased employment opportunities for blacks. The *Griggs* decision permitting such a holding is the result not of a good faith effort to enforce Title VII, but of the determination of the Justices to convert Title VII into what Congress had explicitly assured the country it would not be, a requirement of racial preferences in employment.

Although *Griggs* converts Title VII from a nondiscrimination to a compulsory discrimination measure, Congress has not acted to disavow that result. Instead, following the Court's lead, Congress in 1977 enacted for the first time an "affirmative action" racial quota measure of its own, requiring racial preferences in awarding federally funded public works projects. Racial preferences, therefore, can no longer be condemned simply as the product of judicial misbehavior—although they almost surely would not exist except for judicial misbehavior, as in *Bakke*—they must be considered on their own merits.

America can be said to have been born not only in glory as a land of freedom, but also in sin as a land of slavery. Racial prejudice remains our most serious and intractable domestic problem, an ominous cloud overhanging American freedom and prosperity. Our peace and security, to say nothing of our ideals, require that we act to improve the situation of the black underclass. Doing so requires finding a means to improve their employment opportunities, because both blacks and whites must be given the opportunity to prosper. The granting of racial preferences in employment, however, will almost certainly hinder rather than advance that objective. Racial preferences necessarily make our industries less competitive in an increasingly competitive world. Increased employment opportunities for those at the bottom of the economic ladder require that we remain competitive. More important, what blacks in lower economic classes require most, like everyone else, is respect: both self-respect and the respect of others. Granting racial preferences undermines the ability of blacks to attain such respect.

Perhaps the most serious consequence of racial preferences, however, is that their justification requires continuing insistence that America is a racist nation, and that blacks cannot expect or be expected to succeed on their own merits. This is not only untrue but is also the worst message society could convey. It teaches that ambition, self-discipline, responsibility, and effort are not relevant to black success, that the most important studies for blacks are studies insisting on their victimization, and that the skill they most need to acquire is skill in protest. Such teaching is a prescription for black self-destruction and for the incitement of racial conflict in which blacks cannot ultimately prevail.

I do not believe that racial preferences and quotas can ever be made acceptable to the vast majority of the American people. It may be an inherent defect of policy recommendations by professors of constitutional law that they tend, along with other academics, to be so high-minded and self-sacrificing—having abandoned pursuit of personal gain in the interest of public service—that they lose touch with the mass of their less elevated fellow citizens. I differ from my professional colleagues in accepting the propriety of the pursuit of self-interest, if for no other reason than that it is inevitable. Despite their insistence that America is a racist nation, proponents of racial preferences seem simultaneously to assume a level of altruism or, at least, of acceptance of racial guilt on the part of most Americans that I am sure does not exist. The imposition of racial preferences in employment, therefore, can serve only to create the interracial hostility that proponents of preferences assert already exists and use to justify such preferences. The result is a vicious and potentially disastrous cycle of racial hostility.

The only good news I can offer is that this problem is not really difficult to solve. As with so many of our problems, all that is necessary is the repeal of legislation. Nearly

one million employment discrimination claims were filed
with the EEOC between 1965 and 1983, more than
175,000 settlements were reached in the administrative
process, nearly 60,000 lawsuits were filed, and these figures, it is said, "only begin to suggest the social effects
generated by Title VII." What these figures most clearly
suggest is that the principal social effect generated by Title
VII, as revised by the Supreme Court in *Griggs*, is virtually
endless employment opportunities for lawyers. If a better
world is a world with fewer lawyers, to repeal Title VII
would be to make a significant improvement in human
welfare. Racial discrimination in employment is undoubtedly a very bad thing, but that does not establish that a law
against it is needed or, on the whole, useful.

But the repeal of Title VII is, of course, entirely wishful
and unrealistic. There is no possibility that Title VII (or
any other "civil rights" measure) will be repealed. On the
contrary, Congress and the President are moving to undo
the Supreme Court's recent efforts to put modest limits on
the racially discriminatory effects of *Griggs*. The bad news
is that there is no guarantee that this nation will survive,
and if it tears itself apart in the near future, it will surely
be because of the enhanced racial consciousness and conflict that is the inevitable result of our present course on
"civil rights." Perhaps America will then finally have paid
the full price for the terrible mistake of bringing in Africans
in chains.

PART THREE

PERSONAL PERSPECTIVES

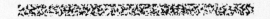

THE DEATH OF THE PROFANE

Patricia J. Williams

Patricia J. Williams is associate professor of law at the
University of Wisconsin Law School. Her writing has appeared in the *Village Voice* and *The New York Times Book
Review*. "The Death of the Profane" first appeared in 1991
in her book *The Alchemy of Race and Rights*.

Buzzers are big in New York City. Favored particularly by
smaller stores and boutiques, merchants throughout the
city have installed them as screening devices to reduce the
incidence of robbery: if the face at the door looks desirable,
the buzzer is pressed and the door is unlocked. If the face
is that of an undesirable, the door stays locked. Predictably,
the issue of undesirability has revealed itself to be a racial
determination. While controversial enough at first, even
civil-rights organizations backed down eventually in the
face of arguments that the buzzer system is a "necessary
evil," that it is a "mere inconvenience" in comparison to
the risks of being murdered, that suffering discrimination
is not as bad as being assaulted, and that in any event it is
not all blacks who are barred, just "seventeen-year-old
black males wearing running shoes and hooded sweat-
shirts."

The installation of these buzzers happened swiftly in New York; stores that had always had their doors wide open suddenly became exclusive or received people by appointment only. I discovered them and their meaning one Saturday in 1986. I was shopping in SoHo and saw in a store window a sweater that I wanted to buy for my mother. I pressed my round brown face to the window and my finger to the buzzer, seeking admittance. A narrow-eyed white teenager wearing running shoes and feasting on bubble gum glared out, evaluating me for signs that would pit me against the limits of his social understanding. After about five seconds, he mouthed "We're closed," and blew pink rubber at me. It was two Saturdays before Christmas, at one o'clock in the afternoon; there were several white people in the store who appeared to be shopping for things for *their* mothers.

I was enraged. At that moment I literally wanted to break all the windows of the store and *take* lots of sweaters for my mother. In the flicker of his judgmental gray eyes, that saleschild had transformed my brightly sentimental, joy-to-the-world, pre-Christmas spree to a shambles. He snuffed my sense of humanitarian catholicity, and there was nothing I could do to snuff his, without making a spectacle of myself.

I am still struck by the structure of power that drove me into such a blizzard of rage. There was almost nothing I could do, short of physically intruding upon him, that would humiliate him the way he humiliated me. No words, no gestures, no prejudices of my own would make a bit of difference to him; his refusal to let me into the store—it was Benetton's, whose colorfully punnish ad campaign is premised on wrapping every one of the world's peoples in its cottons and woolens—was an outward manifestation of his never having let someone like me into the realm of his reality. He had no compassion, no remorse, no reference to me; and no desire to acknowledge me even at the estranged level of arm's-length transactor. He saw me only as one who would take his money and therefore could not conceive that I was there to give him money.

In this weird ontological imbalance, I realized that buying something in that store was like bestowing a gift, the gift of my commerce, the lucre of my patronage. In the wake of my outrage, I wanted to take back the gift of appreciation that my peering in the window must have appeared to be. I wanted to take it back in the form of unappreciation, disrespect, defilement. I wanted to work so hard at wishing he could feel what I felt that he would never again mistake my hatred for some sort of plaintive wish to be included. I was quite willing to disenfranchise myself, in the heat of my need to revoke the flattery of my purchasing power. I was willing to boycott Benetton's, random white-owned businesses, and anyone who ever blew bubble gum in my face again.

My rage was admittedly diffuse, even self-destructive, but it was symmetrical. The perhaps loose-ended but utter propriety of that rage is no doubt lost not just to the young man who actually barred me, but to those who would appreciate my being barred only as an abstract precaution, who approve of those who would bar even as they deny that they would bar *me*.

The violence of my desire to burst into Benetton's is probably quite apparent. I often wonder if the violence, the exclusionary hatred, is equally apparent in the repeated public urgings that blacks understand the buzzer system by putting themselves in the shoes of white storeowners— that, in effect, blacks look into the mirror of frightened white faces for the reality of their undesirability; and that then blacks would "just as surely conclude that [they] would not let [themselves] in under similar circumstances." (That some blacks might agree merely shows that some of us have learned too well the lessons of privatized intimacies of self-hatred and rationalized away the fullness of our public, participatory selves.)

On the same day I was barred from Benetton's, I went home and wrote the above impassioned account in my journal. On the day after that, I found I was still brooding, so I turned to a form of catharsis I have always found healing. I typed up as much of the story as I have just told, made a big poster of it, put a nice colorful border around it, and, after Benetton's was truly closed, stuck it to their big sweater-filled window. I exercised my First-Amendment right to place my business with them right out in the street.

So that was the first telling of this story. The second telling came a few months later, for a symposium on Excluded Voices sponsored by a law review. I wrote an essay summing up my feelings about being excluded from Benetton's and analyzing "how the rhetoric of increased privatization, in response to racial issues, functions as the rationalizing agent of public unaccountability and, ultimately, irresponsibility." Weeks later, I received the first edit. From the first page to the last, my fury had been carefully cut out. My rushing, run-on rage had been reduced to simple declarative sentences. The active personal had been inverted in favor of the passive impersonal. My words were different; they spoke to me upside down. I was afraid to read too much of it at a time—meanings rose up at me oddly, stolen and strange.

A week and a half later, I received the second edit. All reference to Benetton's had been deleted because, according to the editors and the faculty adviser, it was defamatory; they feared harassment and liability; they said printing it would be irresponsible. I called them and offered to supply a footnote attesting to this as my personal experience at one particular location and of a buzzer system not limited to Benetton's; the editors told me that they were not in the habit of publishing things that were unverifiable. I could not but wonder, in this refusal even to let me file an affadavit, what it would take to make my experience verifiable. The testimony of an independent white by-stander (a requirement in fact imposed in U.S. Supreme Court holdings through the first part of the century)?

Two days *after* the piece was sent to press, I received copies of the final page proofs. All reference to my race had been eliminated because it was against "editorial policy" to permit descriptions of physiognomy. "I realize," wrote one editor, "that this was a very personal experience, but any reader will know what you must have looked like when standing at that window." In a telephone conversation to them, I ranted wildly about the significance of such an omission. "It's irrelevant," another editor explained in a voice gummy with soothing and patience; "It's nice and poetic," but it doesn't "advance the discussion of any principle. . . . This is a law review, after all." Frustrated, I accused him of censorship; calmly he assured me it was not. "This is just a matter of style," he said with firmness and finality.

Ultimately I did convince the editors that mention of my race was central to the whole sense of the subsequent text; that my story became one of extreme paranoia without the information that I am black; or that it became one in which the reader had to fill in the gap by assumption, presumption, prejudgment, or prejudice. What was most interesting to me in this experience was how the blind application of principles of neutrality, through the device of omission, acted either to make me look crazy or to make the reader participate in old habits of cultural bias.

That was the second telling of my story. The third telling came last April, when I was invited to participate in a law-school conference on Equality and Difference. I retold my sad tale of exclusion from SoHo's most glitzy boutique, focusing in this version on the law-review editing process as a consequence of an ideology of style rooted in a social text of neutrality. I opined:

Law and legal writing aspire to formalized, color-blind, liberal ideals. Neutrality is the standard for assuring these ideals; yet the adherence to it is often determined by reference to an aesthetic of uniformity, in which difference is simply omitted. For example, when segregation was eradicated from the American lexicon, its omission led many to actually believe that racism therefore no longer existed. Race-neutrality in law has become the presumed antidote for race bias in real life. With the entrenchment of the notion of race-neutrality came attacks on the concept of affirmative action and the rise of reverse discrimination suits. Blacks, for so many generations deprived of jobs based on the color of our skin, are now told that we ought to find it demeaning to be hired, based on the color of our skin. Such is the silliness of simplistic either-or inversions as remedies to complex problems.

What is truly demeaning in this era of double-speak-no-evil is going on interviews and not getting hired because someone doesn't think we'll be comfortable. It is demeaning not to get promoted because we're judged "too weak," then putting in a lot of energy the next time and getting fired because we're "too strong." It is demeaning to be told what we find demeaning. It is very demeaning to stand on street corners unemployed and begging. It is downright demeaning to have to explain why we haven't been employed for months and then watch the job go to someone who is "more experienced." It is outrageously demeaning that none of this can be called racism, even if it happens only to, or to large numbers of, black people; as long as it's done with a smile, a handshake, and a shrug; as long as the phantom-word *race* is never used.

The image of race as a phantom-word came to me after I moved into my late godmother's home. In an attempt to make it my own, I cleared the bedroom for painting. The following morning the room asserted itself, came rushing and raging at me through the emptiness, exactly as it had been for twenty-five years. One day filled with profuse and overwhelming complexity, the next day filled with persistently recurring memories. The shape of the past came to haunt me, the shape of the emptiness confronted me each time I was about to enter the room. The force of its spirit still drifts like an odor throughout the house.

The power of that room, I have thought since, is very like the power of racism as status quo: it is deep, angry, eradicated from view, but strong enough to make everyone who enters the room walk around the bed that isn't there, avoiding the phantom as they did the substance, for fear of bodily harm. They do not even know they are avoiding; they defer to the unseen shapes of things with subtle responsiveness, guided by an impulsive awareness of nothingness, and the deep knowledge and denial of witchcraft at work.

The phantom room is to me symbolic of the emptiness of formal equal opportunity, particularly as propounded by President Reagan, the Reagan Civil Rights Commission, and the Reagan Supreme Court. Blindly formalized constructions of equal opportunity are the creation of a space that is filled in by a meandering stream of unguided hopes, dreams, fantasies, fears, recollections. They are the presence of the past in imaginary, imagistic form—the phantom-roomed exile of our longing.

It is thus that I strongly believe in the efficacy of programs and paradigms like affirmative action. Blacks are the objects of a constitutional omission which has been incorporated into a theory of neutrality. It is thus that omission is really a form of expression, as oxymoronic as that sounds: racial omission is a literal part of original intent; it is the fixed, reiterated prophecy of the Founding Fathers. It is thus that affirmative action is an affirmation; the affirmative act of hiring—or hearing—blacks is a recognition of individuality that re-places blacks as a social statistic, that is profoundly interconnective to the fate of blacks and whites either as subgroups or as one group. In this sense affirmative action is as mystical and beyond-the-self as an initiation ceremony. It is an act of verification and of vision. It is an act of social as well as professional responsibility.

The following morning I opened the local newspaper, to find that the event of my speech had commanded two columns on the front page of the Metro section. I quote only the opening lines: "Affirmative action promotes prejudice by denying the status of women and blacks, instead of affirming them as its name suggests. So said New York City attorney Patricia Williams to an audience Wednesday."

I clipped out the article and put it in my journal. In the margin there is a note to myself: eventually, it says, I should try to pull all these threads together into yet another law-review article. The problem, of course, will be that in the hierarchy of law-review citation, the article in the newspaper will have more authoritative weight about me, as a so-called "primary resource," than I will have; it will take precedence over my own citation of the unverifiable testimony of my speech.

I have used the Benetton's story a lot in speaking engagements at various schools. I tell it whenever I am too tried to whip up an original speech from scratch. Here are some of the questions I have been asked in the wake of its telling:

Am I not privileging a racial perspective, by considering only the black point of view? Don't I have an obligation to include the "salesman's side" of the story?

Am I not putting the salesman on trial and finding him guilty of racism without giving him a chance to respond to or cross-examine me?

Am I not using the store window as a "metaphorical fence" against the potential of his explanation in order to represent my side as "authentic"?

How can I be sure I'm right?

What makes my experience the real black one anyway?

Isn't it possible that another black person would dis- agree with my experience? If so, doesn't that render my story too unempirical and subjective to pay any attention to?

Always a major objection is to my having put the poster on Benetton's window. As one law professor put it: "It's one thing to publish this in a law review, where no one can take it personally, but it's another thing altogether to put your own interpretation right out there, just like that, uncontested, I mean, with nothing to counter it."

THE CIVIL RIGHTS ACT: WHITE MEN'S HOPE

Julian Bond

Julian Bond is a television commentator and authority on the civil rights movement. During the 1960s he was communications director for the Student Nonviolent Coordinating Committee (SNCC). Later he was elected to the Georgia House of Representatives and Georgia State Senate. He was narrator for Parts I and II of the PBS television documentary *Eyes on the Prize*. "The Civil Rights Act: White Men's Hope" first appeared in *The New York Times,* June 26, 1990.

President Bush and Congress have overlooked an important reason why they should immediately enact the Civil Rights Act of 1990: to help white men overcome their feelings of inferiority.

Let me explain. Many whites and some blacks now argue that preferential racial treatment creates deep-seated feelings of deficiency and mediocrity in its beneficiaries. They warn that race-conscious practices, in hiring or education, cast suspicion on the competence of those given an advantage.

But if that is so, we need the new Civil Rights Act more

than ever, to overcome the sense of inferiority that has afflicted American white men for years.

Think of it. For decades, white men have known they've received favored, front-of-the-line positions in jobs, education, and the benefits of a race-conscious society.

Without having to compete with minorities or women, any white man, no matter what his qualifications, had a head start. All he needed was membership in the favored race and sex.

The knowledge that maids, porters, garbage collectors, unemployed teenagers, and cotton pickers were suspicious of their credentials took a heavy psychic toll on white American males. Some even chose to remain unemployed rather than take a job or a place in a prestigious university solely because of their race.

"How would you feel," one said, "if everyone knew you had your job just because you were white?"

Social scientists say white male inferiority complexes began to diminish with the passage of early civil rights laws in the 1960s, and when blacks and women began to enter the work force in large numbers.

But even relaxing the discrimination—which had reserved jobs as diverse as Supreme Court Justice, professional baseball manager, big city mayor, U.S. Naval officer, professional quarterback, talk show host, serial killer, and newspaper columnist and publisher for white men exclusively—did little to ease the cruel intimations of mediocrity that ran rampant among white males.

These feelings of inadequacy began to return during the Reagan years. Some white men adopted a victim complex, blaming the federal government and the courts for mistreating them. Last year's Supreme Court decisions were the final straw.

The Court made it harder for minorities to sue against white privilege and harder for women to litigate employment rules that discriminated against them. It guaranteed a return to favored status for white males.

"It's all I can take," a white investment banker said. "I'm sure my gardener was laughing at me as I drove into town this morning. Then the waiter at the club had a funny smirk on his face. I've had it, I tell you!" the anguished Anglo-Saxon mourned.

If President Bush has any compassion, he will move swiftly to remove the awful stigma of race.

These victims have suffered long enough. Free white men!

"IF YOU HADN'T BEEN MEXICAN"

Ruben Navarrette, Jr.

Ruben Navarrette, Jr., is the author of *A Darker Shade of Crimson: Odyssey of a Harvard Chicano*. His writing has also appeared in the *San Francisco Chronicle, Fresno Bee,* and *Kansas City Star*. "If You Hadn't Been Mexican" first appeared in the *Los Angeles Times,* May 12, 1991.

Their young eyes stare at me with a hint of skepticism, and perhaps a bit of anger. With more courage than common sense I have come as a guest speaker to a government class at the high school I attended not long ago. Invited to defend an educational program that is continually under siege by those who want racial equity without sacrifice, I have come to confront an old friend—Allan Bakke.

It was six years ago, as a high-school senior in this brown and white town, that I first met the spirit of the thirty-three-year-old NASA engineer who, a decade earlier, had decided to become a doctor. After being rejected by twelve medical schools, he had challenged the admissions policy at UC Davis's medical school. Bakke charged that the school's special admissions program, which reserved sixteen of a hundred places for "economically and educa-

129

tionally disadvantaged" applicants, violated his Fourteenth Amendment right to equal protection.

Though, in 1978, the U.S. Supreme Court, by 5–4, eventually ordered his admission to Davis, it also allowed— indeed encouraged—colleges and universities to consider the race and gender of its applicants to bring diversity and racial parity to U.S. higher education. Taking his place in history beside Linda Brown and James Meredith, Bakke was catapulted to the dubious position of poster boy for a new kind of racial injustice. For opponents of affirmative action, the issue was clear: Bakke was the blond, blue-eyed victim of a new kind of discrimination—reverse discrimination.

None of this seemed important to me at the beginning of my senior year in high school, when I was setting my sights on applying to some top colleges.

Not everyone shared my confidence. In the middle of the application process, my high-school principal counseled me not to bite off more than I could chew. Diplomatically, he said that it was "fine" that I was applying to schools like Harvard, Yale, and Princeton, but that I should also consider applying to Fresno State nearby "just in case." I thanked him and promptly disregarded his advice.

Rebuffed, he cast the first spear of a bitter attack that was to be taken over by my Anglo classmates and maintained through spring. "You may be right," he conceded with insincerity. "After all, [in the admissions process] your race should help you a lot." In five minutes, he had dismissed four years of hard work and perfect grades in favor of a more race-conscious explanation of why I would eventually be admitted to each of the schools I applied to.

My white classmates, many with grades not as good as mine and reeling from rejections by the schools that were admitting me, were far more direct. "Now, you know if you hadn't been Mexican . . ." one said. "Reverse discrimination," another charged. And it was then that I met Bakke.

He was there in the eyes of my classmates, who clutched in their fists letters of rejection from such schools as Stanford and UC Berkeley. "It's not fair," I remember one saying. "They turned me down because I was white."

I half expected to find huge clusters of Mexican students at Harvard, but I was one of only thirty-five Mexican Americans at the welcoming luncheon. Did this signify the alleged "darkening" of higher education?

Part of youth is ignorance of the world outside your window. Yet, the furor over perceived "reverse discrimination" is not limited to high-school seniors. A few weeks ago, a friend of mine who is a graduate of Yale stormed into the law firm where she works after a lunchtime argument with the managing partner. The partner had blatantly charged that "the only reason" my friend had been admitted to Yale was because she was Mexican American and a woman— the dreaded "double whammy." He had dismissed not only her near-perfect grades in high school but also her equally outstanding marks at Yale.

The stories of angry white Americans in search of whipping boys—and girls—could go on without end.

This is the legacy with which I entered the high-school government class and confronted Bakke. "Granted, racial discrimination was wrong back then [presumably pre–civil rights movement]," a student conceded. "But now that that's over with, shouldn't we get rid of affirmative action? And if we don't, aren't we just creating new victims?"

The first time I'd heard this line was from Nathan Glazer, a professor of mine at Harvard, who some say coined the phrase *reverse discrimination*. Once a society has liberated its employment and educational opportunities and fully met the burden of its democratic principles, Glazer argues, any further tampering with the laws of appropriation through race-preference programs constitutes impermissible "reverse discrimination."

Fair enough. My dispute with my old professor and those who yell "foul" at the mere mention of the phrase *affirmative action,* because they instinctively consider it to be nothing more than reverse discrimination, is that American society has not yet reached Glazer's wonderful window of equal educational and employment opportunity.

I suggested to the students that they needed only to look at their immediate surroundings. Sanger is, I reminded them, 72.8 percent Mexican American. The fire chief, the police chief, the mayor, the city attorney, the city manager, and a majority of the City Council are white. The dropout rate of Latino students from the school system that produced me is consistent with the distressing national figure of 50–60 percent. Only 29 percent of the senior class of a public-school system that is nearly 80 percent Latino is considered "eligible" to enter UC directly after graduation. On average, less than 5 percent do.

Of the nearly 200 teachers employed by the Sanger Unified School District, an estimated 10 percent are Latino. Never in the hundred-year history of the district has there been a Latino principal of its only high school or a Mexican-American superintendent of schools. As for the hiring body, the local school board, it is all white.

Nationally, thousands of towns like Sanger in the American Southwest, with bigger cities often faring not much better, have produced distressing economic gaps between Latinos and non-Latinos. The Census Bureau recently reported that 23.4 percent of Latino families live in poverty, compared with 9.2 percent of non-Latino families. About 30 percent of male Latino workers are concentrated in lower-paying jobs, compared with 19.5 percent of non-Latino workers. The median income of Latino families is $23,400, compared with $35,200 for non-Latino families.

Clearly, no matter how slick and seductive the rhetoric about the suffering of "new victims," the reality of American society is that, as we enter the year 2000, we have not yet ended the suffering of our old victims. It is against this backdrop of economic disempowerment and educational neglect of the nation's Latino population, along with tragically similar statistics for African Americans, that charges of "reverse discrimination" are best and most honestly considered.

I confess that much of this is new for me. In the recent past, when I wrote or lectured about affirmative action or when I assigned readings to my students on the subject, I had intended to criticize the program and the way it is implemented on most college campuses. Though we share the same target, the important difference between my view and those who embrace Bakke is that, while they attack the preferential treatment of minorities because they believe it does "too much" to address the racial inequity that still exists in our society, I attack it because I continue to believe that it does not do enough to correct that inequality.

The door of educational opportunity, opened only a crack to minorities by two decades of preferential treatment, is sending a draft that is already giving many Americans a bit of a cold, and they are seeking to close it before their condition worsens. That is unfortunate, given the fact that my colleagues and I are determined to kick down that archaic barrier once and for all.

Now that we have found your library and have discovered your books, it will be difficult for us to forget what was learned in those pages. Now that we have finally been invited to dine in restaurants never open to our parents and have discovered in them a buffet of delicacies, we hope you will not be offended if we engage in a bit of conspicuous consumption and serve ourselves a second helping. Like the English language, these opportunities are mine now and I will not give them back.

High-school seniors and others will continue to feel wronged by what they do not understand. I am sympathetic to their plight; I know firsthand the sting of rejection.

Still, it is inconsistent, and indeed immoral, for us as a nation dedicated to the principle of genuine equality to, on the one hand, anguish over what the President has called "the crisis in Hispanic education" and, at the same time, to rationalize the rejection of our sons and daughters by attacking students who somehow miraculously succeed in the face of desperate odds. Webster himself could provide no better definition of the word *qualified*.

BENEATH THE GLASS CEILING

Julie Hessler

Julie Hessler's writing has appeared in the Minneapolis *Star Tribune, City Pages,* and *Iowa Woman.* "Beneath the Glass Ceiling" was written for *Debating Affirmative Action.*

They are everywhere: page after page of high-powered women in high-status careers leading board meetings, tracking down hot stories, introducing legislation. Assertive women clad in chic tailored suits, swinging smart briefcases wherein lies the stuff of mergers and acquisitions, the stuff that, before affirmative action and the equal rights movement, was restricted largely to the domain of men.

With their serious hair, à la Melanie Griffith in *Working Girl,* these women aren't merely grasping for the glass ceiling, they've damn near shattered it. At least it looks that way in magazines like *Glamour* and *Mademoiselle.*

I don't own their clothes or their careers. Like more than half of all working women in the United States, I'm part of a nebulous category which the U.S. Department of Labor terms "sales, support, and service." When I go to work each morning, it's to a job, not a career. I work with my hands: I'm a secretary, ninety words per minute.

Although I have both a B.A. and a graduate degree, I've been a secretary for nearly all my adult working life. I am, in a sense, following my mother's footsteps. She never intended to make a career as a secretary (she'd been an elementary schoolteacher), but after leaving the state in which her teaching license was valid, after having children and being out of the professional work force for many years, the typing skills she'd first learned in high school were a quick and relatively easy way of landing a part-time job. Part-time eventually turned into full-time and for the past thirteen years she's worked as a secretary for an adoption agency.

Typing—now word processing—has been my sure thing, too, a skill I can fall back on when the job market is tight. After college I worked as a data-entry clerk for a nonprofit agency and later as a secretary-receptionist. In the late 1980s, after completing a graduate writing degree, I took a job as a secretary at a state university. Teaching and writing jobs were scarce, student loans loomed in the distance; my quick hands paid the bills and came with health insurance.

But these jobs often come with little else besides a steady paycheck and some benefits. The world of work that I inhabit often seems stuck in a 1950s time warp. Women still comprise 99 percent of all secretaries and many of our duties still include making coffee, fussing over details for the next office party, enduring questions such as "Did you make these cookies or are you one of those feminists who don't believe in baking?"

Actually, I'm one of those feminists who believe strongly in affirmative action. But on a day-to-day basis, as I three-hole-punch a knee-high stack of paper or make one hundred double-sided copies that He Needs Now, the whole idea seems, at best, distant.

I've never seen the glass ceiling, much less gotten close

enough to touch it. My expectations are lower. I would settle for less: I'd like to be able to step out to the restroom without having to notify my supervisor and to have a lunch hour rather than a forty-five-minute lunch break.

When I was a college freshman, I listed "computers" as one of my potential career choices. I have spent much of my professional life working with computers, although not in the way I had first imagined.

A 1989 study reports that even in such fields as science and engineering, where women are now actively recruited, many of the jobs are still clearly defined as "men's jobs" and "women's jobs." While men are often encouraged to experiment with technology and explore the intricacies of computers, women, in effect, are simply encouraged to push the buttons or to type on the keyboard.

Despite affirmative action, more than half of all working women (59 percent) are still doing most of the jobs they have always done—selling, supporting, serving—while earning only seventy-four cents per every dollar earned by working men.

So where does the revolution begin? At the federal level, with continued affirmative action programs like that of the City of San Francisco, which has begun to level the employment playing field for women.

In 1984, the City of San Francisco enacted an ordinance providing "affirmative action for minority, women, and locally owned businesses in city contracting." Provisions of the ordinance gave 5 percent bidding preference to these groups for contracts under $50,000.

The ordinance was intended to alleviate what the city described as "historic discrimination against minorities and women, often officially sanctioned and enforced by government from the inception of our Republic to the present."

When Associated General Contractors challenged the validity of the ordinance, a U.S. District Court upheld it.

Associated General Contractors appealed that decision in 1986, arguing that the preferences violated federal civil rights laws and the equal protection clause of the Fourteenth Amendment of the U.S. Constitution. In 1987, the U.S. Court of Appeals, Ninth Circuit, struck down the "provisions of the ordinance giving preference to minority-owned business," ruling that "race-conscious remedies must be narrowly tailored to eliminate consequences of past discrimination."

In the case of discrimination against women, however, a broader scope of justice was allowed. The Court wrote that "fields where women are not disadvantaged . . . are still the exceptions." For "gender-based statutes" the Court concluded that such narrow tailoring was not yet required and preference for women-owned businesses was upheld.

The Court wrote that "many of the disadvantages women have suffered result from stereotypes concerning their proper roles and abilities," something that women have likely known all along. Affirmative action is for many women what George Bush might have called a vision thing: as we see more and more women enter the murky world of nontraditional jobs—as building contractors, as astronauts, as attorney general—these stereotypes are shattered, and the roles and possibilities available to all of us are recast and expanded.

But what about those of us already working in so-called traditional women's jobs? The Ninth Circuit suggests that in regard to gender equality, we may be part of the problem because "in some industries the participation of women may be so high that encouraging further participation may well reinforce harmful stereotypes."

The Ninth Circuit is only half right. The stereotypes we as a nation need to abandon come not from the jobs but from the attitudes, both economic and cultural, that we have toward women's work. The revolution women like me need begins with an economy that has plans for us. In addition to affirmative action, this revolution will require a new vision altogether, one in which the "gender" of our jobs has no bearing upon our salaries or our worth.

We cannot afford to settle for less. We must, instead, ask for more—loudly and in large numbers. Until then, bumping up against a glass ceiling is a luxury we can only imagine.

THE CANDIDATE: INSIDE ONE AFFIRMATIVE ACTION SEARCH

G. Kindrow

G. Kindrow is the pseudonym of a professor at a large midwestern university. Details in this article were changed to protect confidentiality. "The Candidate: Inside One Affirmative Action Search" first appeared in *Lingua Franca*, April 1991.

SEPTEMBER 23, 1989. The first faculty meeting of the term for the Department of English at Midwestern State. One of our assistant professors was denied tenure last year, and, given the financial constraints on the university, we were anxious to find out whether we would be able to replace him. The chair of the department told us the following: "The dean has authorized a search at the assistant professor level for a 'minority' candidate."

Instantly the questions began. "What if we make a good-faith search and fail to come up with a suitable minority candidate? Can we then hire a nonminority candidate?" "Does the search include women or just ethnic minorities?" "What counts as a minority?" The answers: "No, women do not count." "I don't know exactly how *minority* is being defined." "I don't know what would happen if we searched and failed to find a minority candidate." The department asked the chair to try and get some answers, from the dean, to the latter questions.

Most of my colleagues—largely liberal/left ideologically and disillusioned Democrats politically—were sympathetic to the need to have minorities and women on the faculty. The university, after all, had a substantial black and Hispanic undergraduate presence, and we believed that, in pedagogic terms, it was important for undergraduates to see that members of their community could be successful academics.

To this end, the department had been quite conscious of the need to hire women—who, as a consequence, were represented at all ranks, including full professor. Some years ago we had a black assistant professor who left when he received a better offer from an eastern university. All this had been done without any specific pressure from the administration, other than the symbolic need to get approval from the Affirmative Action Office before any official offer went out. This approval was easily obtained by showing that we had advertised in places that would be the natural starting point for minority and women job-seekers.

Many of us, myself included, felt at this point that it would be good if we could find a suitable minority candidate but that we were not prepared to make any concessions about quality. Others were prepared to lower standards, on the grounds either that the traditional standards were biased toward "masculine," "Eurocentric" criteria or that it was more important to provide a minority "role model" than to keep the same standards.

All of us agreed on one thing: that it was going to be very difficult to come up with a suitable candidate. While we are a highly ranked department, we are not in the same class as Michigan and Harvard. And with the total pool of suitable minority Ph.D.'s dismayingly small and heavily recruited, especially by elite institutions, this was a severe liability.

Since time was running short (the annual conference for professors of English, which served as the main interviewing occasion for hiring, was in December, just three months away), we decided to put an ad in the principal English-literature-association newsletter for job hunters. In doing so, we made our first affirmative action compromise: Although we had specific needs in certain areas, we decided not to limit the search by area. Quite simply, to do so would have reduced the minority-candidate pool to minuscule, or even nonexistent, size. The advertisement could not exclude nonminority candidates from applying. It could only state that "Midwestern State is an Affirmative Action/ Equal Opportunity employer. Minority candidates are especially encouraged to apply." Note: Many academic job advertisements carry as a matter of course the "minorities urged to apply" tag, so there was no real way for a candidate to know what the real situation was.

In addition to placing an ad in our association newsletter, the chair placed an ad in a magazine I'll call *Black Opportunity*, a newsletter aimed specifically at listing jobs for minority candidates. In addition, we wrote letters to the major Ph.D.-granting departments asking them to recommend any minority candidates coming on the job market. Finally, a number of us who had minority friends in various departments called them and asked them to recommend minority faculty who already had jobs.

A search committee, of which I was a part, was set up to screen the forthcoming applications. In the current tight job market, we would receive about three hundred applications for this job.

OCTOBER 15. We now had answers to some of the questions our chairman had taken to the dean. Blacks,

"Hispanic-surnamed" persons, and Native Americans counted as minorities; East Indians and Asians did not. Thus, the first absurdity emerged. Someone born in Argentina to a Jewish family named Mendoza would count. A "boat person" from Vietnam would not. The question of what would happen if we did not find a suitable minority candidate was left highly ambiguous by the dean. But the underlying message seemed to be, "Don't count on the position being available."

Applications began to arrive.

OCTOBER 17. In a conversation in the hall, the chair told me that he had gotten a bill from *Black Opportunity* for the advertisement we had placed. It was for three hundred dollars—approximately five times the cost of the advertisement in our association newsletter. This "academic mugging" seemed to me disgraceful, if also a nice lesson in affirmative action economics. To add insult to injury, when the chair asked the dean to pay for the cost of the ad (the departmental operating budget was ludicrously low and could not afford such a sum), the dean refused, with the helpful words "caveat emptor." So much for the "administrative commitment" to minority hiring.

NOVEMBER 2. I am screening the applications, which consist of a transcript of the candidate's grades, a curriculum vitae, three letters of reference, a cover letter, and a written sample of the candidate's research. A problem emerges: How do you tell who is a minority candidate? The applications, quite reasonably, have no place to indicate race. While names single out Hispanics—although a colleague and I spent most of an afternoon trying to figure out from clues in the vitae whether the clearly Romance-language surname of a candidate indicated he was Italian or Hispanic—they are no help for blacks. One looks for subtle, or not so subtle, clues. If the candidate has an undergraduate degree from a largely black school; if the candidate is working on a Ph.D. that involves minority issues; if the candidate belongs to a primarily minority professional organization; if the candidate was born in Ethiopia; if the thesis supervisor is wily enough to somehow get in a reference (not so easy without being open to charges of patronizing or racist behavior).

I usually checked with one of my black professional acquaintances. The grapevine is sufficiently accurate that they are almost always able to make a positive identification. Only once did I actually have to call a department to ask bluntly if a candidate was black (he wasn't); it concerned an applicant from Princeton, and one of our assistant professors had heard that "a black" was applying from there.

At the same time as the applications were coming in, we began to call candidates who had been identified as minorities, asking them to apply.

NOVEMBER 10. At this stage, looking day after day at applications from hopeful Ph.D.'s, I began to develop moral qualms. Basically, I was screening them for indications of race, not scholarship. It was as simple as the two piles of applications on my desk: one for minority candidates, another for nonminorities.

My equivocal moral position soon took on a more personal cast. A candidate at another school where I had been a visiting professor called me to inquire about the job. While he was otherwise quite promising, I knew that he really did not stand a chance of even getting an interview. How much of the situation ought I to reveal? After some thought I decided that if someone asked me whether the job was a "real one"—i.e., competitive in the normal way— I would tell the truth: The position had been "designated" by the dean as a minority position; it was extremely unlikely that a nonminority person would be hired. On the other hand, if I were not asked point-blank, I would maintain silence about the limitations of the search. I would not volunteer information.

NOVEMBER 15. The search committee began to make a short list of candidates to invite for interviews at our annual association conference. Given the time and faculty available, we figured we could interview fourteen people, but it was clear that we didn't have fourteen potential minority interviewees. In fact, we had about twenty minority applications in all, about half of whom were just not qualified. We decided on four people to be interviewed, all blacks, as it turned out, and none from this year's crop of Ph.D.'s. Rather, they were faculty members in tenure-track jobs. If we hired, we were going to be raiding other institutions. (The remaining ten interviews were scheduled with nonminority men and women.)

The list was brought to the department for general discussion. The discussion on the minorities was brief. There was general agreement that these candidates looked like reasonable bets—and, in any case, there were no other options. The candidates had Ph.D.'s from Princeton, Penn, CUNY, Rutgers. There was more animated discussion about the nonminority candidates, mainly because, in these cases, field was an issue.

DECEMBER 28–30. Nobody who hasn't sat in a stuffy hotel room for nine hours a day of job interviews can fully appreciate the horror of it all. I am not sure whether it is worse for the faculty or for the candidates. They, after all, get to talk about their work. We have to listen to nine minilectures a day. After the first few interviews, the attention lags. Virtually everybody was worse in person than on paper, which was inevitable, given the implausibility of their letters of recommendation: Every applicant was the "best in years." (This was true, in one professor's letter, for each of three candidates he was recommending.)

One candidate, however, the man from Rutgers, actually proved more lively, more acute, and wittier than his letters suggested. He displayed a wide range of learning and an analytical mind, impressing the entire committee. Of course, we now had to read his work in more detail and he had to come give a paper to the department, but so far, so good. In addition, two other minority candidates were possibilities. Neither had done particularly well at the interview, but they both seemed to be good teachers and their letters were impressive. Among the nonminorities there were also two or three strong candidates.

That same day, one of the nonminority candidates we had interviewed, an extremely promising young professor from a major graduate department, cornered me in the hall. He was currently in an unhappy academic position that left him little time for research, in spite of which he had just had a book published by Stanford University Press. He was desperate to get another position, and he knew we had nobody in his area of expertise in our department. "How did I do? Do you think I will get an invitation to campus?" Following my policy of not revealing more than I had been explicitly asked, I told him that while he had done well in the interview, the department would make the decision about whom to invite to campus, we had various needs and priorities, blah, blah, blah. But I knew that when he got the standard rejection letter he would blame himself for not doing better in the interview, not getting that extra letter of recommendation. I don't know if he would have felt better if I had said, "You're not going to get an interview. You're white." But *I* would have.

JANUARY 5, 1990. The first faculty meeting after the holidays. The interviewing committee makes its report. We decide to invite three black candidates to campus; a fourth is held in reserve. The man from Rutgers came, he saw, he conquered. His paper was interesting and thoughtful. He held up well under questioning, not overly defensive but holding his ground. The other two candidates more or less repeated their disappointing interviews. All three saw the dean, who did his best to persuade them of the virtues of the Midwest and of Midwestern State in particular.

JANUARY 10. Informal gossip in the hall serves as a commodities exchange for reputation. Wednesday: A is up three, B down one and a quarter. Thursday: A down a half, C up one and an eighth. The politically sophisticated are reading the candidates' work in preparation for the great debate to take place on January 12—the departmental meeting at which we will decide on a recommendation to make to the dean.

JANUARY 12. A startling development. The dean was so impressed with two of the people on the short list that he has given us permission to hire both of them if we so choose. A freebie.

We go around the room and get everyone's impressions. It becomes clear that the first offer is noncontroversial. Indeed it is unanimous: the man from Rutgers. He is in a field that we do not cover now. He is clearly highly qualified. He is not an American black (he's a West Indian), but that's the dean's worry. What about the second offer? Here things turn slightly nasty (in an academic way). It becomes clear that the people in his area do not think that he is good enough. They have read his work and do not think it original or well argued. But, the argument from the opposition goes, we can't be sure that he isn't good enough.

Why not hire him and let the tenure process decide that issue? Meanwhile we have an extra member of the faculty. How can it hurt?

But others, the majority, see another scenario as more convincing. In six years this person will have a long publication list in respectable journals. He will have made the academic contacts to get good letters of recommendation. He will have made himself useful around campus. At that point, given that he is black, it will be impossible for the university to deny him tenure—no matter what the judgment of his peers. So if we think now that the person is unlikely to produce excellent work, we must not make the appointment in the first place. Ultimately, that is the decision of the department. Ironically, in this case the candidate's race worked against him. Had he been white, many would have been willing to give him the benefit of the doubt, to give him the benefit of a trial period. But political realities made that impossible. It's also true that had he been white, he would not have made it to the interview stage.

To his credit, the dean does not question the decision of the department. The search is over. Now it is a matter of wooing.

JANUARY 17. I learn in the hall from the chair that the dean has made the candidate the following offer. (As with my disclosure-upon-request policy, the details of the offer are made known only to those who ask.) He will enter at a salary $4,000 greater than any other assistant professor, including those who had been in rank for five years longer, including an assistant professor who is nationally recognized as a "rising star." He is offered a research fund of $10,000 a year for three years. Unlike other research funds awarded to professors in the department, this money could be used for summer salary. He will have a reduced teaching load for his first year.

JANUARY 27. The candidate, who was teaching at a state university in the Northwest, accepted. The score is Midwest 1, Northwest 0.

NOVEMBER 1, 1990. Now that it's all over, what is my view of how affirmative action works in the university context? It certainly does not conform to the picture painted by the opponents of "quotas." No unqualified individual was forced upon a department against its better judgment, at the cost of passing up much better qualified nonminority candidates. Nor is it the case that the department had "internalized" the process so that, without being forced to, it voluntarily lowered its standards as a means to a good end. On the other hand, I do think that we were lucky: the outcome easily could have been worse. If we had been faced with the choice of the number-two candidate and a dean who said it was that person or the position goes back to the college, what would the department have done?

Had this been a color-blind competition, our winning candidate would almost certainly not have made it to the interviewing stage, where his talents were able to show. He was not from a major graduate department, his letters were not from major figures, and he was not teaching in a major department. These factors would have led to his being lost in the shuffle of nearly three hundred applications. His being black got him an interview.

In fact, since the candidate did not come from a major English department, and since his letters of recommendation were not from important people in his area, many of us worried that we had made a wrong decision even after he was hired. Sometime later, in conversation with a friend at Cambridge, one of the major figures in the area, the candidate's name came up in conversation and I was relieved to hear his work praised.

As to our good fortune, one has to remember that what was fortunate for us was unfortunate for Northwest, and not of any overall benefit to minorities on campus. The total number of blacks in faculty positions was the same after the search as before. I believe that, due to the demographic makeup of Midwest, the "role model" function is more important here than at Northwest. But, to a large extent, the search for minority candidates is a game of national musical chairs. The result is that blacks at existing institutions get wooed away by impressive offers from institutions higher in the prestige hierarchy. It is a zero-sum game, with one institution losing minority presence for every one that gains.

Meanwhile, the procedure has real costs for those non-minority candidates who thought they were in an open competition and who lost out. And it inevitably breeds bitterness and envy on their part. My own view is that we should adopt a truth-in-advertising policy. We now limit applicants by field, by rank, and de facto by quality of graduate school. If we believe it is desirable to hire a black or a woman (whether as rectification for past injustices or to serve as a role model or to just provide fresh perspectives in the discipline), why not just say so? I don't know about the legality of such an advertisement, but morally speaking it seems to me the right thing to do.

RACIAL PREFERENCES? SO WHAT?

Stephen L. Carter

Stephen L. Carter is William Nelson Cromwell Professor
of Law at Yale University Law School. He was a law clerk
for Supreme Court Justice Thurgood Marshall and is the
author of *The Culture of Disbelief*. "Racial Preferences?
So What?" is excerpted from his *Reflections of an Affirmative Action Baby*. This excerpt first appeared in *The Wall
Street Journal*, September 13, 1989.

Those of us who have graduated from professional school
over the past fifteen to twenty years and are not white travel
a career path that is frequently bumpy with suspicions that
we did not earn the right to be where we are. We bristle
when others raise what might be called the affirmative
action question—"Did you get into a school because of a
special program?" That prickly sensitivity reveals a rarely
mentioned cost of racial preferences. The cost I have in
mind is to the psyches of the beneficiaries themselves, who
simultaneously want racial preferences to be preserved and
to force the world to pretend that no one benefits from
them. And therein hangs a tale.

For law students at the leading law schools, the autumn
brings the recruiting season, the idyllic weeks when law

firms from around the country compete to lavish lunches and dinners and other attentions upon them, all with the professed goal of obtaining the students' services—perhaps for the summer, perhaps for a longer term. This year, however, the nation's largest firm, Baker & McKenzie, has been banned from interviewing students at the University of Chicago Law School, and is on probation—that is, enjoined to be on its best behavior—at some others.

The immediate source of Baker & McKenzie's problems was a racially charged interview that a partner in the firm conducted last fall with a black third-year Chicago law student. The interviewer evidently suggested that other lawyers might call her "nigger" or "black bitch," and wanted to know how she felt about that. Perhaps surprised that she played golf, he observed that "there aren't too many golf courses in the ghetto." He also made a comment suggesting that students admitted under a racially conscious affirmative action program were less qualified than students admitted in any other way.

The law school reacted swiftly, and the firm was banned from campus. Because I am black myself, and teach in a law school, I suppose the easiest thing for me to do would be to clamor in solidarity for suspension or worse.

Yet I find myself strangely reluctant to applaud the school's action. Instead, I am disturbed rather than excited by the vision of law schools' circling the wagons to defend their minority students against insensitive remarks. The Chicago action is part of a trend on campuses across the nation to punish those who utter remarks deemed disparaging to racial and ethnic groups. At the many schools that are considering forbidding such remarks, the comments are referred to as "harassment" (which in many cases they certainly are)—evidently in an effort to show that it is conduct, not speech, for which punishment is proposed.

It strikes me as paradoxical that universities, traditionally bastions of free thought, should suddenly be taking the lead in punishing speech because they find it offensive. But it is not my intention to defend the interviewer, most of whose reported questions and comments were inexplicable and inexcusable. I am troubled, however, by my suspicion that there would still have been outrage—not as much, but some—had the interviewer asked only the affirmative action question.

I suspect this because in my own student days, something over a decade ago, when an interviewer from a major law firm in Washington addressed this very question to a Yale student who was not white, the student voices—including my own—howled in protest. But with the passing years, I have come to wonder whether our anger might not have been misplaced.

To be sure, the question was boorish. And because the interviewer had a grade record and résumé right in front of him, it was probably irrelevant as well. But lots of interviewers ask questions that meet the tests of boorishness and irrelevance.

At Yale a decade ago, we called the question racist. I have heard it said that the Baker & McKenzie interviewer's question on affirmative action was racist. I also understand that at least one university is considering a proposal that would deem it harassment per se for a (white?) student to question the qualifications of nonwhite classmates. But we can't change either the truths or the myths about racial preferences by punishing those who speak them.

This clamor for protection from the affirmative action question is the best evidence of the terrible psychological pressure that racial preferences put on their beneficiaries. Indeed, it sometimes seems as though the programs are not supposed to have any beneficiaries—or at least, that no one is permitted to suggest that they have any.

And that's ridiculous. If one supports racial preferences

in professional school admissions, one must be prepared to treat them like any other preference in admissions. One must believe that they make a difference, that is, that some students would not be admitted if the preferences did not exist. This is not a racist observation. It is not normative in any sense. It is simply a fact. A good deal of emotional underbrush might be cleared away were the fact simply conceded, and made the beginning, not the end, of any discussion of preferences.

For once it is conceded that the programs have beneficiaries, it follows that some of us who are professionals and are not white must be among them, and supporters of preferences must stop pretending otherwise. Rather, some large segment of us must be willing to meet the affirmative action question head-on, to say, "Yes, I got into law school because of racial preferences. So what?"—and, having said it, must be ready with a list of what we have accomplished with the opportunities that the preferences provided.

Now, this is a costly concession, because it carries all the baggage of the battle over the relationship between preferences and merit. I take no position on that dispute here, but I do think that the bristling when the question is raised suggests a deep-seated fear that the dichotomy might be real. In any case, it is not racism or harassment to point out that racial preferences make a difference. And if admitting that preferences make a difference leaves a funny aftertaste in the mouths of proponents, they might be more comfortable fighting against preferences rather than for them.

For my part, the matter is simple: I got into law school because I'm black. And I can prove it.

As a senior at Stanford, I applied to about a half dozen law schools. Yale, where I would ultimately enroll, came through fairly early with an acceptance. So did all but one of the others. The last school, Harvard, dawdled and dawdled. Finally, toward the end of the admission season, I received a letter of rejection.

Then, within days, two different Harvard officials and a professor contacted me by telephone to apologize. They were quite frank in their explanation for the "error." I was told by one official that the school had initially rejected me because "we assumed from your record that you were white." (The words have always stuck in my mind, a tantalizing reminder of what is expected of me.) Suddenly coy, he went on to say that the school had obtained "additional information that should have been counted in your favor"—that is, Harvard had discovered the color of my skin. And if I had already made a deposit to confirm my decision to go elsewhere, well, that, I was told, would "not be allowed" to stand in my way should I enroll at Harvard.

Naturally, I was insulted by this miracle. Stephen Carter, the white male, was not good enough for the Harvard Law School; Stephen Carter, the black male, not only was good enough, but rated agonized telephone calls urging him to attend. And Stephen Carter, color unknown, must have been white: How else would he have achieved what he did in college? Except that my college achievements were obviously not sufficiently spectacular to merit acceptance had I been white. In other words, my academic record was too good for a black Stanford undergraduate but not good enough for a white Harvard Law student. Because I turned out to be black, however, Harvard was quite happy to scrape me from what it apparently considered the bottom of the barrel.

My objective is not to single out Harvard for special criticism; on the contrary, I make no claim that a white student with my record would have been admitted to any of the leading law schools. The insult that I felt came from the pain of being reminded so forcefully that I was good enough for a top law school only because I happened to be black.

Naturally, I should not have been insulted at all; that is what racial preferences are for—racial preference. But I was insulted and went off to Yale instead, even though I have now and had then absolutely no reason to imagine that Yale's judgment was based on different criteria than Harvard's. Because Yale is far more selective, the chances are very good that I was admitted at Yale for essentially the same reason that I was admitted at Harvard—the color of my skin made up for evident deficiencies in my academic record.

So I am unable to fool myself: Without that leg up, the thumb on the scale, the extra points due to skin color—choose your own metaphor—I would not be where I am today. And I, too, must be able to say, "So what?" and go on from there.

Whatever the pain it might cause, the affirmative action question, whether at Yale more than a decade ago or at Chicago last year, should come as no surprise. And if those of us who have benefited from racial preferences are not prepared to treat the question in a serious manner, to admit to the advantage that we have been given, then we are not after all the beneficiaries of affirmative action: We are its victims.

PART FOUR

THE POLITICAL ARENA

RACE-NEUTRAL PROGRAMS AND THE DEMOCRATIC COALITION

William Julius Wilson

William Julius Wilson is Lucy Flower Distinguished Service Professor of Sociology at the University of Chicago. His books include *The Declining Significance of Race* and *The Truly Disadvantaged*. "Race Neutral Programs and the Democratic Coalition" first appeared in *The American Prospect*, Spring 1990.

The election of Ron Brown as the first black chairman of the Democratic National Committee triggered a new round of soul-searching among Democrats. Was the party committing political suicide by becoming too strongly identified with the aspirations of minority voters? Had America become so mired in racism that whites would desert the Democrats because blacks seemed to be running things?

My answer to these questions is an empathic "No." Many white Americans have turned, not against blacks, but against a strategy that emphasizes programs perceived to benefit only racial minorities. In the 1990s the party needs to promote new policies to fight inequality that differ from court-ordered busing, affirmative action programs, and antidiscrimination lawsuits of the recent past. By stressing coalition politics and race-neutral programs such

159

as full employment strategies, job skills training, comprehensive health care, reforms in the public schools, child care legislation, and prevention of crime and drug abuse, the Democrats can significantly strengthen their position. As Chairman Brown himself has emphasized, reinforcing Democratic loyalty among minorities and reaching out to reclaim white support are not mutually exclusive.

Such a change of emphasis is overdue. In the 1960s efforts to raise the public's awareness and conscience about the plight of black Americans helped to enact civil rights legislation and affirmative action programs. However, by the 1980s the civil rights strategy of dramatizing black disadvantage was backfiring. The "myth of black progress" theme, frequently invoked to reinforce arguments for stronger race-specific programs, played easily into the hands of conservative critics of antibias policies. The strategy reinforced the erroneous impression that federal antidiscrimination efforts had largely failed, and it overlooked the significance of complex racial changes since the mid-1960s. It also aroused concern that Democratic politicians' sensitivity to black complaints had come at the expense of the white majority.

The tortuous struggles of the 1960s produced real gains. To deny those achievements only invites demoralization among both black and white advocates of racial justice. Yet the movement for racial equality needs a new political strategy for the 1990s that appeals to a broader coalition and addresses many problems afflicting minorities that originated in racist practices but will not be solved by race-specific remedies.

Differential Rates of Black Progress

As we entered the 1980s, the accomplishments of the civil rights struggle were clearly registered in the rising number of blacks in professional, technical, managerial, and administrative positions. Progress was evident also in the increasing enrollment of blacks in colleges and universities and the growing number of black homeowners. These increases were proportionately greater than those for whites. On the other hand, among the disadvantaged segments of the black population, especially the ghetto underclass, many dire problems—poverty, joblessness, family breakup, educational retardation in inner-city public schools, increased welfare dependence, and drug addiction—were getting even worse.

The differential rates of progress in the black community persisted through the 1980s. Family incomes among the poorest of the poor reveal the pattern. From 1978 to 1987, the number of blacks with incomes under half the poverty line (below $4,528 for a three-person family in 1987, adjusting for inflation) increased by 69 percent. In 1978 only one of every three poor blacks fell below half the poverty line, but by 1987 the proportion rose to 45 percent. The average poor black family in 1986 and 1987 slipped further below the poverty level than in any year since the Census Bureau started collecting such data in 1967. While the average income of the lowest fifth of black families in the United States was dropping 24 percent, the average income of the highest fifth of black families was climbing by more than $3,000 and that of the top 5 percent by almost $9,000. Upper-income whites are considerably wealther than upper-income blacks, but in 1987 the highest fifth of black families secured a record 47.4 percent of the total black income, compared to the 42.9 percent share of total white family income received by the highest fifth of white families.

So while income inequality widened generally in America during the 1980s, it widened even more dramatically among black Americans. If we are to fashion remedies for black poverty, we need to understand the origins and dynamics of inequality in the black community. Without disavowing the accomplishments of the civil rights movement, black leaders and liberal policy makers now need to focus on remedies that will make a difference to the poor.

Progress and Protest

Before the emergence of activist black protest, the professionals of the National Association for the Advancement of Colored People (NAACP), working mainly through the courts, achieved important victories in the drive for civil rights. Prior to 1960, the NAACP publicly defined the racial problem as legal segregation in the South and set as its major goal the end of all state-enforced segregation—as the civil rights slogan then had it, "free by 1963." In landmark Supreme Court decisions, the NAACP won legal mandates to improve the conditions of black Americans. Most important, of course, was the 1954 Supreme Court ruling against mandatory school segregation, which overturned the "separate but equal" doctrine and authoritatively defined blacks as first-class citizens.

Important and necessary as these victories were, it soon became apparent that they were not sufficient. Jim Crow regimes in the South ingeniously circumvented the new rulings and made it apparent to black leaders that they had defined both the problem and the goal too narrowly. The problem, as they now saw it, was token compliance with the newly created mandates; the goal they now set was the end of both de jure and de facto segregation.

Despite Southern white resistance, black expectations of continued racial progress continued rising. Not only had the Supreme Court ruled in favor of desegregation; the federal government was growing more sensitive to the condition of black America for two reasons.

The first was international. When the new African regimes broke up the old colonial empires, both the West and the Soviet bloc began competing for influence in the new states. Racial violence and animosities in the United States were now more embarrassing to federal officials than in the past. As a result, Southerners, who had enjoyed significant autonomy in handling racial matters prior to World War II, came under closer national scrutiny.

The increased voting power of blacks in national elections was also a factor. Since the elections of the 1920s, civil rights advocates had monitored the voting records of congressmen and policies of presidents. The lure of the black vote sometimes prompted politicians to support racial equality, as did the Democratic and Progressive candidates of 1928. At other times, politicians granted token concessions in the hope of preserving or gaining black support, as did President Franklin D. Roosevelt in 1940 when he increased black participation in the armed forces, though still within segregated units.

As early as the forties, the black vote was substantial enough in pivotal Northern states to decide close national elections. In 1948 President Truman recognized that to defeat his favored Republican opponent, Thomas E. Dewey, he needed strong black support. For the first time since Reconstruction, the status of blacks emerged as a central presidential campaign issue. Much to the chagrin of its Southern members, the Democratic party adopted a civil rights plank as part of its 1948 platform. That same year, satisfying a demand black leaders introduced eight years earlier, President Truman issued an executive order banning racial segregation in the armed forces. Despite a Dixiecrat walkout from the party, the strategy worked: black voters helped Truman narrowly defeat Dewey. The black vote also provided the margin of victory for Kennedy in 1960, and it almost defeated Nixon again in 1968.

* * *

In the 1960s, as blacks increased their political resources, white resistance to complete desegregation intensified and black support for protest action mushroomed. For a brief period, the nonviolent resistance strategy proved highly effective, particularly in forcing local governments and private agencies to integrate facilities in Southern cities and towns. The nonviolent demonstrations also pressed the federal government into passage of civil rights legislation in 1964 and voting rights legislation in 1965.

Nonviolent protest was successful for several reasons. The demands accompanying the protests—for example, "end discrimination in voting"—tended to be fairly specific and hard to oppose in principle. The remedies were also relatively straightforward and did not require immediate sacrifices by most whites, which reduced white political backlash in areas outside the South. Federal officials were receptive not only because they saw the international attention these developments were receiving. They recognized the political resources blacks had developed, including the growing army of Northern whites sympathetic to the civil rights movement and to direct action protests.

The demands of the civil rights movement reflected a general assumption by black leaders in the 1960s that the government could best protect the rights of minority groups not by formally bestowing rewards and punishments based on group membership, but by using antidiscrimination measures to enhance individual freedom. The movement was particularly concerned about access to education, employment, voting, and public accommodations. So from the 1950s to 1970, the emphasis was on freedom of choice; the role of the state was to prevent the formal categorization of people on the basis of race. Antibias legislation was designed to eliminate racial discrimination without considering the proportion of minorities in certain positions. The underlying principle was that individual merit should be the sole determining factor in choosing among candidates for positions. Because civil rights protests clearly upheld this basic American principle, they carried a degree of moral authority that leaders such as Martin Luther King, Jr., repeatedly and effectively invoked.

It would have been ideal if programs based on the principle of freedom of individual opportunity were sufficient to remedy racial inequality. Long periods of racial oppression can result, however, in a system of inequality that lingers even after racial barriers come down. The most disadvantaged minority individuals, crippled by the cumulative effects of both race and class subjugation, disproportionately lack the resources to compete effectively in a free and open market. Conversely, the members of a minority group who stand to benefit most from the removal of racial barriers are the ones who least need extra help.

Eliminating racial barriers creates the greatest opportunities for the better trained, talented, and educated members of minority groups because they possess the most resources to compete. Those resources reflect a variety of advantages—family stability, financial means, peer groups, and schooling—provided or made possible by their parents.

By the late 1960s a number of black leaders began to recognize this dilemma. In November 1967, for example, Kenneth B. Clark said, "The masses of Negroes are now starkly aware of the fact that recent civil rights victories benefited a very small percentage of middle-class Negroes while their predicament remained the same or worsened." Simply eliminating racial barriers was not going to be enough. As the late black economist Vivian Henderson put it in the NAACP journal *The Crisis,* "If all racial prejudice and discrimination and all racism were erased today, all the ills brought by the process of economic class distinction and economic depression of the masses of black people would remain."

Accordingly, black leaders and liberal policy makers began to emphasize the need not only to eliminate active discrimination, but also to counteract the effects of past racial oppression. Instead of seeking remedies only for individual complaints of discrimination, they sought government-mandated affirmative action programs to ensure adequate minority representation in employment, education, and public programs.

However, as the political scientist James Fishkin has argued, if the more advantaged members of minority groups benefit disproportionately from policies that embody the principle of equality of individual opportunity, they also profit disproportionately from policies of preferential treatment based solely on their racial group membership. Why? Again simply because minority individuals from the most advantaged families tend to be disproportionately represented among those of their racial group most qualified for preferred status, such as college admissions, higher-paying jobs, and promotions. Thus policies of preferential treatment are likely to improve further the socioeconomic positions of the more advantaged without adequately remedying the problems of the disadvantaged.

To be sure, affirmative action was not intended solely to benefit the more advantaged minority individuals. As William L. Taylor, the former director of the U.S. Civil Rights Commission, has stated, "The focus of much of the [affirmative action] effort has been not just on white collar jobs, but also on law enforcement, construction work, and craft and production in large companies—all areas in which the extension of new opportunities has provided upward mobility for less advantaged minority workers." Taylor also notes that studies show that many minority students entering medical schools during the 1970s were from families of low income.

Affirmative action policies, however, did not really open up broad avenues of upward mobility for the masses of disavantaged blacks. Like other forms of "creaming," they provided opportunities for those individuals from low socio-economic backgrounds with the greatest educational and social resources. Recent data on income, employment opportunities, and educational attainment confirm that relatively few individuals who reside in the inner-city ghettos have benefited from affirmative action.

During the past two decades, as I have argued previously in *The Truly Disadvantaged* (1987), urban minorities have been highly vulnerable to structural changes in the economy, such as the shift from goods-producing to service-producing industries, the increasing polarization of the labor market into low-wage and high-wage sectors, innovations in technology, and the relocation of manufacturing industries out of the central city. These shifts have led to sharp increases in joblessness and the related problems of highly concentrated poverty, welfare dependency, and family breakup, despite the passage of antidiscrimination legislation and the creation of affirmative action programs. In 1974, for example, 47 percent of all employed black males ages twenty to twenty-four held blue-collar, semiskilled operative and skilled-craft positions, which typically earned wages adequate to support a family. By 1986 that figure plummeted to 25 percent. A survey I have directed, randomly sampling residents from poor Chicago neighborhoods, revealed that Puerto Rican men up to age forty-five and black men under age thirty-six have borne the brunt of job losses due to deindustrialization.

However, I do not advance the foregoing arguments to suggest that race-specific programs were inefficacious. They clearly helped to bring about a sharp increase in the number of blacks entering higher education and gaining professional and managerial positions. But neither policies based on the principle of equality of individual opportunity, nor policies that call for preferential group treatment, such as affirmative action, will do much for less advantaged blacks because of the combined effects of past discrimination and current structural changes in the economy. Now more than ever we need broader solutions than those we have employed in the past.

Toward a New Political Strategy

Full employment policies, job skills training, comprehensive health-care legislation, educational reforms in the public schools, child care legislation, and crime and drug abuse prevention programs—these are the race-neutral policies likely to begin making a difference for the poor, black and white.

When presenting this argument to academic audiences, I am frequently told that such programs would face general opposition not only because of their cost, but also because many whites have become disenchanted with the black movement and its calls for intensified affirmative action.

These programs should be presented, however, not as ways to address the plight of poor minorities (though they would greatly benefit from them), but as strategies to help all groups, regardless of race or economic class. After all, Americans across racial and class lines continue to be concerned about unemployment and job security, declining real wages, escalating medical costs, the sharp decline in the quality of public education, the lack of good child care, and crime and drug trafficking in their neighborhoods.

Public opinion surveys reflect these concerns. For the

last several years national opinion polls consistently reveal strong public backing for government labor market strategies, including training efforts to enhance employment. A 1988 Harris poll indicated that almost three quarters of the respondents would support a tax increase to pay for child care. A 1989 Harris poll reports that almost nine out of ten Americans would like to see fundamental change in the U.S. health-care system. And recent surveys conducted by the National Opinion Research Center at the University of Chicago reveal that a substantial majority of Americans want more money spent to improve the nation's schools and to halt rising crime and drug addiction.

Programs that expand employment opportunities and job skills training, improve public education, provide adequate child and health care, and reduce neighborhood crime and drug abuse could alleviate many problems of poor minorities that cannot be successfully attacked by race-specific measures alone. In the 1990s the best political strategy for those committed to racial justice is to promote these programs for all groups in America, not just minorities.

Race-Neutral Programs and Coalition Politics

"The economic future of blacks in the United States," Vivian Henderson argued in 1975, "is bound up with that of the rest of the nation. Policies, programs, and politics designed in the future to cope with the problems of the poor and victimized will also yield benefits to blacks. In contrast, any efforts to treat blacks separately from the rest of the nation are likely to lead to frustration, heightened racial animosities, and a waste of the country's resources and the precious resources of black people."

Henderson's warning seems to be especially appropriate in periods of economic stagnation, when public support of programs targeted for minorities—or associated with real or imagined material sacrifice on the part of whites—seems to wane. The economy was strong when affirmative action programs were introduced during the Johnson administration. When the economy turned down in the 1970s, the public's view of affirmative action turned increasingly sour.

Furthermore, as Joseph A. Califano, Johnson's staff assistant for domestic affairs, observed in 1988, such programs were generally acceptable to whites "only as a temporary expedient to speed blacks' entry into the social and economic mainstream." But as years passed, many whites "saw continuing such preferences as an unjust insistence by Democrats that they do penance for an era of slavery and discrimination they had nothing to do with." They also associated the decline in public schools, not with broader changes in society, but with "forced integration."

The Democrats also came under fire for their support for Great Society programs that increasingly and incorrectly acquired the stigma of being intended for poor blacks alone. Virtually separate medical and legal systems developed in many cities. Public services became identified mainly with blacks, private services mainly with whites. In an era of ostensible racial justice, many public programs ironically seemed to develop into a new and costlier form of segregation. White taxpayers saw themselves as being forced to pay for medical and legal services for minorities that many of them could not afford to purchase for their own families.

From the New Deal to the 1960s, the Democrats were able to link Keynesian economics and middle-class prosperity with programs for integrating racial minorities and the poor into the American mainstream. "In periods of great economic progress when [the incomes of the middle classes] are rising rapidly," argues Lester Thurow, "they are willing to share some of their income and jobs with those less fortunate than themselves, but they are not willing to reduce their real standard of living to help either minorities or the poor."

As the economic situation worsened, Ronald Reagan was able to convince many working- and middle-class Americans that the decline in their living standards was attributable to expensive and wasteful programs for the poor (and implicitly for minorities). When Reagan was elected to office in 1980, the New Deal coalition collapsed; the principal groups supporting the Democratic ticket with wide majorities were blacks, Hispanics, and the poor, who represent only a quarter of the American population.

What are the implications for the Democratic party? After losing three straight presidential elections, the Democrats are reexamining their programs and approaches to voters, partly in the hope of recapturing support from disaffected whites who voted for Reagan and Bush. Those steps ought to involve the development of race-neutral programs. Consider, for example, one issue likely to be at the core of new domestic programs—the future of the American work force.

Social scientists, corporate leaders, and government officials have all expressed concerns about the potential weakening of America's competitive position if we fail to confront the growing shortage of skilled workers. These concerns have led to a heightened awareness of the consequences of poverty, poor education, and joblessness. Many of the new jobs will require higher levels of training and education at the very time when our public schools are graduating too many students who can barely read or write. The 1987 U.S. Department of Labor Study, "Workforce 2000," pointed out that for demographic reasons members of minority groups will necessarily fill a majority of the new jobs in the next decade.

A major policy initiative to improve the quality of the work force would open up opportunities for the minorities who are heavily represented among the educational have-nots. But such an initiative would also open opportunities for others, and it should draw general support because of concerns over the devastating effects a poorly trained work force will have on the entire economy.

Nonracial Affirmative Action

However, even if minorities would benefit disproportionately from new race-neutral initiatives to combat the problems and consequences of social inequality, are there not severe problems in the inner-city ghetto that can only be effectively addressed by creative programs targeted on the basis of race? For example, Roger Wilkins has argued persuasively that the cumulative effects of racial isolation and subjugation have made the plight of the black poor unique. Many inner-city children have a solo parent and lack educational support and stability in their home; Wilkins contends that they need assistance to enable them to become capable adults who can provide their children with emotional and educational support. Accordingly, he maintains that special social service programs are needed for inner-city (presumably, minority) schools.

No serious initiative to improve the quality of the work force could ignore problems such as poverty, social isolation, and family instability, which impede the formal education of children and ultimately affect their job performance. Service programs to meet these needs could easily fit into an overall race-neutral initiative to improve America's work force. To be sure, this component of the larger initiative would be introduced only in the most disadvantaged neighborhoods, but the neighborhoods would not have to be racially defined. Poor minorities need not be treated separately from the rest of the nation in a national effort to enhance the skill levels of the labor force.

It is particularly important for blacks and other minorities to recognize that they have a stake in the formation of a Democratic coalition that would develop race-neutral initiatives. Only with multiracial support could programs of social and economic reform get approved in Congress. Black voters who are dubious about this approach ought to be reminded of the success of the Jesse Jackson presidential campaign. By highlighting problems plaguing all groups in America, the Jackson campaign drew far more support from white working- and middle-class voters than most political observers thought possible.

The Positive Effects of Race-Neutral Policies

My emphasis on race-neutral programs should be clearly distinguished from the neoconservative critique of affirmative action that attacks both racial preference and activist social welfare policies. The former is said to be antidemocratic, the latter economically counterproductive to minorities. My approach, in contrast, supports the alliance between activist government and racial justice in three key respects—as guarantor of civil rights, as custodian of coalition politics, and as sponsor of race-neutral strategies that advance the well-being of America's neediest along with that of America as a whole. For those who came of age in the 1970s, it seems paradoxical that this goal is now best achieved via race-neutral approaches. Yet, a society without racial preference has, of course, always been the long-term goal of the civil rights movement.

An emphasis on coalition politics that features progressive, race-neutral policies could have two positive effects. It could help the Democratic party regain lost political support, and it could lead to programs that would especially benefit the more disadvantaged members of minority groups—without being minority policies.

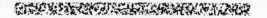

JUST SAY LATINO

Linda Chavez

Linda Chavez is John M. Olin Fellow at the Manhattan
Institute for Policy Research and a former executive direc-
tor of the U.S. Commission on Civil Rights. She is the
author of *Out of the Barrio: Toward a New Politics of
Hispanic Assimilation.* "Just Say Latino" first appeared in
The New Republic, March 22, 1993.

It's been two years since Latin and black youth rampaged
through a Washington, D.C., neighborhood, burning and
looting local businesses and attacking police. The three-
day riot in Mount Pleasant was sparked when a black D.C.
policewoman shot a Salvadoran man, who she claimed
threatened her with a knife as she attempted to arrest him
for drinking in public. Now the U.S. Commission on Civil
Rights, in a report last month, has determined that the way
to prevent such violent outbreaks in the future is for the
mostly black D.C. government to establish an affirmative
action program for hiring Latinos for city jobs and provide
Hispanics with a proportional share of city social services.
The commission's recommendations echo the increasingly
militant demands of Latino advocates for such entitlements.

They couldn't be more foolish. Although affirmative action sounds like a natural way to tackle the problems many Latinos experience in D.C. and other cities, it's a very rough stick to use on a very complex problem. Crudely ascribing the difficulties of a disparate racial grouping to discrimination and recommending group preferences as an anodyne are likely to drive an even deeper wedge between Hispanic citizens and noncitizens and exacerbate already tense relations between blacks and Hispanics. The major problem Hispanics face throughout the country is not discrimination by city officials, but the fact that so many of them are new immigrants—often illegal aliens—without much education.

The huge increase in the Hispanic population nationwide (53 percent from 1980 to 1990) is largely the result of a massive influx of immigrants from Latin America. Immigrants make up about half the nation's adult Latino population and constitute most of D.C.'s Latino population. Though accurate figures are hard to come by, the Census Bureau estimates that the D.C. metropolitan area is now home to some quarter-million Hispanics; 33,000 live in the District, making up roughly 5 percent of the city's population. Most are immigrants from El Salvador, Guatemala, and a handful of other Latin countries. Very few were originally admitted legally to the United States. Many have subsequently acquired permanent status as a result of the amnesty provisions of the Immigration Reform and Control Act of 1986, and many more remain illegal aliens.

Given these realities, the Civil Rights Commission's demand that the D.C. government simply hire more Hispanics in order "to eliminate any discriminatory practices" is a little absurd. "Discriminatory practices" are not what is keeping them out. Their illegal status is a far more salient fact than their race. And their poor education is an even more salient fact than their illegality. On average,

Latino immigrants to the United States have had seven years of school, making it difficult for them even to qualify for government jobs.

Nevertheless, the Civil Rights Commission insists on seeing the matter in purely racial terms. The target number for Latinos in government jobs is based on a population figure that includes both legal *and* illegal immigrants. In its fixation on quotas, the commission simply ignores the enormous problem of illegal immigration and implicitly urges the D.C. government to do what Zoe Baird was dismissed for trying to do.

Elsewhere, the commission explicitly urges privileges for illegal Latinos. It upbraids the University of the District of Columbia for requiring proof of residency in order to qualify for in-state tuition. But in this the commission is only following the lead of Latino civil rights organizations. Like the Civil Rights Commission, Latino advocacy groups generally look upon the problems Latino immigrants face as obstacles of racial discrimination rather than barriers that result from their illegal status. Consequently, the Mexican American Legal Defense and Education Fund (MALDEF) and other advocacy groups have increasingly pressed immigrants' claims, winning benefits through judicial and state and local administrative action.

One of MALDEF's first and most important victories in this new arena was a successful Supreme Court case, *Plyler v. Doe* (1982), which established the right to free public education for illegal aliens. Since then many jurisdictions have expanded educational benefits for illegal aliens to include eligibility for in-state college tuition as well. New Mexico's board of education has gone one step further, extending alien benefits literally across the border by requiring local school districts to provide free public education to children who reside in neighboring Mexico but take chartered buses into New Mexico border towns to attend school. A variety of federal and state court decisions has also mandated unemployment compensation and disability benefits for illegal aliens, even though it is illegal for an employer to hire them in the first place. For these people, rights are plentiful; but their civic responsibilities to work and contribute to society are actually illegal.

Other welfare benefits for immigrants have become a heavy burden for states like California and Texas, home to one third of all legally admitted immigrants and an even larger share of illegal aliens. A recent Los Angeles County study found that illegal immigrants accounted for nearly $310 million a year in county spending on social services. Even where jurisdictions deny direct welfare payments to illegal immigrants, their U.S.-born children are nonetheless eligible. About 10 percent of California's welfare recipients are such children, whose parents, ineligible themselves, receive the checks on their children's behalf. Perhaps to ensure a political constituency to maintain such benefits, Latino advocates have recently sought and won voting rights for immigrants (regardless of legal status) in local elections in some jurisdictions, including the Washington suburb of Takoma Park, Maryland.

All of this activity has one immediate outcome: it has angered other Latinos and black Americans. Though few black or Hispanic leaders are willing to discuss it publicly, tensions between blacks and Hispanics have risen recently, fueled by competition over affirmative action programs and jobs. In little more than a decade, Hispanics will replace blacks as the largest minority group in the country, in part because of the continued flow of Hispanic immigrants. Already, Hispanics are winning the race for jobs, at least in the private sector. Recent studies by the Urban Poverty and Family Structure Project at the University of Chicago show that many employers already prefer hiring Hispanic immigrants over black Americans. By extending privileges to illegal immigrants under the guise of civil rights, liberals are likely to make this tension even more explosive. Far from preventing another Mount Pleasant, affirmative action might actually provoke one.

Latino citizens are just as angry as blacks, and appear no more likely than blacks or whites to favor special treatment for Hispanic immigrants, however politically correct and despite the claims of advocacy groups that purport to speak for all Latinos. According to the Latino National Political Survey, the most comprehensive opinion study of its kind ever done, U.S. citizens of Hispanic origin—like most other Americans—think there are already too many immigrants in the United States. It found that 75 percent of Mexican-Americans share that view, as do 70 percent of Puerto Ricans and 65 percent of Cuban-Americans, compared to about 74 percent of non-Hispanic whites. What's more, a majority of all Hispanic citizens oppose giving preference to those who want to immigrate from Latin America over immigrants from other areas; and a majority of both Mexican-Americans and Puerto Ricans believe that employers should hire citizens over noncitizens. This sentiment is nothing new among ethnic groups. The descendants of early waves of German Jews who came to the United States during the 1800s, for example, were wary of the Eastern European Jews who arrived at the beginning of this century, fearful that the newcomers would erode their hard-won status.

Hispanic advocacy groups are betting that all Hispanics will gain if the pool of Latinos eligible to receive benefits is expanded to include immigrants, legal and illegal. But clearly, the Civil Rights Commission should not implicitly encourage employers to break the law. Unfortunately, the commission has surrendered to the entitlements mentality and fails to see that Hispanics—including many new legal immigrants—are succeeding the old-fashioned way, through hard work and individual effort.

As for D.C.'s angry illegal aliens, it may sound harsh, but affirmative action programs can't resolve their legal status. They should make their way by the age-old methods of illegal immigrants—self-help, self-education, and eventual assimilation. If they broke the law to arrive here, they cannot expect the law immediately to privilege them over actual citizens of whatever race. This traditional path of assimilation has one other benefit: it is likely to avert, rather than incite, the racial wars that are now bubbling in our inner cities.

THE POLITICS OF DIVERSION: BLAME IT ON THE BLACKS

William Greider

William Greider is the author of *Secrets of the Temple: How the Federal Reserve Rules the Country* and *Who Will Tell the People: The Betrayal of American Democracy*. He was assistant managing editor of *The Washington Post*. "The Politics of Diversion: Blame It on the Blacks" first appeared in *Rolling Stone*, September 5, 1991.

If a foreigner relied only on the media for a current impression of America, he would see a nation obsessed with race. From books and magazines, from reporting on the higher realms of political conflict, he would conclude that the country's biggest problem is not the recession or failing banks, not the global competition for jobs or declining family incomes, but blacks and their privileged position in the American system.

Blacks are in the news again—but this time they're being portrayed not as righteous citizens victimized by racism who are making just claims on America's guilty conscience but as pampered interlopers using their political influence to deprive other citizens—white citizens—of their rights. On college campuses, it is said, black students are bullying their peers and professors into silence. In the workplace, blacks are accused of taking unfair advantage of their skin color to win jobs and promotions.

Preparing the ground for his reelection campaign, George Bush has railed loudly against quotas, the summer's hot issue, refusing to compromise on civil-rights legislation with even the moderate senators in his own party. To blunt the charge that he is playing race politics, Bush has nominated to the Supreme Court a black lawyer who opposes racial preferences in hiring and college admissions, even though he has personally benefited from them.

People should be judged, Clarence Thomas has said, "on the basis of what they can do and not on the basis of irrelevant personal characteristics." Perhaps most whites believe this is how the system works, or at least how it ought to work. Most blacks (and Hispanics and many women of all races) have a lifetime of personal experiences that tells them differently. "Irrelevant personal characteristics" like race or gender still often decide who gets in the door, who gets the job or the promotion.

It seems truly bizarre that a nation confronted by so many deep economic disorders should be informed—relentlessly, it seems, by the major media—that "affirmative action" is the destructive force that demands our attention. Why now? None of the aggravations caused by affirmative action programs—and there are real aggravations—is new. And none of the supposed benefits for blacks has been suddenly enlarged. The benefits have, in fact, been shrinking for at least a decade.

Notwithstanding the "race-conscious" admissions policies of colleges, black college enrollment peaked in 1980 and has declined since then (mainly because federal tuition aid was cut by the Reagan administration at the same time family incomes were faltering). Black unemployment, now approaching 13 percent, is rising faster than white unemployment (now at 5.8 percent), which hardly suggests a job market tilted in favor of blacks. As for affirmative action programs, the conservative Republican Supreme Court is dismantling them case by case, an assault that will continue regardless of whether Thomas wins confirmation or even whether Bush wins reelection.

So why exactly have politicians and the press seized on affirmative action? I detect a whiff of old-fashioned scapegoating in this born-again obsession with race—a way to change the subject from what's really hurting people. The impulse is deeply rooted in American politics: Whenever things are going badly, whenever people are losing their jobs and social decline is visible, it's easier to blame the troubles on racial minorities—especially those who have made some advancement—than it is to confront the leaders who are responsible or the powerful economic interests aligned with them. Tolerant people sometimes become resentful when they themselves are in need and the government isn't helping them.

That's the grotesque politics of this season: No one, not even the Democrats, wants to talk much about the recession and the deeper economic problems that are gradually eroding living standards for ordinary Americans. No one has a plan to deal with the long-term losses facing the American middle class, white and black. Instead, let's just talk about whether blacks are getting more than their share.

If the arguments over quotas sound stale, it's because these arguments have been around for over twenty years (and originated when the Nixon administration first devised quotas to integrate labor unions). The language of racial politics has been cleaned up a lot, thanks to the moral force of the civil-rights movement, so that no one speaks directly about keeping "them" in their place, as race-baiting politicians did even a generation ago in some parts of the country.

Today racial messages are delivered in slick TV images. Bush used Willie Horton, the black rapist, in 1988 as a device to agitate white fears and resentment. Senator Jesse Helms won reelection in 1990 with a nasty little commercial called "White Hands, Black Hands," a visual depiction of blacks taking the good life from whites. There will be more of this, for sure, in 1992, wherever GOP candidates think it is needed to win.

The Democratic party has paid dearly for its defense of antidiscrimination programs. Some groups within the party, such as the conservative Democratic Leadership Council, would like to placate white voters by throwing the programs over the side. They don't quite have the nerve to say it so directly, because if loyal black voters were alienated, the Democrats would be in even deeper trouble. A new book, *Chain Reaction,* by *Washington Post* reporter Thomas B. Edsall, takes a similar stance. Edsall recounts in authoritative detail how for twenty-five years the GOP has used race as the wedge to dislodge white working-class voters from their natural home in the Democratic party. His book seems to argue that Democrats can never win back the presidency unless they dump affirmative action. But in the end, like the DLC, Edsall stops just short of recommending abandonment.

The race issue is usually framed as a high-minded discussion of American values. There is an obvious conflict, it seems, between the idea of political equality and the programs that give a leg up to some citizens on the basis of their skin color, whether it is for jobs or college admissions. The critics of affirmative action piously proclaim that the goal of civil rights should be a "color-blind society" that rewards people solely on the basis of individual merit. All they seek is a "level playing field" for everyone. Who can be against that?

What the critics don't like to talk about is the fundamental success of affirmative action, visible in large and small towns across the country. Walk into any bank and you'll see that some of the tellers are black—a perfectly normal sight, though a generation ago it wasn't, in either the North or the South. White customers, bankers reasoned, would feel uncomfortable handing their money to blacks. Banks did not even hire blacks as guards, since black men carrying guns made whites nervous too.

But the integration of banking proceeded rather swiftly in the early seventies (the GOP was in the White House) once the federal government announced that, henceforth, companies seeking federal contracts had to demonstrate they were equal-opportunity employers. For banks this rule was especially threatening because it meant they might become ineligible to receive huge federal deposits. Rather abruptly, bankers decided that white customers were mature enough to deal with black hands.

Police and fire departments, likewise, were overwhelmingly white twenty-five years ago, even in cities like Washington, D.C. Women, of course, were not considered physically capable of those two occupations or dozens of others reserved for men, usually white men. Today most big-city fire and police forces are substantially integrated by race and gender, and the appointment of black chiefs is regarded as almost routine, even in some cities where blacks aren't the majority.

The results of affirmative action are expressed most clearly in the rise of the black middle class. In 1960, according to Edsall's book, 48 percent of all black families were poor; by 1980, 70 percent of black families weren't poor. They were middle class or higher, and many had moved to the suburbs, seeking the same things as prospering white families—good schools, pleasant surroundings, the security of homeownership.

Not all of this progress, of course, can be traced directly to affirmative action, but the enforcement of civil-rights laws stimulated a broad opening of opportunities for people with talent and ambition who had been excluded because of race. Even employers who were not yet feeling the law's heat changed their hiring practices. To imagine that any of this would have happened without the forceful intervention of government requires a deep innocence about race and privilege in America.

The social costs of affirmative action have been inescapably borne by real people—mainly white men. The rancor is shared by the white police officer who didn't make sergeant even though his test score was higher than that of the black who got the promotion, by the white student who didn't get into the Ivy League college trying to expand its minority enrollment, by the middle manager in business who sees blacks and women in his office advancing while his career is stalled.

The current argument is that intervention has gone too far and developed standards that amount to "reverse discrimination." Most critics prefer to concentrate their case on blacks—the minority that arouses the most intense hostilities—but their arguments, if they prevail, would also strip the legal protections against discrimination from a long list of other groups—women, Hispanics and other racial minorities, the elderly, the handicapped, homosexuals.

The issue was joined concretely in 1989 when the new conservative majority on the Supreme Court reversed portions of a 1971 ruling, *Griggs v. Duke Power Company*, that prevented companies from using employment-test scores to evaluate candidates if the tests were not based on necessary qualifications for the job. You don't need an engineering degree to turn valves on a boiler or a Ph.D. in accounting to be a bookkeeper. When Democrats in Congress proceeded to pass a new civil-rights bill to restore the old legal standard, Bush jumped in with his "quota" argument. Democrats declared themselves against "quotas," too, since that's not really what the dispute is about.

The central issue is this: Should entry hurdles be lowered for black applicants in order to ensure that employers reverse the patterns of their past discrimination? As a practical matter, *Griggs* allowed employers to set minimum qualifications for a job—applicable to blacks and everyone else—but not simply to pick those who had made the highest test scores.

Naturally, that seems unfair to the people who scored the highest, but if companies are free to concoct testing that is only vaguely related to the actual work requirements and then to pick only the top scorers, the exclusion of blacks will be virtually guaranteed—even though they may be fully capable of doing the job in question. The Supreme Court's reversal of *Griggs* effectively invites such employment practices.

Critics of affirmative action are morally offended by all this because it seems to contradict the cherished idea of meritocracy. This ideal is widely realized in American life—everyone knows someone, perhaps even him- or herself, whose individual success proves the case. But another, unacknowledged employment system exists too—interwoven with the meritocracy—that relies not on individual merit but on who you know, where you came from, what you look like, or lots of other personal qualities that have nothing to do with capability. Young people seem to understand this well enough; they spend enormous energy on "networking"—making personal connections that will advance their careers.

To take another obvious example, the police departments of several large American cities did not become overwhelmingly Irish because cops were recruited solely on merit. In New York City, for instance, the common wisdom for generations held that the Irish had the police, the Italians had the sanitation department, and the Jews had the school system. Everyone understood how these preference systems worked, but they were never written down on paper or formalized in law.

Given their distinctive minority status, blacks were not only excluded by those tribal patronage systems (and similar ones in trade unions) but also denied the political power to create such networks for themselves. In a sense, affirmative action was a way of formally extending to racial minorities the same kind of helpful political ladder that other groups had informally used before them.

Middle-class white Americans without any special ethnic identity also benefited from such preferences and still do. Informal quotas existed in college admissions long before affirmative action was invented for blacks. I should know: As a white middle-class male, I was admitted to an Ivy League school many years ago partly because I came from a tiny high school in Ohio—and helped the Midwest quota.

If that university had picked only the applicants with the highest SATs, its enrollment would have been dominated by the East Coast prep schools. It would certainly not have included me. I had a second advantage: A classmate of mine, a good guy with an unimpressive academic record but the son of a prominent alumnus, was applying to the same school. If they took him, I figured, they'd have to take me, too, and I was right. As it turned out, we were both in over our heads, but we managed to do the work—sort of—and to graduate, though not with any great distinction.

Clarence Thomas is a more uplifting example of the same practical reality. Thomas grew up poor in south Georgia, bright and ambitious but utterly without the resources and connections that are so helpful. He was admitted to Yale Law School in 1971 under lower admissions standards devised for minority students, but ones based on a straightforward question: Were they capable of doing the work? "We didn't want anyone who would fail," one Yale professor told *The New York Times*.

In Thomas's case, Yale's gamble clearly paid off. His academic work was not especially dazzling, but his subsequent career has been impressive enough to get him nominated to the Supreme Court at the age of forty-three. Though he now opposes "race conscious" remedies, Thomas long ago acknowledged that without affirmative action, "God only knows where I would be today."

The right question, I think, is the one Yale asked—can the applicant do the work?—and that ought to be the general standard for affirmative action of every sort. Confining selection to the highest test scores would actually create higher barriers for disadvantaged racial minorities than other groups faced in earlier eras when they were trying to get a foot in the door.

Test scores are useful, but they're not a reliable basis for determining a person's quality, much less for advancing social equity. If conservatives insist on such a standard, they are going to collide with their own hypocrisies. If a meritocracy requires the highest test scores, then that standard ought to apply to everything. That would mean, for example, no more preferential admissions for the children of important alumni, no more hiring of the boss's nephew, no more networking to find jobs. A true meritocracy would mean—good grief!—that colleges couldn't admit talented athletes with lousy scores when more gifted students were being turned away. Not even conservatives want a playing field that level.

In fact, this preoccupation with "level playing fields" sounds extremely out of touch with reality in an era when government is executing billion-dollar bailouts for certain bankers and doling out gargantuan tax favors for wealthy campaign contributors and ignoring the general distress of working people everywhere, white and black, men and women.

The cruel paradox of affirmative action is that its very success may have unwittingly accelerated the social deterioration in inner-city ghettos—blacks who, between crime and drugs and teenage pregnancy, always seem to be in the news. When blacks were rigidly segregated in the same part of town, the poorest children at least had visible role models in their own communities—striving, hardworking middle-class people who were the church leaders and civic activists.

The triumph of some black families inevitably left others behind—up against the same problems of poverty and social disarray but with fewer strong figures needed to hold their communities together. The ones left behind are the principal source of the white resentment and fear—not affirmative action, not the black people who have succeeded in getting ahead.

"I believe that the exodus of middle- and working-class families from many ghetto neighborhoods removes an important 'social buffer' that could deflect the full impact of the kind of prolonged and increasing joblessness that plagued inner-city neighborhoods," sociologist William Julius Wilson has written. "The very presence of these families during such periods provides mainstream role models that help keep alive the perception that education is meaningful, that steady employment is a viable alternative to welfare, and that family stability is the norm, not the exception."

Affirmative action does not reach those people mired in self-destructive behavior, and it was folly to imagine that it ever could. As Wilson and others have argued for more than a decade, the core element in the inner-city decay is economic loss—the changing labor market that has eliminated millions of low-skill jobs, the downward pressures on wages at the bottom of the ladder. This diagnosis is well documented by now, but it is not what political leaders want to hear, because it suggests a dramatic reversal in economic priorities—a politics focused on defending wages and jobs.

New economic policies along those lines would, of course, benefit not just poor blacks but struggling whites as well. Since no one wants to talk in those terms, the losses are likely to continue for both, and as standards of living decline further, the troubled racial climate may become even more exacerbated. And some politician will try to profit by promising, via coded messages, to put uppity blacks back in their place.

AFFIRMATIVE RACISM

Charles Murray

Charles Murray is Bradley Fellow at the American Enterprise Institute in Washington, D.C. He is author of *Losing Ground: American Social Policy, 1950–1980* and *In Pursuit: Of Happiness and Good Government.* "Affirmative Racism" first appeared in *The New Republic,* December 31, 1984.

A few years ago, I got into an argument with a lawyer friend who is a partner in a New York firm. I was being the conservative, arguing that preferential treatment of blacks was immoral; he was being the liberal, urging that it was the only way to bring blacks to full equality. In the middle of all this he abruptly said, "But you know, let's face it. We must have hired ten blacks in the last few years, and none of them has really worked out." He then returned to his case for still stronger affirmative action, while I wondered what it had been like for those ten blacks. And if he could make a remark like that so casually, what remarks would he be able to make some years down the road, if by that time it had been fifty blacks who hadn't "really worked out"?

My friend's comment was an outcropping of a new

racism that is emerging to take its place alongside the old. It grows out of preferential treatment for blacks, and it is not just the much-publicized reactions, for example, of the white policemen or firemen who are passed over for promotion because of an affirmative action court order. The new racism that is potentially most damaging is located among the white elites—educated, affluent, and occupying the positions in education, business, and government from which this country is run. It currently focuses on blacks; whether it will eventually extend to include Hispanics and other minorities remains to be seen.

The new racists do not think blacks are inferior. They are typically longtime supporters of civil rights. But they exhibit the classic behavioral symptom of racism: they treat blacks differently from whites, because of their race. The results can be as concretely bad and unjust as any that the old racism produces. Sometimes the effect is that blacks are refused an education they otherwise could have gotten. Sometimes blacks are shunted into dead-end jobs. Always, blacks are denied the right to compete as equals.

The new racists also exhibit another characteristic of racism: they *think* about blacks differently from the way they think about whites. Their global view of blacks and civil rights is impeccable. Blacks must be enabled to achieve full equality. They are still unequal, through no fault of their own (it is the fault of racism, it is the fault of inadequate opportunity, it is the legacy of history). But the new racists' local view is that the blacks they run across professionally are not, on the average, up to the white standard. Among the new racists, lawyers have gotten used to the idea that the brief a black colleague turns in will be a little less well rehearsed and argued than the one they would have done. Businessmen expect that a black colleague will not read a balance sheet as subtly as they do.

Teachers expect black students to wind up toward the bottom of the class.

The new racists also tend to think of blacks as a commodity. The office must have a sufficient supply of blacks, who must be treated with special delicacy. The personnel problems this creates are more difficult than most because whites barely admit to themselves what's going on.

What follows is a foray into very poorly mapped territory. I will present a few numbers that explain much about how the process gets started. But the ways that the numbers get translated into behavior are even more important. The cases I present are composites constructed from my own observations and taken from firsthand accounts. All are based on real events and real people, stripped of their particularities. But the individual cases are not intended as evidence, because I cannot tell you how often they happen. They have not been the kind of thing that social scientists or journalists have wanted to count. I am writing this because so many people, both white and black, to whom I tell such stories know immediately what I am talking about. It is apparent that a problem exists. How significant is it? What follows is as much an attempt to elicit evidence as to present it.

As in so many of the crusades of the 1960s, the nation began with a good idea. It was called "affirmative action," initiated by Lyndon Johnson through Executive Order 11246 in September 1965. It was an attractive label and a natural corrective to past racism: actively seek out black candidates for jobs, college, or promotions, without treating them differently in the actual decision to hire, admit, or promote. The term originally evoked both the letter and the spirit of the order.

Then, gradually, affirmative action came to mean something quite different. In 1970 a federal court established the legitimacy of quotas as a means of implementing Johnson's executive order. In 1971 the Supreme Court ruled that an employer could not use minimum credentials as a prerequisite for hiring if the credential acted as a "built-in headwind" for minority groups—even when there was no discriminatory intent and even when the hiring procedures were "fair in form." In 1972 the Equal Employment Opportunity Commission acquired broad, independent enforcement powers.

Thus by the early 1970s it had become generally recognized that a good-faith effort to recruit qualified blacks was not enough—especially if one's school depended on federal grants or one's business depended on federal contracts. Even for businesses and schools not directly dependent on the government, the simplest way to withstand an accusation of violating Title VII of the Civil Rights Act of 1964 was to make sure not that they had not just interviewed enough minority candidates, but that they had actually hired or admitted enough of them. Employers and admissions committees arrived at a rule of thumb: If the blacks who are available happen to be the best candidates, fine; if not, the best available black candidates will be given some sort of edge in the selection process. Sometimes the edge will be small; sometimes it will be predetermined that a black candidate is essential, and the edge will be very large.

Perhaps the first crucial place where the edge applies is in admission to college. Consider the cases of the following three students: John, William, and Carol, seventeen years old and applying to college, are all equal on paper. Each has a score of 520 in the mathematics section of the Scholastic Aptitude Test, which puts them in the top third—at the 67th percentile—of all students who took the test. (Figures are based on 1983 data.)

John is white. A score of 520 gets him into the state

university. Against the advice of his high school counselor, he applies to a prestigious school, Ivy U., where his application is rejected in the first cut—its average white applicant has math scores in the high 600s.

William is black, from a middle-class family who sent him to good schools. His score of 520 puts him at the 95th percentile of all blacks who took the test. William's high school counselor points out that he could probably get into Ivy U. William applies and is admitted—Ivy U. uses separate standards for admission of whites and blacks, and William is among the top blacks who applied.

Carol is black, educated at an inner-city school, and her score of 520 represents an extraordinary achievement in the face of terrible schooling. An alumnus of Ivy U. who regularly looks for promising inner-city candidates finds her, recruits her, and sends her off with a full scholarship to Ivy U.

When American universities embarked on policies of preferential admissions by race, they had the Carols in mind. They had good reason to be optimistic that preferential treatment would work—for many years, the best universities had been weighting the test scores of applicants from small-town public schools when they were compared against those of applicants from the top private schools, and had been giving special breaks to students from distant states to ensure geographic distribution. The differences in preparation tended to even out long-standing and successful tradition of preferential treatment.

In the case of blacks, however, preferential treatment ran up against a large black-white gap in academic performance combined with ambitious goals for proportional representation. This gap has been the hardest for whites to confront. But though it is not necessary or even plausible to believe that such differences are innate, it is necessary to recognize openly that the differences exist. By pretending they don't, we begin the process whereby both the real differences and the racial factor are exaggerated.

The black-white gap that applies most directly to this discussion is the one that separates blacks and whites who go to college. In 1983, for example, the mean Scholastic Aptitude Test score for all blacks who took the examination was more than 100 points below the white score on both the verbal and the math sections. Statistically, it is an extremely wide gap. To convert the gap into more concrete terms, think of it this way: in 1983, the same Scholastic Aptitude Test math score that put a black at the fiftieth percentile of all blacks who took the test put him at the sixteenth percentile of all whites who took the test.

These results clearly mean we ought to be making an all-out effort to improve elementary and secondary education for blacks. But that doesn't help much now, when an academic discrepancy of this magnitude is fed into a preferential admissions process. As universities scramble to make sure they are admitting enough blacks, the results feed the new racism. Here's how it works:

In 1983, only 66 black students nationwide scored above 700 in the verbal section of the Scholastic Aptitude Test, and only 205 scored above 700 in the mathematics section. This handful of students cannot begin to meet the demand for blacks with such scores. For example, Harvard, Yale, and Princeton have in recent years been bringing an aggregate of about 270 blacks into each entering class. If the black students entering these schools had the same distribution of scores as that of the freshman class as a whole, then every black student in the nation with a verbal score in the 700s, and roughly 70 percent of the ones with a math score in the 700s, would be in their freshman classes.

The main problem is not that a few schools monopolize

the very top black applicants, but that these same schools have much larger implicit quotas than they can fill with those applicants. They fill out the rest with the next students in line—students who would not have gotten into these schools if they were not black, who otherwise would have been showing up in the classrooms of the nation's less glamorous colleges and universities. But the size of the black pool does not expand appreciably at the next levels. The number of blacks scoring in the 600s on the math section in 1983, for example, was 1,531. Meanwhile, 31,704 nonblack students in 1983 scored in the 700s on the math section and 121,640 scored in the 600s. The prestige schools cannot begin to absorb these numbers of other highly qualified freshmen, and they are perforce spread widely throughout the system.

At schools that draw most broadly from the student population, such as the large state universities, the effects of this skimming produce a situation that confirms the old racists in everything they want most to believe. There are plenty of outstanding students in such student bodies (at the University of Colorado, for example, 6 percent of the freshmen in 1981 had math scores in the 700s and 28 percent had scores in the 600s), but the skimming process combined with the very small raw numbers means that almost none of them are black. What students and instructors see in their day-to-day experience in the classroom is a disproportionate number of blacks who are below the white average, relatively few blacks who are at the white average, and virtually none who are in the first rank. The image that the white student carries away is that blacks are less able than whites.

I am not exalting the SAT as an infallible measure of academic ability, or pointing to test scores to try to convince anyone that blacks are performing below the level of whites. I am simply using them to explain what instructors and students already notice, and talk about, among themselves.

They do not talk openly about such matters. One characteristic of the new racism is that whites deny in public but acknowledge in private that there are significant differences in black and white academic performance. Another is that they dismiss the importance of tests when black scores are at issue, blaming cultural bias and saying that test scores are not good predictors of college performance. At the same time, they watch anxiously over their own children's test scores.

The differences in academic performance do not disappear by the end of college. Far from narrowing, the gap separating black and white academic achievement appears to get larger. Various studies, most recently at Harvard, have found that during the 1970s blacks did worse in college (as measured by grade point average) than their test scores would have predicted. Moreover, the black-white gap in the Graduate Record Examination is larger than the gap in the Scholastic Aptitude Test. The gap between black and white freshmen is a bit less than one standard deviation (the technical measure for comparing scores). Black and white seniors who take the Graduate Record Examination reveal a gap of about one and a quarter standard deviations.

Why should the gap grow wider? Perhaps it is an illusion—for example, perhaps a disproportionate number of the best black students never take the examination. But these are also reasons for suspecting that in fact blacks get a worse education in college than whites do. Here are a few of the hypotheses that deserve full exploration.

Take the situation of William—a slightly above-average student who, because he is black, gets into a highly competitive school. William studies very hard during the first year. He nonetheless gets mediocre grades. He has a choice. He can continue to study hard and continue to get mediocre grades, and be seen by his classmates as a black who cannot do very well. Or he can explicitly refuse to engage in the academic game. He decides to opt out; and his performance gets worse as time goes on. He emerges from college with a poor education and is further behind the whites than he was as a freshman.

If large numbers of other black students at the institution are in the same situation as William, the result can be group pressure not to compete academically. (At Harvard, it is said, the current term among black students for a black who studies like a white is "incognegro.") The response is not hard to understand. If one subpopulation of students is conspicuously behind another population and is visibly identifiable, then the population that is behind must come up with a good excuse for doing poorly. "Not wanting to do better" is as good as any.

But there is another crucial reason why blacks might not close the gap with whites during college: they are not taught as well as whites are. Racist teachers impeding the progress of students? Perhaps, but most college faculty members I know tend to bend over backward to be "fair" to black students—and that may be the problem. I suggest that inferior instruction is more likely to be a manifestation of the new racism than the old.

Consider the case of Carol, with outstanding abilities but deprived of decent prior schooling: she struggles the first year, but she gets by. Her academic skills still show the aftereffects of her inferior preparation. Her instructors diplomatically point out the more flagrant mistakes, but they ignore minor lapses, and never push her in the aggressive way they push white students who have her intellectual capacity. Some of them are being patronizing (she is doing quite well, considering). Others are being prudent: teachers who criticize black students can find themselves being called racists in the classroom, in the campus newspaper, or in complaints to the administration.

The same process continues in graduate school. Indeed, because there are even fewer blacks in graduate schools than in undergraduate schools, the pressures to get black students through to the degree, no matter what, can be still greater. But apart from differences in preparation and ability that have accumulated by the end of schooling, the process whereby we foster the appearance of black inferiority continues. Let's assume that William did not give up during college. He goes to business school, where he gets his master's degree. He signs up for interviews with the corporate recruiters. There are one hundred persons in his class, and Willam is ranked near the middle. But of the five blacks in his class, he ranks first (remember that he was at the ninety-fifth percentile of blacks taking the Scholastic Aptitude Test). He is hired on his first interview by his first-choice company, which also attracted the very best of the white students. He is hired alongside five of the top-ranking white members of the class.

William's situation as one of five blacks in a class of one hundred illustrates the proportions that prevail in business schools, and business schools are by no means one of the more extreme examples. The pool of black candidates for any given profession is a small fraction of the white pool. This works out to a twenty-to-one edge in business; it is even greater in most of the other professions. The result, when many hiring institutions are competing, is that a major gap between the abilities of new black and white employees in any given workplace is highly likely. Everyone needs to hire a few blacks, and the edge that "being black" confers in the hiring decision warps the sequence of hiring in such a way that a scarce resource (the blacks with a given set of qualifications) is exhausted at an artificially high rate, producing a widening gap in comparison with the remaining whites from which an employer can choose.

The more aggressively affirmative action is enforced, the greater the imbalance. In general, the first companies to hire can pursue strategies that minimize or even eliminate the difference in ability between the new black and white employees. IBM and Park Avenue law firms can do very well, just as Harvard does quite well in attracting the top black students. But the more effectively they pursue these strategies, the more quickly they strip the population of the best black candidates.

To this point I have been discussing problems that are more or less driven by realities we have very little hope of manipulating in the short term except by discarding the laws regarding preferential treatment. People do differ in acquired abilities. Currently, acquired abilities in the white and black populations are distributed differently. Schools and firms do form a rough hierarchy when they draw from these distributions. The results follow ineluctably. The dangers they represent are not a matter of statistical possibilities, but of day-to-day human reactions we see around us.

The damage caused by these mechanistic forces should be much less in the world of work than in the schools, however. Schools deal in a relatively narrow domain of skills, and "talent" tends to be assigned specific meanings and specific measures. Workplaces deal in highly complex sets of skills, and "talent" consists of all sorts of combinations of qualities. A successful career depends in large part upon finding jobs that elicit and develop one's strengths.

At this point the young black professional must sidestep a new series of traps laid by whites who need to be ostentatiously nonracist. Let's say that William goes to work for the XYZ Corporation, where he is assigned with another management trainee (white) to a department where much of the time is spent preparing proposals for government contracts. The white trainee is assigned a variety of scut work—proofreading drafts, calculating the costs of minor items in the bid, making photocopies, taking notes at conferences. William gets more dignified work. He is assigned portions of the draft to write (which are later rewritten by more experienced staff), sits in on planning sessions, and even goes to Washington as a highly visible part of the team to present the bid. As time goes on, the white trainee learns a great deal about how the company operates, and is seen as a go-getting young member of the team. William is perceived to be a bright enough fellow, but not much of a detail man and not really much of a self-starter.

Even if a black is hired under terms that put him on a par with his white peers, the subtler forms of differential treatment work against him. Particularly for any corporation that does business with the government, the new employee has a specific, immediate value purely because he is black. There are a variety of requirements to be met and rituals to be observed for which a black face is helpful. These have very little to do with the long-term career interests of the new employee; on the contrary, they often lead to a dead end as head of the minority-relations section of the personnel department.

Added to this is another problem that has nothing to do with the government. When the old racism was at fault (as it often still is), the newly hired black employee was excluded from the socialization process because the whites did not want him to become part of the group. When the new racism is at fault, it is because many whites are embarrassed to treat black employees as badly as they are willing to treat whites. Hence another reason that whites get on-the-job training that blacks do not: much of the early training of an employee is intertwined with menial assignments and mild hazing. Blacks who are put through these routines often see themselves as racially abused (and when a black is involved, old-racist responses may well have crept in). But even if the black is not unhappy about the process, the whites are afraid that he is, and so protect him from it. There are many variations, all having the same effect: the black is denied an apprenticeship that the white has no way of escaping. Without serving the apprenticeship, there is no way of becoming part of the team.

Carol suffers a slightly different fate. She and a white woman are hired as reporters by a major newspaper. They both work hard, but after a few months there is no denying it: neither one of them can write. The white woman is let go. Carol is kept on, because the paper cannot afford to have any fewer blacks than it already has. She is kept busy with reportorial work, even though they have to work around the writing problem. She is told not to worry— there's lots more to being a journalist than writing.

It is the mascot syndrome. A white performing at a comparable level would be fired. The black is kept on, perhaps to avoid complications with the Equal Employment Opportunity Commission (it can be very expensive to fire a black), perhaps out of a more diffuse wish not to appear discriminatory. Everybody pretends that nothing is wrong—but the black's career is at a dead end. The irony, of course, is that the white who gets fired and has to try something else has been forced into accepting a chance of making a success in some other line of work whereas the black is seduced into *not* taking the same chance.

Sometimes differential treatment takes an even more pernicious form: the conspiracy to promote a problem out of existence. As part of keeping Carol busy, the newspaper gives her some administrative responsibilities. They do not amount to much. But she has an impressive title on a prominent newspaper and she is black—a potent combination. She gets an offer from a lesser paper in another part of the country to take a senior editorial post. Her current employer is happy to be rid of an awkward situation and sends along glowing references. She gets a job that she is unequipped to handle—only this time, she is in a highly visible position, and within a few weeks the deficiencies that were covered up at the old job have become the subject of jokes all over the office. Most of the jokes are openly racist.

It is important to pause and remember who Carol is: an extremely bright young woman, not (in other circumstances) a likely object of condescension. But being bright is no protection. Whites can usually count on the market to help us recognize egregious career mistakes and to prevent us from being promoted too far from a career line that fits our strengths, and too far above our level of readiness. One of the most prevalent characteristics of white differential treatment of blacks has been to exempt blacks from these market considerations, substituting for them a market premium attached to race.

The most obvious consequence of preferential treatment is that every black professional, no matter how able, is tainted. Every black who is hired by a white-run organization that hires blacks preferentially has to put up with the knowledge that many of his co-workers believe he was hired because of his race; and he has to put up with the suspicion that in his own mind they might be right.

Whites are curiously reluctant to consider this a real problem—it is an abstraction, I am told, much less important than the problem that blacks face in getting a job in the first place. But black professionals talk about it, and they tell stories of mental breakdowns; of people who had to leave the job altogether; of long-term professional paralysis. What white would want to be put in such a situation? Of course it would be a constant humiliation to be resented by some of your co-workers and condescended to by others. Of course it would affect your perceptions of yourself and your self-confidence. No system that produces such side effects—as preferential treatment must do—can be defended unless it is producing some extremely important benefits.

And that brings us to the decisive question. If the alternative were no job at all, as it was for so many blacks for so long, the resentment and condescension are part of the price of getting blacks into the positions they deserve. But is that the alternative today? If the institutions of this country were left to their own devices now, to what extent would they refuse to admit, hire, and promote people because they were black? To what extent are American institutions kept from being racist by the government's intervention?

It is another one of those questions that are seldom investigated aggressively, and I have no evidence. Let me suggest a hypothesis that bears looking into: that the signal event in the struggle for black equality during the last thirty years, the one with real impact, was not the Civil Rights Act of 1964 or Executive Order 11246 or any other governmental act. It was the civil rights movement itself. It raised to a pitch of acute and lasting discomfort the racial consciousness of the generations of white Americans who are now running the country. I will not argue that the old racism is dead at any level of society. I will argue, however, that in the typical corporation or in the typical admissions office, there is an abiding desire to be not-racist. This need not be construed as brotherly love. Guilt will do as well. But the civil rights movement did its job. I suggest that the laws and the court decisions and the continuing intellectual respectability behind preferential treatment are not holding many doors open to qualified blacks that would otherwise be closed.

Suppose for a moment that I am right. Suppose that, for practical purposes, racism would not get in the way of blacks if preferential treatment were abandoned. How, in my most optimistic view, would the world look different?

There would be fewer blacks at Harvard and Yale; but they would all be fully competitive with the whites who were there. White students at the state university would encounter a cross section of blacks who span the full range of ability, including the top levels, just as whites do. College remedial courses would no longer be disproportionately black. Whites rejected by the school they wanted would quit assuming they were kept out because a less-qualified black was admitted in their place. Blacks in big corporations would no longer be shunted off to personnel-relations positions, but would be left on the main-line tracks toward becoming comptrollers and sales managers and chief executive officers. Whites would quit assuming that black colleagues had been hired because they were black. Blacks would quit worrying that they had been hired because they were black.

Would blacks still lag behind? As a population, yes, for a time, and the nation should be mounting a far more effective program to improve elementary and secondary education for blacks than it has mounted in the last few decades. But in years past virtually every ethnic group in America has at one time or another lagged behind as a population, and has eventually caught up. In the process of catching up, the ones who breached the barriers were evidence of the success of that group. Now blacks who breach the barriers tend to be seen as evidence of the inferiority of that group.

And that is the evil of preferential treatment. It perpetuates an impression of inferiority. The system segments whites and blacks who come in contact with each other so as to maximize the likelihood that whites have the advantage in experience and ability. The system then encourages both whites and blacks to behave in ways that create self-fulfilling prophecies even when no real differences exist.

It is here that the new racism links up with the old. The old racism has always openly held that blacks are permanently less competent than whites. The new racism tacitly accepts that, in the course of overcoming the legacy of the old racism, blacks are temporarily less competent than whites. It is an extremely fine distinction. As time goes on, fine distinctions tend to be lost. Preferential treatment is providing persuasive evidence for the old racists, and we can already hear it sotto voce: "We gave you your chance, we let you educate them and push them into jobs they couldn't have gotten on their own and coddle them every way you could. And see: they still aren't as good as whites, and you are beginning to admit it yourselves." Sooner or later this message is going to be heard by a white elite that needs to excuse its failure to achieve black equality.

The only happy aspect of the new racism is that the corrective—to get rid of the policies encouraging preferential treatment—is so natural. Deliberate preferential treatment by race has sat as uneasily with America's equal-opportunity ideal during the post-1965 period as it did during the days of legalized segregation. We had to construct tortuous rationalizations when we permitted blacks to be kept on the back of the bus—and the rationalizations to justify sending blacks to the head of the line have been just as tortuous. Both kinds of rationalization say that sometimes it is all right to treat people of different races in different ways. For years, we have instinctively sensed this was wrong in principle but intellectualized our support for it as an expedient. I submit that our instincts were right. There is no such thing as good racial discrimination.

PART FIVE

IVORY TOWERS UNDER SIEGE

THE GREAT WHITE MYTH

Anna Quindlen

Anna Quindlen is a columnist for *The New York Times*.
Her books include *Living Out Loud, Thinking Out Loud*,
and a novel, *Object Lessons*. "The Great White Myth"
first appeared in *The New York Times*, January 15, 1992.

In a college classroom, a young white man rises and asks
about the future. What, he wants to know, can it possibly
hold for him when most of the jobs, most of the good
positions, most of the spots in professional schools are
being given to women and, most especially, to blacks?

The temptation to be short, sarcastic, incredulous in
reply is powerful. But you have to remember that kids learn
their lessons from adults. That's what the mother of two
black children who were sprayed with white paint in the
Bronx said last week about the assailants, teenagers who
called her son and daughter "nigger" and vowed they would
turn them white. "Can you imagine what they are being
taught at home?" she asked.

A nation of laws, we like to believe that when they are
changed, attitudes will change along with them. This is
naive. America continues to be a country whose people are

211

obsessed with some spurious pecking order. Leaving, at the bottom, blacks to be taught at ages twelve and fourteen through the utter humiliation of having their faces cleaned with paint thinner that there are those who think that even white in a bottle is better than not white at all.

Each generation finds its own reasons to hate. The worried young white men I've met on college campuses in the last year have internalized the newest myth of American race relations, and it has made them bitter. It is called affirmative action, a.k.a. the systematic oppression of white men. All good things in life, they've learned, from college admission to executive position, are being given to black citizens. The verb is ubiquitous: given.

Never mind that you can walk through the offices of almost any big company and see a sea of white faces. Never mind that with all that has been written about preferential treatment for minority law students, only about 7,500 of the 127,000 students enrolled in law school last year were African American. Never mind that only 3 percent of the doctors in this country are black.

Never mind that in the good old days preferential treatment was routinely given to brothers and sons of workers in certain lines of work. Perceptions of programs to educate and hire more black citizens as, in part, an antidote to decades of systematic exclusion have been inflated to enormous proportions in the public mind. Like hot air balloons they fill up the blue sky of the American landscape with the gaudy stripes of hyperbole. Listen and you will believe that the construction sites, the precinct houses, the investment banks are filled with African Americans.

Unless you actually visit them.

The opponents of affirmative action programs say they are opposing the rank unfairness of preferential treatment. But there was no great hue and cry when colleges were candid about wanting to have geographic diversity, perhaps giving the kid from Montana an edge. There has been no national outcry when legacy applicants whose transcripts were supplemented by Dad's alumni status—and cash contributions to the college—were admitted over more qualified comers. We somehow only discovered that life was not fair when the beneficiaries happened to be black.

And so the chasm widens. The old myth was the black American incapable of prosperity. It was common knowledge that welfare was purely a benefits program for blacks; it was common knowledge although it was false. The percentage of whites on public assistance is almost identical to the percentage of blacks.

The new myth is that the world is full of black Americans prospering unfairly at white expense, and anecdotal evidence abounds. The stories about the incompetent black co-worker always leave out two things: the incompetent white co-workers and the talented black ones. They also leave out the tendency of so many managers to hire those who seem most like themselves when young.

"It seems like if you're a white male you don't have a chance," said another young man on a campus where a scant 5 percent of his classmates were black. What the kid really means is that he no longer has the edge, that the rules of a system that may have served his father will have changed. It is one of those good-old-days constructs to believe it was a system based purely on merit, but we know that's not true. It is a system that once favored him, and others like him. Now sometimes—just sometimes—it favors someone different.

EDUCATION: ETHNICITY AND ACHIEVEMENT

Andrew Hacker

Andrew Hacker is professor of political science at Queens College. His books include *The End of the American Era* and *The United States: A Statistical Portrait of the American People*. "Education: Ethnicity and Achievement" is excerpted from his 1992 study, *Two Nations: Black and White, Separate, Hostile, Unequal*.

If affirmative action has had a mixed record in employment, it remains alive and well on the nation's campuses. Until a decade or so ago, conflicts could be construed largely in black and white terms. Now there are more players in the field, with Hispanics and Asians, and women and other groups also making claims. Decisions about college admissions are based on varied views of merit and equity. Two cases illustrate some of the issues that are involved.

- In recent years, the University of Virginia has moved to double its admissions of black students, while cutting back on white enrollments. Recently, it accepted over half the blacks who had applied, but only a quarter of the whites, even though the Scholastic Aptitude Test scores for the black group averaged 240 points lower. An admissions dean admitted, "We take in more in the groups with weaker credentials and make it harder for those with stronger credentials."

• In California, about 33 percent of high school seniors with Asian backgrounds have academic records that qualify them for the state's university system. However, in 1988 they were allotted only 26 percent of the places at the Berkeley campus, and 18 percent at UCLA. Many Asians complained that a ceiling had been set to limit their presence on some campuses, despite their records and qualifications.

Virginia's admission policy for black students is an example of *affirmative action* at work. The Asians objecting to California's plan were asking for an *equal opportunity* to compete fairly with other applicants. The two principles may sound similar, but they can actually be in opposition.

Today, every college and university says it is committed to "equal opportunity" in faculty hiring and student admissions. On its face, the principle would seem unassailable: all applicants should be given full and fair consideration, regardless of age or race or sex, or other characteristics and conditions, including physical disabilities. Under equal opportunity, standards would be set and all would stand the same chance in the competition. If this seems a commonplace now, it was not always the case. In the past, colleges turned down qualified candidates because they were Catholic or Jewish, and in many cases would not even consider blacks. Now, as has been noted, some Asians are protesting that while they have satisfied admissions standards, they are not getting their fair share of college places.

In a similar vein, some whites have complained that blacks with lower test results are given places sought by higher-scoring whites.

"Affirmative action" is rather different from "equal opportunity." No colleges today turn down black applicants who meet their academic criteria. Virtually all schools say they would like to attract even more black students, since small black enrollments have become a matter of embarrassment. At last report, only 3.2 percent of the students at Smith College were black. Bates College in Maine could manage only 2.1 percent, and at the main University of Wisconsin campus at Madison the black proportion was only 1.7 percent. Few schools simply wait for black candidates to apply; almost all mount recruiting drives.

The difficulty has been to find candidates the schools believe are qualified. Not only elite private schools but many state universities want to maintain minimal standards for the people they admit. Hence their quandary when too few black applicants meet those requisites.* To solve this problem, affirmative action programs have moved beyond recruiting drives and offers of financial aid. In other words "action" must mean more than "opportunity"; it has to be able to point to results. To ensure that entering classes will display a certain racial composition, applications from black students are judged by a separate set of standards.

Separate standards can be rationalized in several ways. One argument is that preferential treatment is hardly new. For years, Ivy League colleges acted "affirmatively" by giving places to mediocre students from fashionable prep schools. Or, to cite a current example, since the Massachu-

---

* Of course, black students are not the only group "protected" (the official term) by affirmative action. Most programs also provide for Hispanics and Native Americans. Berkeley has added Filipinos, as well as applicants from low-income families and persons with physical disabilities. The City University of New York, having decided it should have more Italian-Americans on its faculty, is allowed to judge candidates from that group by less stringent standards.

setts Institute of Technology wants its classes to have a certain ratio of women, it admits some who have lower mathematics scores then male applicants. It can also be argued that reserving places for athletes is a variant of affirmative action, as is greater indulgence toward candidates from distant states. The most common practice involves giving favored consideration to the offspring of alumni, even if their records are less impressive than those of other applicants. A recent study of Harvard, for example, found that about 40 percent of alumni children were admitted, compared with 14 percent from less well-connected homes. To be sure, "reasons" can be marshaled to support alumni preference or athletic scholarships or applicants from Alaska.*

Presumably everyone approves of diversity. In the *Bakke* case, which upheld a medical school's affirmative action program, Justice Lewis Powell wrote that institutions should be allowed to assemble a varied student body. In this vein, a report by the Faculty Senate at Berkeley has suggested that the possession of certain ethnic backgrounds could be seen as a "qualification" for admission. The diversity that such students would bring to the campus would, it was argued, make for "a more dynamic intellectual environment and a richer undergraduate experience."

Indeed, one of the most graphic examples of how affirmative action works has been on the Berkeley campus. It is an intricate story, involving at least four ethnic groups. In 1973, an official plan recommended that "each segment of California public higher education shall strive to approximate by 1980 the general ethnic, sexual, and economic composition of the recent high school graduates." Despite

---

* In response to inquiries from the U.S. Department of Education, Harvard officials said that alumni whose children were admitted gave more generously to the university. However, they later confessed that they had no figures to support this supposition.

this goal, a count taken in 1981 found that only 3.8 percent of Berkeley's students were black and only 4.4 percent were Hispanic, whereas students from those two groups together made up 27.2 percent of California's statewide pool of high school graduates. Black and Hispanic enrollments at Berkeley were still two thirds short of the target set eight years earlier.

The reason for this shortfall was not overt discrimination, but the prevailing standards for admission. To be accepted at Berkeley and seven other selective campuses, applicants had to rank in the top 12.5 percent of California's high school graduates, determined by an index combining grades and Scholastic Aptitude Test scores. Unfortunately, few blacks and Hispanics were in that 12.5 percent.

As the table on this page shows, by 1988 only 5 percent of the Hispanics and even fewer of the blacks were eligible for Berkeley. Using these and other figures, the Faculty Senate found that a class admitted solely on academic grounds would be less than 4 percent black and Hispanic. The chief reason was that Berkeley, enjoying its status as

		ETHNICITY AND ADMISSIONS AT BERKELEY (1988–1989)		
Blacks	Hispanics		Whites	Asians
7.9%	19.3%	Ethnicity of California's High School Graduates*	61.1%	8.7%
4.5%	5.0%	Proportion of Each Group Eligible for University	15.8%	32.8%
11.4%	19.6%	Ethnicity of Students Accepted by Berkeley*	38.9%	27.5%
37.5%	43.5%	Graduation Rate for Students in Each Group	71.5%	67.3%

* Totals run across and omit other ethnic groups.

the most selective campus, took only the very top scorers within the group of students eligible for the statewide system. To raise its ratio of Hispanic and black students, it would be necessary to change the admission procedures to allow applicants from these groups to come to Berkeley regardless of where they ranked in the state pool. As a result, in the 1988 entering class, black and Hispanic applicants together were given 31 percent of the places. This was achieved by admitting almost all the black and Hispanic candidates who met the minimal standard. In the past, as many as two thirds of those entrants would have been sent to other colleges in the system, which have lower admission standards.

The total enrollment at Berkeley has remained fairly stable over the past dozen years; so if some groups receive more places, others will get fewer. Of those admitted to the 1988 freshman class, 27.5 percent were Asian, three times their proportion among high school graduates. Even more striking, only 38.9 percent of its places went to whites, who numbered 61.1 percent of the state's high school graduates, and who had received two thirds of the freshmen places just seven years earlier.

Yet it was not easy for white Californians to complain, since their overall scholastic records were not very auspicious; only 15.8 percent of white high school graduates met Berkeley's academic standards. Asians might have been content since, as was noted, their share of the entering class worked out to three times their representation among high school graduates. However, they were not, because a large number of Asians who had suitable academic scores were still rejected by Berkeley. Many claimed in newspaper and television interviews that they had been subjected to a quota system. Equally disturbing to Asian applicants, the number of places based solely on academic criteria, which they had worked to satisfy, had been substantially reduced. The fear of having "too many" Asians seemed to many a replay of policies colleges once had concerning Jews.

Complicating the equation is the fact that most Asians wanted to attend Berkeley or UCLA, rather than less metropolitan campuses like Davis or Santa Cruz. One reason is that many of them have part-time jobs in family businesses and must remain close to their homes. Given their good records and the large numbers applying, there is a likelihood that those campuses could become overwhelmingly Asian. Indeed, in the UCLA class admitted for the fall of 1990, Asian freshmen in fact outnumbered whites.

Since the system is not expanding its enrollment, if more Asians are admitted, then fewer whites or blacks or Hispanics can be let in. Most Asians say that they have no quarrel with affirmative action for those who need it. For their own part, however, they would rather be judged by regular admissions criteria, which ends up pitting them against whites. And that has been happening not only at Berkeley and UCLA. Yale and Harvard, which draw on national pools, now have entering classes which are 13 percent and 15 percent Asian respectively. At Stanford, the figure is close to 20 percent, while at MIT it is close to a quarter.

AVERAGE SAT SCORES OF STUDENTS FROM LOW-INCOME FAMILIES (1990)		
	Number	Score
White	65,599	881
Asian	18,729	832
Hispanic	21,291	738
Black	32,738	692

* * *

It will be interesting to see how white applicants will react as they find fewer college places open to them. At selective undergraduate and professional schools, more will no longer get their first choice. Of course, this need not doom their college plans. Someone who in the past might have got into Berkeley or UCLA can still enroll at Riverside or Santa Barbara, where the competition is less stringent.

White students may grumble about being denied admissions they feel should have been theirs. By and large, however, few have gone public with their complaints. To start, one can't easily object to facing Asian competitors, since they play by the regular rules. (So far there haven't been complaints about recent immigrants' being subsidized by taxes and contributions from native citizens.) At all events, whites still tend to make up the majority of those admitted to competitive schools, so those who find themselves rejected tend to have less impressive records. So they resign themselves to attending Lehigh instead of Amherst, or going to law school at the University of Michigan rather than at Yale.

It remains to be seen how Berkeley's new student body will function in practice. In introductory courses, on one side of the room will be Asians admitted on the academic track. Across from them will be blacks and Hispanics with classroom skills at a rather lower level. It is almost as if two dissimilar colleges were sharing the same campus. Indeed, an earlier Berkeley study of freshmen calculus courses found that whereas only 5 percent of the Asian students failed, half of the black students did.

The real test is how many actually make it to graduation. Even before affirmative action, minority attrition was a cause for concern. Also included in the Berkeley table are the graduation outcomes for students who started as freshmen in 1983. As can be seen, 71.5 percent of the whites and 67.3 percent of the Asians received degrees by 1988. The figures for Hispanics and blacks were 43.5 percent and 37.5 percent.

Studies of attrition suggest that affirmative action programs may do some students a disservice, by placing them in colleges for which they are not properly prepared. Pennsylvania State University has even tried cash incentives to stem the dropout and failure rates. Black students who manage a C+ average have been given awards of $550; higher grades can win them double that. These grants have stirred some controversy, since they are confined to students of one race. Harvard has sought to avoid the attrition problem by ensuring that most of its black students will come from middle-class homes and have attended predominantly white schools. As an admissions officer explained, "It is right for Harvard and better for the students, because there is better adjustment and less desperate alienation."

Most colleges remain committed to their affirmative action programs. Smith College, which now has a 3.2 percent black enrollment, has pledged to double that proportion over the next ten years. Since this step will almost inevitably bring in students who will have difficulty keeping up with their classmates, it seems appropriate to ask why Smith and other schools persist in this kind of effort. The candid answer is that many professors and quite a few students regard the paucity of black faces on their campuses as a cause for shame. To raise the minority presence eases a lot of academic guilt. The fact that the newly admitted students themselves may bear an unfair burden is hardly even mentioned in campus discussions. Even with intensive remedial programs, teenagers from inner-city high schools are unlikely to be lofted to Ivy League levels.

The question frequently arises why affirmative action must specify race. After all, it can be argued, the whole intent of the civil rights drive was to remove race as a factor, since it was long used to bar blacks from enrolling in many colleges. Yet today, preferential policies for blacks mean that some whites are being shunted aside, simply because they are white.

Hence the argument has been made that if a college wants a diverse student body, it could gear preferential admissions and aid to *all* low-income students, regardless of their ethnic origins. And because a higher proportion of black applicants come from families of modest means, they should get more than their share of low-income places and scholarships.

There is only one problem with this proposal. Among the black, white, Asian, and Hispanic school seniors who took the Scholastic Aptitude Test in 1990, a total of 138,357 came from families having incomes under $20,000. The table on page 220 shows how they divided by ethnicity and average SAT scores. Since all 138,357 have similar economic backgrounds, presumably admissions and aid would be allocated according to academic merit. But gauged by SAT scores, low-income whites and Asians would end up with almost all of the "race-blind" awards, since they obviously have better records from a strictly scholastic standpoint. This is why affirmative action that aims at helping blacks must take race into account.

The kinds of abilities the SAT actually evaluates has been the subject of much debate, and some of those issues will be considered momentarily. At this poiint, it can simply be said that doing well on the SAT shows how well students have prepared themselves—and been prepared—for the admissions competition as it currently exists.

The next table gives SAT scores for the four groups, along with some background information about those taking the test. The gap between the average scores of black and white students—almost 200 points—has received a great deal of attention, and need not be belabored here. Further insights can be obtained if the black and white groups are compared not with each other, but with two other cohorts. This approach makes sense, since in terms of parental income and education, the Hispanic and black students taking the SAT have fairly comparable backgrounds. The Asians and whites are also quite similar so far as parental education is concerned.

Yet Hispanics average 66 points higher than blacks, which might be considered surprising since two thirds of the Hispanic students come from families in which English is not the primary language and may not be spoken at all. So it is impressive that they score as well as they do, as their parents are often new to this country or live in Spanish-speaking neighborhoods. That Asians do five points better than whites is at least equally striking, since English is not the principal language in most of their homes and their economic status is relatively modest. And, as is apparent from the depiction on the next page they move further ahead of whites as their economic standing improves.

This is not the first time that immigrants and their offspring have surpassed native residents. Hard work and

		STUDENTS TAKING THE SAT (1990)		
Blacks	Hispanics		Whites	Asians
737	803	Average Scores*	933	938
150	176	Point-Gain: Low to High Income	119	211
40.4%	37.5%	Parents Attended College	60.5%	55.5%
8.0%	67.8%	English Not First Language	5.8%	70.0%
23.3%	25.8%	Family Income over $40,000	56.0%	39.5%
37.9%	37.4%	Family Income under $20,000	10.3%	28.3%

*SAT scores run from a low of 400 to a high of 1,600.

ambition still pay off, as they have in the past. However, there is another factor at work. While today's newly arrived immigrants tend to start out with lower incomes, many of them belonged to the middle class in their countries of origin, and they bring those values with them. Over half of the Asian students taking the SAT have parents who attended college, as do more than a third of the Hispanics. Also, immigrants who arrive today are less beset by culture shock. In the global village of an electronic age, most are prepared for American ways.

The Scholastic Aptitude Test has become the closest thing we have to a national IQ test. So it is best that we be clear about what this three-hour examination measures. Clearly, it does not gauge "intelligence" or "aptitude" in a broad sense. At best, it rates a narrow range of academic-oriented skills. Some have argued that, as much as anything, scores simply reflect how adept people are at taking that kind of test. As it happens, the sponsors of the SAT have known for many years that their test fails to identify how people will do in later life. A follow-up of Yale University graduates revealed that "no significant relation could be found between original scores and . . . honors and standing within their occupations." A similar study concluded that "no consistent relationships exist between Scholastic Aptitude Test scores in college students, and their actual accomplishments in social leadership, the arts, sciences, music, writing, and speech and drama."

Yet SAT scores will convey something about the attitudes and abilities of the nation's teenagers. As was noted earlier, they show how well students have prepared for the admissions competition, which in turn reflects a willingness to adapt to a structure of success set up by the adult society.

Most of us are familiar with the SAT format, in which

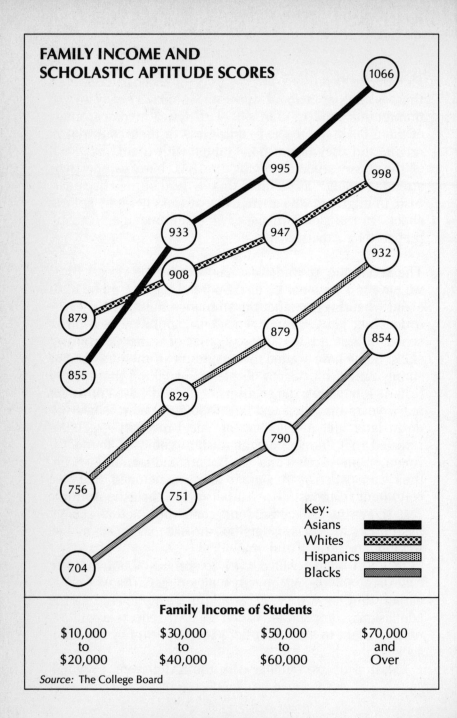

you are asked to pick the correct responses from four or five possible answers. Some are mathematical problems, with several specious solutions. In the reading section, you may be presented with a paragraph on an unfamiliar subject, say, the feeding habits of migratory birds. After taking a minute to read it, you must pick which of several sentences "best describes" the contents of the passage. For each question, there is a single correct answer that the testmakers expect you to identify. For this reason, the SAT has been called "objective," since there is only one set of right answers.

Do the tests discriminate? Quite obviously they do, and not simply along racial lines. First of all, they are biased in favor of people who have a knack for solving puzzles at a one-a-minute rate. Also teenagers drawn to music and the arts are less likely to do well, as are people who eventually prove themselves in the business world. Such disadvantages can be eased for students from better-off homes, who are more apt to attend schools that make a point of preparing them for the multiple-choice method. As has been seen, there is a close association between economic status and SAT scores, and this accounts for much of the variation among ethnic groups.

The record of Asian and Hispanic students would seem to undercut charges that the SAT is basically a "white"—or even a "Western"—test. Of course, it does have a class bias, since much in the verbal portion alludes to information or experiences with which middle-class children are more likely to be familiar. One question once asked which of the following options was most analogous to "runner . . . marathon":

> (a) envoy . . . embassy
> (b) martyr . . . massacre
> (c) oarsman . . . regatta

      (d) referee . . . tournament
      (e) horse . . . stable

Still, a presumption of American life has been that those at lower social levels will come to know about how people above them live, an awareness presumably to be derived from movies and television which depict embassies and regattas. That so many young Asians and Hispanics have shown themselves able to master the SAT would suggest that they have adapted to this "white" world. Nor is it simply that they cram for the tests. Asian high school students have been found twice as likely as whites to take the full academic program recommended by the National Council on Excellence in Education, which includes intensive work in American history and literature.

So it may be more accurate to say that tests like the SAT now reflect not a racial or national corpus of knowledge, but a wider "modern" consciousness. In the past, the word "modern" tended to have white and Western connotations. Today, however, the term has a far broader range. Much of Asia and Latin America have become modernized, to degrees few would have predicted a generation ago. Taiwanese and Costa Rican teenagers arrive in the United States already schooled in advanced mathematics and the multiple-choice method. So "modern" now stands for the mental and structural modes that characterize the developed world. It calls for a commitment to science and technology, as well as skills needed for managing administrative systems. The modern world rests on a framework of communication and finance, increasingly linked by common discourse and rules of rationality. Indeed, evidence from the educational scene suggests that even within this country, young people from immigrant backgrounds are showing themselves to be more "modern" in these commitments and skills than many of their native-born classmates.

Between 1982 and 1988, over half of the top sixty Westinghouse science competition winners were immigrants or the children of immigrants.

Aspiring middle-class Hispanics have outlooks similar to those found among Asians. In fact, the term *Hispanic* underscores the European element in their origins, rather than aboriginal American links or ties to Africa. (An alternative, *Latino,* carries Mediterranean connotations.) In common with Asians, many young Hispanics can pass what someone once called the "telephone test": you cannot identify their ancestry from their accent, something not as easily said for black Americans. For these and related reasons, white Americans are considerably less averse to having Hispanics and Asians as neighbors, or as classmates for their children.

It is striking that black students from better-off homes do not do particularly well on the SAT. Indeed, those whose parents earn between $50,000 and $60,000 barely match Asians from families in the $10,000 to $20,000 range.

Surveys of neighborhoods and schools show that black Americans spend more of their lives in segregated settings than even recent immigrants. One outcome of this isolation is that black Americans have less sustained exposure to the "modern" world than have many members of immigrant groups. Blacks with middle-class jobs and incomes may have greater opportunities to meet and mingle in this world, but those contacts are seldom allowed to develop to the fullest extent. The fact that black modes of perception and expression, which are largely products of segregation, become impediments to performing well on tests like the SAT reveals that racial bias remains latent not only in the multiple-choice method, but in the broader expectations set by the modern world.

SINS OF ADMISSION

Dinesh D'Souza

Dinesh D'Souza is a research fellow at the American
Enterprise Institute and the author of *Illiberal Education:
The Politics of Race and Sex on Campus.* "Sins of Admission" first appeared in *The New Republic,* February 18,
1991.

When Michael Williams, head of the civil rights division of
the Department of Education, sought to prevent American
universities from granting minority-only scholarships, he
blundered across the tripwire of affirmative action, the
issue that is central to understanding racial tensions on
campus and the furor over politically correct speech and
the curriculum.

Nearly all American universities currently seek to
achieve an ethnically diverse student body in order to
prepare young people to live in an increasingly multiracial
and multicultural society. Diversity is usually pursued
through "proportional representation," a policy that attempts to shape each university class to approximate the
proportion of blacks, Hispanics, whites, Asian Americans,
and other groups in the general population. At the Univer-

sity of California, Berkeley, where such race balancing is official policy, an admissions report argues that proportional representation is the only just allocation of privileges for a state school in a democratic society, and moreover, "a broad diversity of backgrounds, values, and viewpoints is an integral part of a stimulating intellectual and cultural environment in which students educate one another."

The lofty goals of proportional representation are frustrated, however, by the fact that different racial groups perform very differently on academic indicators used by admissions officials, such as grades and standardized test scores. For example, on a scale of 400 to 1600, white and Asian-American students on average score nearly 200 points higher than black students on the Scholastic Aptitude Test (SAT). Consequently, the only way for colleges to achieve ethnic proportionalism is to downplay or abandon merit criteria, and to accept students from typically underrepresented groups, such as blacks, Hispanics, and American Indians, over better-qualified students from among whites and Asian Americans.

At Ivy League colleges, for instance, where the median high school grade average of applicants approaches 4.0 and SAT scores are around 1300, many black, Hispanic, and American Indian students are granted admission with grade scores below 3.0 and SATs lower than 1000. Each year state schools such as Berkeley and the University of Virginia turn away hundreds of white and Asian-American applicants with straight As and impressive extracurriculars, while accepting students from underrepresented groups with poor to mediocre academic and other credentials. John Bunzel, former president of San Jose State University, argues that since the pool of qualified minority students is small, selective colleges "soon realize they have to make big academic allowances" if they are going to meet affirmative action targets.

Although universities strenuously deny the existence of quota ceilings for Asians, it is mathematically impossible to raise the percentage of students from underrepresented groups without simultaneously reducing the percentage of students from overrepresented groups. Former Berkeley chancellor Ira Heyman has admitted and apologized for his university's discriminatory treatment of Asians, and this year the Department of Education found the University of California, Los Angeles, guilty of illegal anti-Asian policies. Stanford, Brown, and Yale are among the dozen or so prestigious institutions under close scrutiny by Asian groups.

For Asian Americans, the cruel irony is that preferential admissions policies, which are set up to atone for discrimination, seem to have institutionalized and legitimized discrimination against a minority group that is itself the victim of continuing prejudice in America. Moreover, for Asians, minority quotas that were intended as instruments of inclusion have become instruments of exclusion.

The second major consequence of proportional representation is not an overall increase in the number of blacks and other preferred minorities in American universities, but rather the *misplacement* of such students throughout higher education. In other words, a student who might be qualified for admission to a community college now finds himself at the University of Wisconsin. The student whose grades and extracurriculars are good enough for Wisconsin is offered admission to Bowdoin or Berkeley. The student who meets Bowdoin's or Berkeley's more demanding standards is accepted through affirmative action to Yale or Princeton. Somewhat cynically, one Ivy League official terms this phenomenon "the Peter Principle of university admissions."

Aware of the fact that many affirmative action students are simply not competitive with their peers, many colleges offer special programs in remedial reading, composition, and basic mathematics to enable disadvantaged students to keep pace. But enrollment in such programs is generally poor: students who are already experiencing difficulties with their regular course load often do not have the time or energy to take on additional classes. Consequently, the dropout rate of affirmative action students is extremely high. Figures from the Department of Education show that blacks and Hispanics are twice as likely as whites and Asians to drop out for academic reasons. A recent study of 1980 high school graduates who entered four-year colleges found that only 26 percent of black and Hispanic students had graduated by 1986.

Even taking into account other factors for leaving college, such as financial hardship, the data leave little doubt that preferential admissions seriously exacerbate what universities euphemistically term "the retention problem." An internal report that Berkeley won't release to the public shows that, of students admitted through affirmative action who enrolled in 1982, only 22 percent of Hispanics and 18 percent of blacks had graduated by 1987. Blacks and Hispanics not admitted through preferential programs graduated at the rates of 42 and 55 percent respectively.

Although most universities do everything they can to conceal the data about preferential admissions and dropout rates, administrators will acknowledge the fact that a large number of minority students who stay in college experience severe academic difficulties. These classroom pressures, compounded by the social dislocation that many black and Hispanic students feel in the new campus environment, are at the root of the serious racial troubles on the American campus.

* * *

It is precisely these pressures that thwart the high expectations of affirmative action students, who have been repeatedly assured by college recruiters that standards have not been abridged to let them in, that they belong at the university, indeed, that they provide a special perspective that the school could not hope to obtain elsewhere. Bewildered at the realities of college life, many minority students seek support and solace from others like them, especially older students who have traveled the unfamiliar paths. Thus begins the process of minority separatism and self-segregation on campus, which is now fairly advanced and which has come as such a surprise to universities whose catalogs celebrate integration and the close interaction of diverse ethnic groups.

Distinctive minority organizations, such as Afro-American societies and Hispanic student organizations, provide needed camaraderie, but they do not provide academic assistance to disadvantaged students. Instead, they offer an attractive explanation: classroom difficulties of minorities are attributed not to insufficient academic preparation, but to the pervasive atmosphere of bigotry on campus. In particular, both the curriculum and testing systems are said to embody a white male ethos that is inaccessible to minorities.

Through the political agitation of minority organizations, many black and Hispanic students seek to recover a confident identity and sense of place on campuses where they otherwise feel alienated and even inadequate. Consequently, minority activists at several universities now have elaborate campaigns to identify and extirpate bigotry, such as racism hotlines and mandatory consciousness-raising sessions directed at white students. In addition, activists demand that "institutional racism" be remedied through greater representation of blacks and Hispanics among administrators and faculty. The logical extreme of this trend is a bill that Assemblyman Tom Hayden has introduced in the California legislature that mandates not just proportional admissions but equal pass rates for racial groups in state universities.

Both survey data and interviews with students published in *The Chronicle of Higher Education* over the past few years show that many white students who are generally sympathetic to the minority cause become weary and irritated by the extent of preferential treatment and double standards involving minority groups on campus. Indeed, racial incidents frequently suggest such embitterment; at the University of Michigan, for example, the affirmative action office has been sent a slew of posters, letters, poems—many racist—objecting specifically to special treatment for blacks and deriding the competence of minority students at the university. An increasing number of students are coming to believe what undergraduate Jake Shapiro recently told the *MacNeil-Lehrer NewsHour:* "The reason why we have racial tensions at Rutgers is they have a very strong minority recruitment program, and this means that many of my friends from my hometown were not accepted even though they are more qualified."

Other students have complained that universities routinely recognize and subsidize minority separatist organizations, black and Hispanic fraternities, and even racially segregated residence quarters while they would never permit a club or fraternity to restrict membership to whites. A couple of American campuses have witnessed the disturbing rise of white student unions in bellicose resistance to perceived minority favoritism on campus.

A new generation of university leaders, weaned on the protest politics of the 1960s, such as Nannerl Keohane of Wellesley, James Freedman of Dartmouth, and Donna Shalala of the University of Wisconsin-Madison, are quite happy to attribute all opposition to resurgent bigotry. Some of this may be true, but as thoughtful university leaders and observers are now starting to recognize, administration policies may also be playing a tragic, counterproductive role. A redoubling of those policies, which is the usual response to racial tension, is not likely to solve the problem and might make it worse.

If universities wish to eliminate race as a factor in their students' decision-making, they might consider eliminating it as a factor in their own. It may be time for college leaders to consider basing affirmative action programs on socioeconomic disadvantage rather than ethnicity. This strategy would help reach those disadvantaged blacks who desperately need the education our colleges provide, but without the deleterious effects of racial head-counting. And it would set a color-blind standard of civilized behavior, which inspired the civil rights movement in the first place.

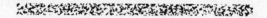

DIVERSITY AND EXCELLENCE IN HIGHER EDUCATION

Chang-Lin Tien

Chang-Lin Tien is chancellor of the University of California at Berkeley. "Diversity and Excellence in Higher Education" is based on his keynote address at "The Mutuality of Excellence and Equity Conference" at the University of Southern California, March 13, 1991.

Today, as all of us in the university community are aware, a debate rages in campuses across the country. Can you refine admissions standards to diversify undergraduate populations without sacrificing academic standards? Doesn't the question of preserving academic standards assume greater importance at the graduate level? Do scholarships and financial aid programs that assist ethnic minorities unfairly discriminate against white students? As competition for qualified faculty becomes more intense, can universities afford to pay attention to the recruitment of women and ethnic minorities? These are the questions that ignite passionate discourse inside our faculty senates, department meetings, administrative parleys, classroom corridors, and campus coffeehouses.

In the 1990s, I believe the focus of our questions must

shift. We can no longer afford to ask: Should we—or can we—diversify at the undergraduate, graduate, and faculty levels? Instead, the question for higher education is: How can we diversify? How can we make diversity work?

The 1990 United States Census figures are a solid base for building the case that excellence in higher education is impossible without equity. The census confirms that California is rapidly becoming a state where there is no ethnic majority. By 1990, ethnic minorities represented 43 percent of the state population. A decade earlier, in 1980, ethnic minorities comprised just a third of the population.

For the past ten years, the fastest growing groups were Hispanics, Chicanos, Latinos, Asians, and Pacific Islanders. There was an impressive 69 percent jump in the Hispanic population. For Asians and Pacific Islanders, the totals more than doubled. Ethnic minorities enjoy a numerical edge in 115 California cities. And at least three counties—Los Angeles, San Francisco, and Imperial—have no majority population.

What does this sweeping sociodemographic transformation signify for higher education? The ethical, educational, economic, and political realities of this decade demand that we strive to diversify. We must seek to serve all segments of our multicultural society. Our colleges and universities must reflect the new face of our state and our nation.

The arguments for diversification are just as compelling as they are numerous. But I believe academics would concur on our central mission. We share the immense responsibility of preparing future generations of leaders who will shape the fate of America in the twenty-first century.

Who will be the future leaders of California and the nation? Increasingly universities will frame the answer to this all-important question. With the breathtaking speed of advances in human knowledge, education will assume increasing importance in all professions. The captains of industry, government, science, and education will require advanced knowledge. Those with limited academic skills will find themselves locked out of the system.

As a result, whenever colleges and universities fail to fully serve any ethnic or cultural groups, the problem is far greater than limiting educational opportunities for a portion of the population. The lack of a college education in the twenty-first century will effectively shut people out of the social and economic mainstream. In short, if we fall down on the job, we will set in motion the forces that lead to a form of apartheid almost as pervasive and insidious as the strictest segregation in South Africa.

So far, I have concentrated on the *ethical* considerations for diversifying campuses. But let us turn now to the educational merits of diversity. In the event that some segments of the population are not represented on campuses, all students suffer. It is not misplaced idealism, charitable zeal, or adherence to a politically correct line that compels me to make this statement. In practical terms, we are doing a second-rate job if we fail to prepare students for work in a multicultural society. This preparation is impossible without strong representation of minorities and women in the faculty, in the staff, and in the student body.

Consider just a few examples of the demand for multicultural understanding in different fields. The medical student who plans to set up practice in east Los Angeles needs to learn how to interpret the way her patients perceive and describe symptoms, patients whose families come from Mexico, Guatemala, El Salvador, Korea, China, Taiwan, and Japan.

The journalism student who aspires to one of California's major dailies—such as the *Los Angeles Times, San Jose Mercury News,* the *San Francisco Chronicle,* or others—must be versed in interviewing and reporting on all constituencies. The story about flooding in a Central Valley farm town will be based on accounts from Mexican field hands. The story about new directions in Silicon Valley electronics will require interviews with engineers born in Taiwan and India.

The business administration major who hopes to climb the corporate ladder will head a work force predominated by women and ethnic minorities. The education student will one day teach classes populated by youngsters of different ethnic and language backgrounds. The law student whose sights are set on political office must become familiar with the needs of a multicultural electorate in order to win votes.

You don't have to be a demographer to read the population trends. And you don't have to be an academic visionary to decipher the bottom line for higher education. We must incorporate in higher education the unique talents, understanding, experiences, knowledge, and perceptions of all the minorities who will constitute the majority population of the twenty-first century. Otherwise, our graduates will be ill prepared to function in this multicultural society.

There is another, equally important facet to the merits of diversity in higher education. Women and minorities stimulate new directions and advances in research. People of diverse backgrounds tend to shape different questions and apply different methods to find the answers.

Already the examples are numerous. In legal education, the addition of women scholars opened the field of feminist jurisprudence, which uses new methodologies and new perspectives in shaping answers. Another new area of legal scholarship is critical race theory. African-American, Hispanic, and Asian-American scholars are questioning the legal treatment of racial and ethnic groups and exploring the implications of this treatment on the entire system of justice.

Women's studies brings a new perspective to economics, agriculture, sociology, and anthropology. The synergy of women and ethnic minorities in traditional disciplines has breathed new vitality into the social sciences and humanities as well. Research and instruction in literature, art, and history no longer stick to interpretations of novels and individual historical events. Instead, more scholars delve into the historical context of literature and the arts. In the study of history, the popular culture is considered an important element, as well as the stories of everyday people.

If the educational reasons for diversifying campuses are compelling, the economic arguments are equally strong. No society can afford to throw away the talents of a large segment of its population. And the value of a highly trained, diverse work force soars in an era of fast-growing international investment. Moreover, California is strategically situated for business exchange with the Pacific Rim. Japanese retail banking interests in the U.S. are concentrated in California. Also on the rise are investments in the state from South Korea, Taiwan, Hong Kong, and Singapore. Failure to tap into our human resources would be dangerously shortsighted; the talents of California's diverse population are needed more than ever to meet the challenges of a diversified marketplace.

But no matter how educators respond to the sociodemographic transformation, universities will diversify sooner or later. If we fail to take the lead, elected politicians are sure to take over. That is a political reality. Already the 1990 census figures have prompted predictions of political redistricting, which is leading to increased minority representation in the state legislature and congressional delegation. And minority or not, all lawmakers in a democracy understand the basic political rule of survival: Keep your constituency happy. With their increased political clout, minority Californians can—and should—demand that colleges and universities serve them.

Although state and federal lawmakers cannot legislate what we teach or how we teach, they hold the power of the purse strings—a formidable form of influence indeed. The University of California, California State University, and community college campuses rely heavily on state funding. At the state and federal level, the availability of student grants and financial aid affects both public and private universities. Finally, consider the immense authority of funding agencies in the arts, humanities, and sciences. Whenever a major national foundation gives extra consideration to projects that further opportunities for ethnic minorities, the repercussions are felt in laboratories and classrooms across the country.

Higher education in California has passed the point in history when we can ask whether campuses ought to diversify. The ethical, educational, economic, and political realities compel us instead to concentrate on how best to incorporate women and ethnic minorities. By saying this, I do not mean to imply the process will be simple and straightforward. It is a complex challenge that demands our best thinking and long-term commitment. But the potential dividends from success are extensive and exciting.

Our experiences at Berkeley, I believe, offer valuable insights into the process of diversification. An Academic Senate committee of faculty, students, and admissions office representatives researched the freshman admissions process and developed a blueprint for selecting top scholars who reflect the diversity of this state. This plan of action fine-tunes admissions standards and extends the concept of diversity. Greater consideration in freshman admissions is given to low-income students of all races. And, for the first time, Berkeley is giving special consideration to older students who seek a college education after starting a career or family.

Despite the overall success of student admissions policies at Berkeley, not everyone likes or supports affirmative action. But concern over access and fairness of admissions policies is hardly surprising when competition for admissions is intense. We have learned the immense value of active communications in dispelling mistaken notions and addressing concerns.

What are some of the common myths about affirmative action at Berkeley? The first is that academic quality at Berkeley has declined as the student population has diversified. In fact, the reverse is true. Of the freshmen admitted to our campus, 95 percent continue to rank among the top 12.5 percent of the statewide high-school graduates.

More important, our academic standards are higher than ever and each entering class is more talented than the last. For example, the mean Scholastic Aptitude Test score was 1220 for our new freshmen in fall 1992. This mean score is 100 points higher than a decade ago, a significant increase.

Some critics might argue this overall trend obscures disparities. They might question whether higher scores of whites and Asians account for the overall increase. But that simply is not true. The test scores of other minorities have increased as well.

We have done an analysis of Scholastic Aptitude Test scores and high-school grade-point averages of our entering first-year students, breaking our freshman classes into quintiles. When we compared the scores and grades of all groups to those ten years ago, the recent scores were higher in each quintile. So all segments of our freshman class are stronger than their counterparts of a decade ago.

The second myth about Berkeley admissions is that diversity is limited to race and ethnicity. But our new admissions policies also assure that our doors are open to low-income students, older students, immigrant students, disabled students, students with special talents, and students from rural and urban areas alike.

The fall 1992 freshman class included students from fifty-one of California's fifty-eight counties. Nearly one in four freshmen—23 percent—came from families with annual incomes less than $30,000. And 17 percent of this class were immigrants who resided in California, not international students who come here just to study.

The third myth is that affirmative action in admissions is nothing more than an entitlement program for middle-class minorities. In contrast, the median family income for Chicano freshmen in the fall 1992 class was $31,000, less than half the median $77,000 income for incoming white students. The median income was $44,000 for African Americans and $50,000 for Asian Americans.

The disparity in educational background is just as striking. While nearly 70 percent of the parents of white students have a postgraduate degree, the highest level of parental education was high school or less for 49 percent of Chicano students enrolling in fall 1992. And 41 percent of African-American students came from families where parents do not have four-year college degrees.

The fourth myth is that a diverse student population, once admitted to the university, will not succeed academically. Again, this is not the case at Berkeley. A study done of the entering classes in 1948 and 1949 found that less than half of the students graduated in five years or less. In the 1970s, the graduation rates climbed to almost sixty percent. In the entering class of 1986, seven of ten students graduated in five years' time. This is a big jump—

from 50 percent in the late 1940s, to 60 percent in the 1970s, to 70 percent today.

In the 1940s and 1950s, the overwhelming majority of students were white. In contrast, less than half the entering class of 1986 were white. About 20 percent were Asian American, 12 percent were Chicano or Latino, 8 percent were African American, 6 percent were Filipino, and 9 percent did not report their race or ethnicity.

Moreover, the graduation rates for all ethnic groups have improved significantly. For the class that entered in 1986, the five-year graduation rate was, according to the 1991–92 "Student Retention Update" put out by the Berkeley Office of Student Research, African Americans, 46 percent; American Indians, 47 percent; Chicanos, 56 percent; Latinos, 59 percent; Filipinos, 63 percent; whites, 76 percent; and Asians other than Filipino, 78 percent.

Now that we enjoy an outstanding, diverse undergraduate population, can we pat ourselves on the back for a job well done? Absolutely not. Deep-seated social change— especially when it involves affirmative action—touches off many reverberations. We know that while some students gain self-esteem and a sense of cultural identity at Berkeley, others report that they never had close interactions with students from different racial or ethnic groups. We need to make the same kind of commitment to minimizing racial isolation as we have to increasing racial diversity.

Yes, the 1990s pose formidable challenges for the leaders in higher education who believe in the mutuality of excellence and equity. But I take heart in the understanding that these goals are neither new nor radical. They have garnered the attention of academic leaders for many, many decades. As University of California President Daniel Coit Gilman pointed out in his inaugural address in 1872, "It is not the University of Berlin nor of New Haven which we are to copy . . . but it is the University of this state. It must be adapted to this people, to their public and private schools, to their peculiar geographical position, to the requirements of their new society and their undeveloped resources."

WHO'S THE REAL AFFIRMATIVE ACTION PROFITEER?

John Larew

John Larew is a former chairman of the *Harvard Crimson*. "Who's the Real Affirmative Action Profiteer?" first appeared in *The Washington Monthly*, June 1991.

Growing up, she heard a hundred Harvard stories. In high school, she put the college squarely in her sights. But when judgment day came in the winter of 1988, the Harvard admissions guys were frankly unimpressed. Her academic record was solid—not special. Extracurriculars, interview, recommendations? Above average, but not by much. "Nothing really stands out," one admissions officer scribbled on her application folder. Wrote another, "Harvard not really the right place."

At the hyperselective Harvard, where high school valedictorians, National Merit Scholarship finalists, musical prodigies—11,000 ambitious kids in all—are rejected annually, this young woman didn't seem to have much of a chance. Thanks to Harvard's largest affirmative action program, she got in anyway. No, she wasn't poor, black, disabled, Hispanic, Native American, or even Aleutian. She got in because her mom went to Harvard.

Folk wisdom at Harvard holds that "Mother Harvard does not coddle her young." She sure treats her grandkids right, though. For more than forty years, an astounding one fifth of Harvard's students have received admissions preference because their parents attended the school. Today, these overwhelmingly affluent white children of alumni—"legacies"—are three times more likely to be accepted to Harvard than high school kids who lack that handsome lineage.

Yalies, don't feel smug: Offspring of the Old Blue are two and a half times more likely to be accepted than their unconnected peers. Dartmouth this year admitted 57 percent of its legacy applicants, compared to 27 percent of nonlegacies. At the University of Pennsylvania, 66 percent of legacies were admitted last year—thanks in part to an autonomous "office of alumni admissions" that actively lobbies for alumni children before the admissions committee. "One can argue that it's an accident, but it sure doesn't look like an accident," admits Yale Dean of Admissions Worth David.

If the legacies' big edge seems unfair to the tens of thousands who get turned away every year, Ivy League administrators have long defended the innocence of the legacy stat. Children of alumni are just smarter; they come from privileged backgrounds and tend to grow up in homes where parents encourage learning. That's what Harvard Dean of Admissions William Fitzsimmons told the campus newspaper, the *Harvard Crimson,* when it first reported on the legacy preference last year. Departing Harvard President Derek Bok patiently explained that the legacy preference worked only as a "tie-breaking factor" between otherwise equally qualified candidates.

Since Ivy League admissions data is a notoriously classified commodity, when Harvard officials said in previous years that alumni kids were just better, you had to take them at their word. But then federal investigators came along and pried open those top-secret files. The Harvard guys were lying.

This past fall, after two years of study, the U.S. Department of Education's Office for Civil Rights (OCR) found that, far from being more qualified or even equally qualified, the average admitted legacy at Harvard between 1981 and 1988 was significantly *less* qualified than the average admitted nonlegacy. Examining admissions office ratings on academics, extracurriculars, personal qualities, recommendations, and other categories, the OCR concluded that "with the exception of the athletic rating, [admitted] nonlegacies scored better than legacies in *all* areas of comparison."

Exceptionally high admit rates, lowered academic standards, preferential treatment . . . hmmm. These sound like the cries heard in the growing fury over affirmative action for racial minorities in America's elite universities. Only no one is outraged about legacies.

• In his recent book, *Preferential Policies,* Thomas Sowell argues that doling out special treatment encourages lackluster performance by the favored and resentment from the spurned. His far-ranging study flits from Malaysia to South Africa to American college campuses. Legacies don't merit a word.

• Dinesh D'Souza, in his celebrated jeremiad *Illiberal Education,* blames affirmative action in college admissions for declining academic standards and increasing racial tensions. Lowered standards for minority applicants, he hints, may soon destroy the university as we know it. Lowered standards for legacies? The subject doesn't come up.

• For all his polysyllabic complaints against preferential admissions, William F. Buckley, Jr. (Yale '50) has never bothered to note that son Chris (Yale '75) got the benefit of a policy that more than doubled his chance of admission.

With so much silence on the subject, you'd be excused for thinking that in these enlightened times hereditary preferences are few and far between. But you'd be wrong. At most elite universities during the eighties, the legacy was by far the biggest piece of the preferential pie. At Harvard, a legacy is about twice as likely to be admitted as a black or Hispanic student. As sociologists Jerome Karabel and David Karen point out, if alumni children were admitted to Harvard at the same rate as other applicants, their numbers in the class of 1992 would have been reduced by about 200. Instead, those 200 marginally qualified legacies outnumbered all black, Mexican-American, Native American, and Puerto Rican enrollees put together. If a few marginally qualified minorities are undermining Harvard's academic standards as much as conservatives charge, think about the damage all those legacies must be doing.

Mind you, colleges have the right to give the occasional preference—to bend the rules for the brilliant oboist or the world-class curler or the guy whose remarkable decency can't be measured by the SAT. (I happened to benefit from a geographical edge: It's easier to get into Harvard from West Virginia than from New England.) And until standardized tests and grade-point averages perfectly reflect the character, judgment, and drive of a student, tips like these aren't just nice, they're fair. Unfortunately, the extent of the legacy privilege in elite American colleges suggests something more than the occasional tie-breaking tip. Forget meritocracy. When 20 percent of Harvard's student body gets a legacy preference, aristocracy is the word that comes to mind.

A Caste of Thousands

If complaining about minority preferences is fashionable in the world of competitive colleges, bitching about legacies is just plain gauche, suggesting an unhealthy resentment of the privileged. But the effects of the legacy trickle down. For every legacy that wins, someone—usually someone less privileged—loses. And higher education is a high-stakes game.

High school graduates earn 59 percent of the income of four-year college graduates. Between high school graduates and alumni of prestigious colleges, the disparity is far greater. A *Fortune* study of American CEOs shows the usual suspects—graduates of Yale, Princeton, and Harvard—leading the list. A recent survey of the Harvard Class of 1940 found that 43 percent were worth more than $1 million. With some understatement, the report concludes, "A picture of highly advantageous circumstances emerges here, does it not, compared with American society as a whole?"

An Ivy League diploma doesn't necessarily mean a fine education. Nor does it guarantee future success. What it *does* represent is a big head start in the rat race—a fact Harvard will be the first to tell you. When I was a freshman, a counselor at the Office of Career Services instructed a group of us to make the Harvard name stand out on our résumés: "Underline it, boldface it, put it in capital letters."

Of course, the existence of the legacy preference in this fierce career competition isn't exactly news. According to historians, it was a direct result of the influx of Jews into the Ivy League during the twenties. Until then, Harvard, Princeton, and Yale had admitted anyone who could pass their entrance exams, but suddenly Jewish kids were outscoring the WASPs. So the schools began to use nonacademic criteria—"character," "solidity," and, eventually, lineage—to justify accepting low-scoring blue bloods over their peers. Yale implemented its legacy preference first, in 1925—spelling it out in a memo four years later: The school would admit "Yale sons of good character and reasonably good record . . . regardless of the number of applicants and the superiority of outside competitors." Harvard and Princeton followed shortly thereafter.

Despite its ignoble origins, the legacy preference has only sporadically come under fire, most notably in 1978's affirmative action decision, *University of California Board of Regents v. Bakke*. In his concurrence, Justice Harry Blackmun observed, "It is somewhat ironic to have us so deeply disturbed over a program where race is an element of consciousness, and yet to be aware of the fact, as we are, that institutions of higher learning . . . have given conceded preferences to the children of alumni."

If people are, in fact, aware of the legacy preference, why has it been spared the scrutiny given other preferential policies? One reason is public ignorance of the scope and scale of those preferences—an ignorance carefully cultivated by America's elite institutions. It's easy to maintain the fiction that your legacies get in strictly on merit as long as your admissions bureaucracy controls all access to student data. Information on Harvard's legacies became publicly available not because of any fit of disclosure by the university, but because a few civil rights types noted that the school had a suspiciously low rate of admission for Asian Americans, who are statistically stronger than other racial groups in academics.

While the ensuing OCR inquiry found no evidence of illegal racial discrimination by Harvard, it did turn up some embarrassing information about how much weight the "legacy" label gives an otherwise flimsy file. Take these comments scrawled by admissions officers on applicant folders:

- "Double lineage who chose the right parents."
- "Dad's [deleted] connections signify lineage of more than usual weight. That counted into the equation makes this

a case which (assuming positive TRs [teacher recommendations] and Alum IV [alumnus interview]) is well worth doing."

- "Lineage is main thing."
- "Not quite strong enough to get the clean tip."
- "Classical case that would be hard to explain to dad."
- "Double lineage but lots of problems."
- "Not a great profile, but just strong enough #'s and grades to get the tip from lineage."
- "Without lineage, there would be little case. With it, we'll keep looking."

In every one of these cases, the applicant was admitted.

Of course, Harvard's not doing anything other schools aren't. The practice of playing favorites with alumni children is nearly universal among private colleges and isn't unheard of at public institutions either. The rate of admission for Stanford's alumni children is "almost twice the general population," according to a spokesman for the admissions office. Notre Dame reserves 25 percent of each freshman class for legacies. At the University of Virginia, where native Virginians make up two thirds of each class, alumni children are automatically treated as Virginians even if they live out of state—giving them a whopping competitive edge. The same is true of the University of California at Berkeley. At many schools, Harvard included, all legacy applications are guaranteed a read by the dean of admissions himself—a privilege nonlegacies don't get.

Little White Elis

Like the Harvard deans, officials at other universities dismiss the statistical disparities by pointing to the superior environmental influences found in the homes of their alums. "I bet that, statistically, [legacy qualifications are] a little above average, but not by much," says Paul Killebrew, associate director of admissions at Dartmouth. "The admitted group [of legacies] would look exactly like the profile of the class."

James Wickenden, a former dean of admissions at Princeton who now runs a college consulting firm, suspects otherwise. Wickenden wrote of "one Ivy League university" where the average combined SAT score of the freshman class was 1,350 out of a possible 1,600, compared to 1,280 for legacies. "At most selective schools, [legacy status] doubles, even trebles the chances of admission," he says. Many colleges even place admitted legacies in a special "Not in Profile" file (along with recruited athletes and some minority students), so that when the school's SAT scores are published, alumni kids won't pull down the average.

How do those kids fare once they're enrolled? No one's telling. Harvard, for one, refuses to keep any records of how alumni children stack up academically against their nonlegacy classmates—perhaps because the last such study, in 1956, showed Harvard sons hogging the bottom of the grade curve.

If the test scores of admitted legacies are a mystery, the reason colleges accept so many is not. They're afraid the alumni parents of rejected children will stop giving to the colleges' unending fund-raising campaigns. "Our survival as an institution depends on having support from alumni," says Richard Steele, director of undergraduate admissions at Duke University, "so according advantages to alumni kids is just a given."

In fact, the OCR exonerated Harvard's legacy preference precisely because legacies bring in money. (OCR cited a federal district court ruling that a state university could favor the children of out-of-state alumni because "defendants showed that the alumni provide monetary support for the university.") And there's no question that alumni provide significant support to Harvard: Last year, they raised $20 million for the scholarship fund alone.

In a letter to OCR defending his legacies, Harvard's Fitzsimmons painted a grim picture of a school where the preference did not exist—a place peeved alumni turned their backs on when their kids failed to make the cut. "Without the fund-raising activities of alumni," Fitzsimmons warned darkly, "Harvard could not maintain many of its programs, including needs-blind admissions."

Ignoring, for the moment, the question of how "needs-blind" a system is that admits one fifth of each class on the assumption that, hey, their parents might give us money, Fitzsimmons's defense doesn't quite ring true. The "Save the Scholarship Fund" line is a variation on the principle of "Firemen First," whereby bureaucrats threatened with a budget cut insist that essential programs rather than executive perks and junkets will be the first to be slashed. Truth be told, there is just about nothing that Harvard, the richest university in the world, could do to jeopardize needs-blind admissions, provided that it placed a high enough priority on them.

But even more unclear is how closely alumni giving is related to the acceptance of alumni kids. "People whose children are denied admission are initially upset," says Wickenden, "and maybe for a year or two their interest in the university wanes. But typically they come back around when they see that what happened was best for the kids." Wickenden has put his money where his mouth is: He rejected two sons of a Princeton trustee involved in a $420 million fund-raising project, not to mention the child of a board member who managed the school's $2 billion endowment, all with no apparent ill effect.

Most university administrators would be loath to take such a chance, despite a surprising lack of evidence of the legacy/largess connection. Fitzsimmons admits Harvard knows of no empirical research to support the claim that diminishing legacies would decrease alumni contributions, relying instead on "hundreds, perhaps thousands of conversations with alumni whose sons and daughters applied."

No doubt some of Fitzsimmons's anxiety is founded: It's only natural for alumni to want their kids to have the same privileges they did. But the historical record suggests that alumni are far more tolerant than administrators realize. Admit women and blacks? *Well, we would,* said administrators earlier this century—*but the alumni just won't have it.* Fortunately for American universities, the bulk of those alumni turned out to be less craven than administrators thought they'd be. As more blacks and women enrolled over the past two decades, the funds kept pouring in, reaching an all-time high in the eighties.

Another significant historical lesson can be drawn from the late fifties, when Harvard's selectiveness increased dramatically. As the number of applications soared, the rate of admission for legacies began declining from about 90 percent to its current 43 percent. Administration anxiety rose inversely, but Harvard's fund-raising machine has somehow survived. That doesn't mean there's *no* correlation between alumni giving and the legacy preference; rather, it means that the people who would withhold their money at the loss of the legacy privilege were far outnumbered by other givers. "It takes time to get the message out," explains Fitzsimmons, "but eventually people start responding. We've had to make the case [for democratization] to alumni, and I think that they generally feel good about that."

Heir Cut

When justice dictates that ordinary kids should have as fair a shot as the children of America's elite, couldn't Harvard and its sister institutions trouble themselves to "get the message out" again? Of course they could. But virtually no one—liberal or conservative—is pushing them to do so.

"There must be no goals or quotas for any special group or category of applicants," reads an advertisement in the right-wing *Dartmouth Review*. "Equal opportunity must be the guiding policy. Males, females, blacks, whites, Native Americans, Hispanics . . . can all be given equal chance to matriculate, survive, and prosper based solely on individual performance."

Noble sentiments from the Ernest Martin Hopkins Institute, an organization of conservative Dartmouth alumni. Reading on, though, we find these "concerned alumni" aren't sacrificing *their* young to the cause. "Alumni sons and daughters," notes the ad further down, "should receive some special consideration."

Similarly, Harvard's conservative *Salient* has twice in recent years decried the treatment of Asian-Americans in admissions, but it attributes their misfortune to favoritism for blacks and Hispanics. What about legacy university favoritism—a much bigger factor? *Salient* writers have twice endorsed it.

What's most surprising is the indifference of minority activists. With the notable exception of a few vocal Asian Americans, most have made peace with the preference for well-off whites.

Mecca Nelson, the president of Harvard's Black Students Association, leads rallies for the hiring of more minority faculty. She participated in an illegal sit-in at an administration building in support of Afro-American studies. But when it comes to the policy that Asian-American activist Arthur Hu calls "a twenty-percent-white quota," Nelson says, "I don't have any really strong opinions about it. I'm not very clear on the whole legacy issue at all."

Joshua Li, former co-chair of Harvard's Asian-American

Association, explains his complacency differently: "We understand that in the future Asian-American students will receive these tips as well."

At America's elite universities, you'd expect a somewhat higher standard of fairness than that—especially when money is the driving force behind the concept. And many Ivy League types *do* advocate for more just and lofty ideals. One of them, as it happens, is Derek Bok. In one of Harvard's annual reports, he warned that the modern university is slowly turning from a truth-seeking enterprise into a money-grubbing corporation—at the expense of the loyalty of its alums. "Such an institution may still evoke pride and respect because of its intellectual achievements," he said rightly. "But the feelings it engenders will not be quite the same as those produced by an institution that is prepared to forgo income, if need be, to preserve values of a nobler kind."

Forgo income to preserve values of a nobler kind—it's an excellent idea. Embrace the preferences for the poor and disadvantaged. Wean alumni from the idea of the legacy edge. And above all, stop the hypocrisy that begrudges the great unwashed a place at Harvard while happily making room for the less qualified sons and daughters of alums.

After 70 years, it won't be easy to wrest the legacy preference away from the alums. But the long-term payoff is as much a matter of message as money. When the sons and daughters of today's college kids fill out *their* applications, the legacy preference should seem not a birthright, but a long-gone relic from the Ivy League's inequitable past.

PART SIX

THE FUTURE

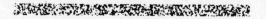

CIVIL RIGHTS AT THE CROSSROADS

Drew S. Days III

Drew S. Days III is solicitor general of the United States. He was assistant attorney general for civil rights in the Carter administration and Alfred M. Rankin Professor of Law, Yale University Law School. "Civil Rights at the Crossroads" first appeared in the inaugural issue of the *Temple Political and Civil Rights Law Review,* Spring 1992.

Toward the end of 1991, the country was treated to a controversy that exemplified, as well as any, the complexities that have beset civil rights in the 1990s. You will recall that a high-ranking black Department of Education official sent a letter to organizers of the upcoming Fiesta Bowl in Arizona informing them that a minority-scholarship plan they were contemplating might violate federal law. Teams from Auburn, in Alabama, and the University of Louisville, in Kentucky, had threatened to pull out of the Bowl to protest Arizona's failure to declare Martin Luther King's birthday a state holiday. In an effort to prevent that from happening, Fiesta Bowl officials committed themselves to setting up $100,000 scholarship funds for minority students at each school. The Department of Education Assistant Secretary announced that it would be a violation of a provision of the 1964 Civil Rights Act that prohibits racial discrimination by recipients of federal financial assistance for either Auburn or Louisville to use the Fiesta Bowl scholarships solely for minority students. He added, however, that the Fiesta Bowl organization, as long as it received no federal funds, could provide scholarships directly to minority students without violating the Civil Rights Act.

As many of you will also remember, the plot thickened when many people, even some members of the Bush cabinet, decried the Department of Education's new rule. The result was a revised policy under which Auburn and Louisville, and other schools presumably, could use funds provided by private organizations, like the Fiesta Bowl, for minority scholarships. However, using their own university monies for such scholarships would still violate the 1964 Act. With the appointment of a new secretary of education, the entire policy was suspended, pending a thorough review. The Department has recently proposed new guidelines for public comment which, if finally approved, would allow funding like that from the Fiesta Bowl sponsors to occur.

I doubt that we have heard the last of this controversy, however. But I do not propose to pursue those issues here. Rather I want to underscore the point that this recent civil rights crisis arose because a black federal official found fault with the fact that organizers of a football game promised to do something to assist minority students in order to prevent a protest against Arizona's refusal to acknowledge Dr. King's birthday from ruining their multimillion-dollar investment. I am certain that Dr. King would not have missed the irony of this situation.

There was a time when civil rights issues were much, much simpler; when it was rather easy to identify which side held the high moral ground. All it took was a pair of eyes and a sense of humanity to understand that black citizens of Birmingham, not Bull Connor with his fire hoses and police dogs, had right on their side and that those marching across the Edmund Pettis Bridge to demand voting rights for blacks in Alabama, not George Wallace's brutal state police, were acting in the finest traditions of the Declaration of Independence and of the Constitution. When Dr. King challenged America to make good on its claim that "all men are created equal" and all who embraced Judeo-Christian principles to acknowledge that blacks, too, were children of God and made in his own image, King's message struck responsive chords throughout the land in a way we have never seen since. The fire hoses are no longer a threat to black citizens of Birmingham who want to enjoy access to public accommodations on a nondiscriminatory basis. And one of the black protesters whose skull stopped a state policeman's riot stick on the Selma march, John Lewis, now serves in the United States House of Representatives. But America has yet to finish the job of ridding its society of the vestiges of a long and sordid history of racial discrimination, particularly in employment, voting, education, and housing.

It has become increasingly difficult, however, to convince many white, and even some black, Americans that achieving further progress in civil rights is still a moral imperative. Memories have faded—naturally or conveniently among some—of the civil rights struggles of the sixties; and many are too young to have any memories at all of that period. Critics of affirmative action are quick to observe that we now have a society in which young whites can honestly claim that they personally never engaged in acts of racial discrimination and young blacks cannot claim to have been the victims of the type of blatant racism that characterized the fifties and sixties.

Moreover, the issues have become, like that of minority scholarships, rather complicated. This is not to say that wrongs do not exist that need to be rectified; it is just harder to explain to the person on the street the nature of the wrong and the necessity of the remedy. It is true that Congress enacted several new pieces of civil rights legislation in the 1980s. But doing so was not easy and even these successes were not necessarily reflective of a widespread national consensus that Congress's actions were right and just. Part of the problem has been that the civil rights efforts have been defensive, rather than offensive, for the past decade, largely as a result of restrictive Supreme Court rulings.

Civil Rights Legislation in the 1980s: Defending the Gains of the 1960s Against an Increasingly Hostile Supreme Court

In 1980, for example, the Court gave a provision of the Voting Rights Act of 1965 a limited reading in striking down lower courts' holdings that Mobile, Alabama's at-large electoral system discriminated against blacks. Congress was able to enact an amendment to the Voting Rights Act in 1982, effectively negating any future impact of the Court's *Mobile* decision. However, it did not do so without a struggle, including overcoming strong Reagan administration approval. Opponents claimed that the Voting Rights Act Amendments of 1982 would result in electoral "quotas" and "proportional representation."

Success in this campaign was attributable to early and effective organization by the civil rights community, both in Congress and at the grass-roots level. But I doubt that many Americans truly understand yet how at-large electoral systems, the very essence of the "one person, one vote" principle (since everyone votes for all the offices at issue), can be racially discriminatory. That they have been in the past and continue to be so in certain parts of the country even today, does not alter the fact that the national consciousness has failed to grasp this reality.

In 1984, the Supreme Court limited the reach of a provision of the 1972 Education Amendments, prohibiting sex discrimination by recipients of federal financial assistance. The ruling's logic applied as well to that provision of the 1964 Civil Rights Act barring racial discrimination at the center of the Fiesta Bowl controversy. Put simply, the issue was whether a recipient of federal funds in one part of its operation could discriminate, nevertheless, in another part of its operation without violating federal law; could a college that received federal funds for its physics program, for example, still engage in sex or racial discrimination in athletics with impunity? I think this issue, if one puts it in terms of a federal recipient's using essentially accounting sleight-of-hand to persist in discriminatory practices, has the potential to take on moral dimensions.

But the actual debate in Congress turned principally on the proper definition of a federally funded "program or activity." And I doubt that the general public ever comprehended the significant impact of the Supreme Court's narrow reading and the importance of a legislative response. Perhaps this explains why it took Congress several attempts, over almost four years, to pass the Civil Rights Restoration Act of 1987. Framed as it was, this issue was unlikely to spur people to march, stand up and be counted, and make their voices heard in support of reform. Civil rights forces were emboldened, however, by the fact that the Restoration Act became law despite President Reagan's veto.

The third piece of civil rights legislation enacted in the 1980s, the Fair Housing Act Amendments of 1988, was not responsive, as such, to restrictive court rulings. However, efforts to amend the original 1968 Act had been ongoing at least since the late 1970s, largely to provide victims of racial discrimination with stronger remedies. The 1988 amendments are largely technical, as well, except in two respects: for the first time housing discrimination against the disabled and families with children was prohibited by federal law.

If one wishes to find a moral imperative in this legislative action, it has to relate to the rights of the disabled. Americans are coming generally to believe, I think, that denying people with disabilities meaningful access to jobs, housing, education, and transportation is no longer acceptable. The recent enactment of the Americans with Disabilities Act of 1990, an omnibus federal law providing significantly expanded opportunities, is further evidence of this changed environment.

The 1988–89 Supreme Court Term and Congress's Response: The Death and Rebirth of Disparate Impact

The Supreme Court in its 1988-89 term, however, set in motion a chain of events that seriously slowed the momentum of civil rights reform. In a series of decisions, the Court significantly narrowed prior interpretations of provisions of both the Civil Rights Act of 1964 and of a civil rights statute that dates from the Reconstruction era. In the latter case, it held that the statute prohibited racial discrimination in the making of employment contracts but not discriminatory practices once the complainant was hired. Put crudely, the Court's reading would preclude a white employer from requiring a black applicant to accept a job with the understanding that he or she would be treated less favorably than whites. But, once hired on a nondiscriminatory basis, the black employee would have no recourse under the Reconstruction Era statute, said the Court, for the employer's racial harassment, for example.

Suffice it to say that this reading was not dictated by the statute's language. Rather, it was in my estimation reflective of a desire by the Court majority to reduce the availability of an alternative cause of action for employment discrimination to that provided by Title VII of the Civil Rights Act of 1964. As a result of this ruling, a black woman, who claimed that she had been told by her supervisor repeatedly that "blacks are known to work slower than whites by nature" because "some animals are faster than other animals" in the course of a pattern of racial harassment, was left empty handed by the Supreme Court. Thereafter, many others with similar claims suffered the same fate, watching their employment discrimination lawsuits filed years before summarily thrown out of court.

More devastating to civil rights enforcement, however, was the Court's decision effectively overruling one of its own precedents of almost eighteen years. To give a bit of history, in 1971 the Court ruled that Title VII of the Civil Rights Act of 1964, which prohibits various forms of employment discrimination, could be violated not only by practices designed to treat persons unfairly because of their race, sex, or national origin. It also prohibited practices that disproportionately burdened racial and ethnic minorities or women unless such practices could be shown genuinely to assess candidates' suitability for the job in question. In the 1971 *Griggs* decision, the Court held that a North Carolina power company could not justify its imposition of a high school diploma requirement or the use of aptitude batteries, both of which presented significant obstacles to black employment or advancement. The Court took special note of the fact that whites who had been hired earlier without their having to meet such requirements were performing quite well in their jobs.

Until 1989, the Supreme Court and lower federal courts had developed a relatively consistent body of law in the "disparate impact" (or discriminatory effect) employment discrimination area. In essence, these precedents held that once plaintiffs established that an employment screening device had a discriminatory impact, the employer's burden was to convince a court that the device was justified in terms of its ability to select qualified employees. Failing to do this, the employer would lose. In its 1989 *Wards Cove* decision, however, the Court in effect both freed the employer in such cases from making a showing of "business-necessity," or "job-relatedness," to use two of the relevant phrases from the earlier case law, and placed the ultimate burden on the plaintiff, of establishing that the screening device violated Title VII. Here is not the place to get into an involved discussion of evidentiary burdens. But, all other things being equal, minority or women plaintiffs who would have won a "disparate impact" employment discrimination case prior to the Court's 1989 decision were likely to lose that case under the new allocation and nature of evidentiary burdens dictated by *Wards Cove.*

Civil rights groups appealed to Congress shortly after these Supreme Court decisions for overruling legislation. The result of this effort was the introduction the following spring of the proposed Civil Rights Act of 1990. That legislation sought not only to address the Supreme Court's narrow readings of the Reconstruction Era and 1964 Civil Rights Acts, but also to strengthen protections for racial minorities and women against employment discrimination. The Bush Administration's initial response was generally unfavorable, however. It agreed in principle that corrective legislation was appropriate to respond to two of the Supreme Court's 1988–89 term decisions, but expressed, by way of its attorney general, overall approval of the Court's rulings.

Beginning in the summer of 1990, President Bush announced his desire to sign a civil rights bill and urged

civil rights groups to work with other administration officials to draft an acceptable piece of legislation. Thus began
a minuet of negotiations involving civil rights groups,
members of Congress, and administration officials that
lasted over several months without meaningful progress.
The ultimate result was that both Houses of Congress
passed legislation, altered in several respects to make it
acceptable to the President. But the President vetoed the
bill and Congress failed to override that veto. Although the
legislation had many parts, the President based his veto
primarily on opposition to provisions having to do with the
restoration of the pre-1989 "disparate impact" test. He
contended that they were designed to establish "employment quotas."

Congress did not give up efforts to pass legislation
overturning the Court's restrictive rulings of the 1988–89
term, however. Those efforts proved ultimately successful
with the passage of the Civil Rights Act of 1991, which
went into effect, with President Bush's signature, in November of last year. Speculation continues to swirl over
how the President, who had condemned Congress's earlier
attempts as "quota" bills, could have found the largely
identical Civil Rights Act of 1991 worthy of support. I find
it plausible that the damage David Duke's campaign for
governor of Louisiana was doing to the Republican party's
image as a conservative, but not racist, political force and
the bruising confirmation fight over Clarence Thomas's
appointment to the Supreme Court persuaded the President that he needed the Civil Rights Act of 1991 to salvage
his reputation as a moderate on race issues. Whether he
will continue to see his support of the 1991 Act as a political
plus as the presidential campaign progresses this year,
only time will tell.

The victory that the Civil Rights Act of 1991 represents
is one that I join many in celebrating. In fact, I would like

to think that I contributed in my own small way to that success. However, I do not think that its passage should cause us to overlook certain basic truths about the current state of civil rights. First, the American people have never fully understood or accepted the importance of the "disparate impact" or discriminatory effect standard in ridding our society of the vestiges of racism and sexism. Even people who claim to be in favor of civil rights advancement often ask, "Why should someone be held to have violated civil rights laws if they had no purpose or intent to discriminate?" There is something very basic to our culture about maintaining a congruence between evil motive and discrimination: no evil motive, no bad actors, no discrimination. This logic, however, places on the most vulnerable in our society the burden, among others, of ferreting out easily hidden and difficult to prove intentional bias and prejudice. Failing that, they must simply accept practices that bar access for them to meaningful participation in the workplace, in housing, and in the political process.

Second, some members of the Supreme Court have never liked the "effects" test in civil rights law and now have a majority to establish that view as law. Those Justices must know that the public will have difficulty grasping the nature of the Court's subtle but basic shift, by way of evidentiary rulings, in the law. Moreover, they are probably aware that the person on the street will not find anything particularly wrong, in any event, with making plaintiffs prove that discrimination exists rather than having employers prove that it does not. I think that we can expect that the Court, even in the face of the Civil Rights Act of 1991, will make other efforts to limit use of the "disparate impact" or "discriminatory effects" approach in civil rights cases.

Third, and finally, the Bush administration was also comfortable with the Supreme Court's shift away from discriminatory effects to discriminatory intent standards in civil rights cases, despite its ultimate decision to support the Civil Rights Act of 1991. Doing away with the "effects" test was one of the central goals of the Reagan administration. Even though it was not fully successful in that respect, its successor administration hoped it might have better luck. The presidential veto and the failure of the override vote on the 1990 bill conveyed a basic message. Given the complexity of the issues dealt with by the Supreme Court in its 1988–89 term rulings and the equal complexity of Congress's attempt to overrule those decisions, the administration could employ a buzzword like *quota* to explain its opposition to civil rights legislation without signficant political cost. Indeed, I think that even many people who consider themselves pro–civil rights had difficulty understanding what all the shouting was about. Very few members of the media, for example, were up to explaining the problem that the Civil Rights Act was designed to address, falling back instead on pat, incorrect characterizations of the bill as an attempt "to make it easier for plaintiffs to win employment discrimination suits."

Without going into the provisions of the proposed Civil Rights Act of 1990 in great detail, let me explain my reason for calling the term *quota* a buzzword in that context. President Bush's position was that the proposed Civil Rights Act of 1990 imposed so heavy a burden on employers to justify screening devices having a disparate impact that they would be inclined to resort to "hiring by the numbers," that is, hiring enough blacks or women to avoid any disparate impact and thereby avoiding a lawsuit. In the first place, the test itself, showing a "significant relationship to successful performance of the job," did not appear to create insurmountable proof problems, given the *Griggs* regime in which employers did succeed in meeting a similar standard. Second, the proposed legislation included, in an effort to allay the President's fears, a specific disclaimer with respect to quota hiring. Third, and finally, there was no credible evidence that quotas had been widely resorted to under the pre-1989 legal regime.

The President, it seems to me, had the duty to establish that American employers, who make business decisions every day because they think they are right despite possible lawsuits, would resort to quota hiring, irrespective of applicants' qualification in this context. Instead, the President placed the burden on civil rights advocates to prove the contrary. Many of these same arguments were raised anew by the Bush administration in opposition to the proposed Civil Rights Act of 1991. In my estimation, the President's ultimate support for that bill represented not a change of heart but rather a change in political strategy.

Civil Rights at the Crossroads: The Future of Affirmative Action in the 1990s and Beyond

I have gone on at some length, I realize, about recent legislative developments. Let me return to Dr. King. We are, in my estimation, at a crossroads with respect to civil rights in this country, very much like that Dr. King confronted in the year or so before he died. What he realized was that his nonviolent approach to attacking discrimination, although extraordinarily effective in striking down blatant segregation in the South and spurring Congress to act, was unlikely to have significant impact upon the lives of millions of blacks without jobs, adequate housing, education, or medical care in the large urban centers in the North, particularly. That was why his attempts to organize in Chicago proved a dismal failure. That was why he went to what turned out to be his last campaign to march with striking sanitation workers in Memphis in April 1968 and why he had organized and planned to lead, had he lived, the Poor People's Campaign and March on Washington for Jobs and Housing. What he sought was recognition of an "economic bill of rights," among other goals.

What Dr. King came to understand was that full equality for blacks in this country will come about only when the civil rights struggle becomes at one with a campaign to ensure that America provides *all* of its citizens with real opportunities to make a living wage, obtain decent housing, receive adequate medical attention, and be meaningfully educated. I do not think that Dr. King's understanding is any less true in 1992 than it was in 1968. This is not to say that blacks, certain other minorities, and women do not have special claims upon the nation for redress. They do. It is not to say that the battles for civil rights waged since 1968 were unjustified or in vain. They were not. Many members of historically discriminated against groups have gained opportunities to better their lives that would not have occurred without federal legislation and successfully litigated civil rights cases.

It is not even to suggest that the fight should be abandoned for congressional legislation to prevent retrenchment by the Supreme Court and to achieve certain incremental advances in civil rights protections. But I do believe that the advances since 1968 for blacks nationally, particularly, appear relatively modest when compared to the major strides in the status of blacks that occurred in the South between the *Brown* decision in 1954 and Dr. King's death in 1968. And, as my earlier comments about recent developments in civil rights were intended to communicate, we may be headed toward a period of ever-diminishing returns in this connection.

Moreover, we have to recognize that massive enforcement of the Civil Rights Act of 1964, the Fair Housing Act of 1968, and the Voting Rights Act of 1965, if such a remarkable state of affairs were to occur, would not alter significantly the lives of millions of black and other minority people who live at, or beyond, the margins of mainstream America. Their tragic lives are chronicled in the increasingly depressing statistics on overall poverty, health care, infant mortality, unemployment, homelessness, crime victimization, drug addiction, and incarceration. One has only to visit areas where blacks and other racial and ethnic minorities tend to be concentrated in our urban centers around the country to grasp the magnitude of these problems. The social infrastructures (churches, clubs, civil centers, unions) have disappeared; those able to achieve some, even shaky, grasp of middle-class life have moved out; social services have fled; and the physical structures often look like Dresden after the Allied bombing raids during the Second World War. William Julius Wilson has accurately described this depressing trend among urban blacks in his book, *The Truly Disadvantaged*.

This reality also helps situate the affirmative action debate that has been raging for at least the last fifteen years, starting with the *DeFunis* case, having to do with a minority admissions program at the University of Washington Law School in 1974, to the recent flap over minority higher education scholarships. The Supreme Court avoided a decision on the merits in *DeFunis*, but almost every year since the *Bakke* decision in 1978, it has had to confront affirmative action challenges of one sort or another. It has been a roller-coaster ride, to put it mildly, with the Court's striking down some programs and upholding others, usually by very close votes, in employment, education, public works contracting, and communications. Given the current makeup of the Supreme Court, I think that we can expect that there will be increasing judicial resistance to programs that rely explicitly on race, national origin, and sex criteria.

Let me emphasize that the Court's treatment of affirmative action programs has had, and will continue to have, profound symbolic importance because it is one measure of how the society views continuing efforts to eradicate the vestiges of discrimination and to transform major institutions that have been "white, male clubs" for too long. We know as students of the law that Supreme Court decisions are about specific cases and are not usually designed to make general pronouncements with respect to conduct not before the Court for consideration.

Nevertheless, its opinions also often set a tone that affects the way in which the average citizen conducts his or her affairs. Consequently, a Supreme Court decision about an affirmative action plan in employment may influence an employer's evaluation of minority or female applicants: do I have to be concerned about the fact that I have no black or female employees? Or is such a consideration irrelevant? Or more irrationally but predictably, are racist or sexist jokes back in fashion or do I still have to watch my language?

But what are the direct consequences of affirmative action decisions? If one talks about programs that have employed race or sex as criteria to remedy findings of discrimination by courts or administrative agencies, I think that large numbers of minorities and women have gained employment or better wages and conditions as a result. Voluntary affirmative action programs in higher education, including scholarship aid, have made it possible for racial minorities to gain access to opportunities that would otherwise have been foreclosed. Similarly, voluntary programs in employment and public contracting have also opened up doors that had previously been locked. However, it should also be noted, not all affirmative action programs have been well-conceived, properly administered, or particularly successful, for that matter. My view is that there continue to be situations that need and justify affirmative action efforts and that support for such programs established under those circumstances ought to continue.

Take, for example, the Fiesta Bowl controversy. What the Department of Education's original policy pronouncement failed to note was that both Auburn, in Alabama, and University of Louisville, in Kentucky, are parts of state higher education systems with proven histories of racial discrimination and segregation. Nor did the press release note that as a remedy for decades of unconstitutional segregation in its university system, Kentucky had during the 1980s submitted to the government a desegregation plan, one component of which was increased financial aid to black students attending white institutions. Also omitted was any mention of the fact that Alabama operated segregated institutions of higher education up through the 1980s, triggering an enforcement suit by the federal government. There are undoubtedly people who would quarrel with the creation of such scholarships even at Auburn and Louisville. But, to me, given the history and context, the rationale is clear and defensible.

The Need for a New Strategy: Enlarging the Pie

Having said all of the foregoing about affirmative action, I want to point out, however, that for most poor minorities and women, affirmative action is of limited significance. Despite what critics of affirmative action have said about "naked quotas," in order to take advantage of special programs for minorities and women, the candidates have to be at least minimally qualified, and when one gets to questions of upper-level jobs or admission to higher education institutions, the so-called minimal qualifications are beyond the reach of the vast majority of poor Americans of any race. So, for all the achievements of affirmative action—viewed by its most enthusiastic supporters—it does not begin even to scratch the surface of the socioeconomic problems that beset most disadvantaged minority groups and women. This leads me to think that affirmative action, although it should continue to have a place in public policy for the time being, cannot be regarded as the core strategy in this respect.

One of the implicit premises of the civil rights effort, once the most obvious forms of racial discrimination had been declared unconstitutional or illegal, was that America offered a limited socioeconomic pie and that, consequently, success for minorities and women probably involved getting a piece of that existing pie, not enlarging it. It was an acceptance of civil rights as a zero-sum game. This operating premise was not necessarily wrongheaded. Certain opportunities have been opened up, but the larger structural issues have been avoided. Congress and the courts have been willing, for example, to restructure the workplace to address racial and sex discrimination, but they have not been willing to ensure full employment.

They have been willing to ensure meaningful participation of minorities in the electoral process, but they have not embraced techniques for expanding generally citizen access to the ballot box. They have been willing to support school desegregation, including educational enhancements in certain cases, but have not acted to ensure that the schools provide training adequate to the demands of our increasingly technological society. Blacks cannot be turned away from certain hospital emergency rooms because of their race, but they can be denied service because they are poor. Employers have to hire minorities and women on a nondiscriminatory basis, but they do not necessarily have to provide health insurance benefits. There are some laudable programs in these respects at the state and local level. But the picture there is generally bleak as well.

I believe, however, that this strategy of sharing a limited pie, rather than working to enlarge the pie, has almost run its course. We should begin focusing on a bigger pie and those individuals and organizations historically identified with the civil rights movement should be at the forefront of this effort. This was the message of Jesse Jackson's Rainbow Coalition. That it was developed in the context of a partisan (indeed, intraparty) debate and personally associated with a somewhat controversial public figure created complications for the message. But, even so, Jackson was able to appeal in the 1988 Democratic primaries increasingly to a widening cross section of the American electorate beyond his original black base—farmers, miners, residents of Appalachia, the young, and the elderly.

It is a message worth working to place in the political mainstream. For we have to recognize that, although there were 9.7 million blacks and 5.5 million people of Spanish origin living below the poverty line in 1987, there were 21.4 million whites in the same predicament. The percentages of members of the two minority groups living below the poverty line were admittedly several times higher than that of whites. But numerically more whites were living in poverty than minorities. My point is that we should not let comparative percentages between whites and minorities obscure the fact that whites, in terms of raw numbers, are a larger group of disadvantaged persons than minorities. Cuts in government financial aid for needy students have taken their toll on the chances of poor white students, as well as of minority students to obtain higher education. Consequently, when one looks at employment and underemployment, health care, adequacy of educational opportunity and housing, this fact has to be kept in mind. It points the way to coalition-building and to a broadened sense of moral imperative.

I am fully aware that there are numerous and vocal

critics of President Johnson's Great Society programs and a feeling abroad in the land—as cities, private businesses, and S&L's contemplate or experience bankruptcy, and the federal deficit rises—that we should be thinking smaller rather than bigger in terms of what government can and should do. I am also aware that strong forces of racism and sexism (just to name a few "isms") will make it difficult to forge the type of socioeconomic coalition I am suggesting. But I think that there is no other alternative. Where there's a will, there's a way, goes the adage. Where will the money come from? The answer may lie in figuring out who got the billions of dollars that used to be in the vaults of failed savings and loans. Where do we find funds to build domed, climatically controlled stadiums? How much do we spend as a nation on cosmetics, fast foods, and candy bars? How were all the multibillion-dollar mergers and acquisitions of the 1980s achieved? Junk bonds are not the full explanation.

Dr. King's Poor People's Campaign did not deserve to die with him. It is as relevant and necessary today as it ever was. It is the turn that civil rights at the crossroads must take.

MULTIRACIAL AFFIRMATIVE ACTION

Viet D. Dinh

Viet D. Dinh is currently clerking for Judge Laurence H. Silberman, U.S. Court of Appeals, D.C. Circuit, and will be clerking for Supreme Court Justice Sandra Day O'Connor. His writing has appeared in *The New York Times* and the *Harvard Law Review*. "Multiracial Affirmative Action" is excerpted from a longer article on the same subject, which first appeared in *Reconstruction*, Vol. 2, No. 2.

In a biracial society with an established history of racial subjugation, entitlements based on race make good theoretical sense. If one race has unjustly exploited the other, the simplest means to rectify the injustice is to give preferences to members of the disadvantaged group. But what happens if we recognize—as we must in the America of the 1990s—that our "biracial" society is really multiracial? The answer, as recent history shows, is that affirmative action entitlements can fan the flames of racial animosity. Each racial and ethnic group looks on the others as competitors rather than allies in the fight for a share of the American pie.

The problem begins with the conflation of two different

conceptions of affirmative action, one looking to race as a proxy for remedial justice and the other looking to race as a component of merit. The traditional theory of affirmative action as a remedy for past injustice is best explicated by President Johnson's two-runner analogy. "You do not take a person who, for years, has been hobbled by chains and liberate him, bring him to the starting line of a race and then say, 'You are free to compete with all others' and still justly believe that you have been completely fair." Affirmative action using race as remedy pushes the newly freed runner up to the point where he can compete on a reasonably equal footing, making up for the head start that the other runners otherwise have had.

In recent years, however, a merit-based conception of race has supplanted this compensatory vision in the affirmative action rhetoric. Proponents of this new formulation argue that ethnic identity is itself a component of merit in our diverse society. Because persons of color have a unique perspective derived from their nonwhite experiences, their color constitutes a meritorious credential. In education a diverse faculty and student body better educates students who otherwise would not be exposed to a multicultural setting. This redefinition of affirmative action is especially appealing as theory, for it escapes the objection that affirmative action, by lowering the formal standard for access to a university, lowers the quality of the admitting school. If race is a component of merit, then the admission of underrepresented minorities actually improves education.

In the multiracial America of the 1990s, I find this latter view problematic. By contrast, I believe that the idea of race as remedy, even with its flaws, does not carry the danger that race as merit does, of pushing our society into a permanent interethnic scramble for racial entitlements.

II

By virtue of the indeterminacy that results when groups rather than individuals are made the source of preferences, affirmative action unavoidably exacerbates tension in a multiracial society like America. Race-as-remedy affirmative action is not immune from this criticism. Race is a poor predictor of societal disadvantage worthy of remedy. A recent Vietnamese immigrant who achieves good marks in high school against remarkable linguistic, cultural, and economic odds may justly wonder why he is denied admission to an elite college merely because he is Asian. He may also look at a lower-achieving black prep school graduate, the son of affluent professionals, and wonder why the latter gained admission merely because of his skin color. Extrapolating from individual wrongs to group remedies necessarily engenders resentment between those who are hurt by and those who benefit from the indeterminacy of such extrapolation.

But in the traditional model of affirmative action, the remedial purpose tempers the indeterminacy of race as a basis for entitlement. Even if the application of group entitlements to *individuals* results in injustice, the recognition that there is a legitimate basis for the group entitlement mitigates the unfairness. Take the poor Asian immigrant and the rich African American. The legitimacy of the latter's claim to the benefit rests on the fact that it is being offered as a remedy for his race—for the fact that he is black. In this case affirmative action remedies the fact that although the African American may be rich and well educated, he would be even richer and better-educated if he were white.

The Asian, of course, may also have a legitimate claim to the benefit by virtue of *his* race, arising from the fact that Asian Americans have also suffered group wrongs. But such a claim cannot trump the African American's for the affirmative action entitlement. Since affirmative action specifically remedies race, the best that can be said is that the claims are equal, and no justification exists to take away the African American's entitlement to favor the Asian.

Such indeterminacy, however, is unacceptable with a merit-based conception of race. Race is proposed as merit based on the value of the perspective that each racial minority brings to the admitting institution. But perspective may not correspond with race. The constituent members of what is bureaucratically deemed to be a "race" may be so radically different from each other that their common categorization is artificial. For example, although I am considered Asian, as a Vietnamese immigrant I may have more in common with a Haitian refugee than with a third-generation Japanese American. Likewise, a recent Somalian immigrant may identify more with his Cambodian neighbors than with Jesse Jackson's prep-school children. To group us into separate races labeled "Asian" and "African" mocks the whole notion of experiential perspective. Even more troubling, such indeterminacy will tend to follow a certain pattern: those minorities who win the intrarace merit contest will tend to be the prep-school-educated elites, who profit from the suffering of less fortunate members of their race.

An analogous problem of indeterminacy further undermines the race-as-merit theory. Up to this point, I have ignored the central question lurking behind the recognition that ours is a multiracial society: "What constitutes a race?" I have done so because generality is acceptable, even desirable from a recipient's perspective, in a remedial system. The broader and more general the definition of the group entitled to remedy, the more entitlements will be available for distribution. In a merit-based system, however, specificity will be the norm because each group that has a plausible claim to be a different "race" will insist on being so categorized in order to gain admission for one of their own.

If one's racial and cultural background forms the basis of merit, then each race and culture must be represented in an institution for it to be truly meritorious. Presumably, no race lacks merit, and all minority voices are equally worthy of inclusion. Neutrality thus requires nothing less than full representation. The atomizing propensity in the definition of race and the respect for neutrality means that nothing short of full representation of a potentially infinite number of "races" will be the practical result of a race-as-merit system in our racially diverse polity. My cultural pride will not be assuaged by the pronouncement that a Chinese professor or student has been deemed to adequately reflect Asian merit. I want a Vietnamese.

Unfortunately, we live in a world of limited resources (which, of course, is the condition that posed the allocative problem in the first place). In a multiracial society, affirmative action fails to provide an acceptable system of priorities to determine which race will get the last position. The call for "a woman of color" to be hired for a position in an all-white institution, for example, provides little guidance as to what color that woman should be. If color determines merit, then neutrality mandates that all women—at least those of color—are equally meritorious and deserving of the position.

III

The second source of interethnic tension arising from affirmative action is the climate of competition along racial lines. This phenomenon differs from group indeterminacy because even if one assumes that racial groups could be deemed "worthy" of entitlements in a determinate and equitable manner, problems arise when there are many such groups equally entitled. Each race brings different and at times conflicting demands to the forum. The need to devote substantial funds to accommodate the many languages in a school's bilingual programs illustrates this difficulty. Where the resource pool is necessarily limited, the groups will naturally compete upon the basis of race, which determines the distribution of such scarce entitlements.

Consider the admission policy of the University of California at Berkeley. In the past two decades, the school has been the model of affirmative action, recruiting and attracting a higher percentage of minority students than most other top-tier academic institutions. But the results are not rosy. The five-year graduation rate for African-American and Hispanic students is significantly lower than for whites or Asian Americans, and the need to admit students who are African American and Hispanic has resulted in an artificial ceiling on admission of Asian-American students. Evidence of the resulting tension includes "nips go home" graffiti on bathroom walls, attacks on black students, and vandalism of the African Students Association offices. In 1988, Berkeley Vice Chancellor Roderic Park said ominously, "It's something everyone's going to face sooner or later. We're just here first."

Such antagonisms arise from the inevitable competition among ethnic groups for a larger share of entitlements. From a remedial perspective, denying such entitlements to Asian Americans in order to admit other minority students cannot be justified. Asian Americans have as valid a claim of racial victimization as other minorities. Just as Africans were brought to America as slaves, Chinese were dragged here as indentured laborers, working in inhumane conditions to build the railroads that became the lifeline of America. Official acts, such as the Chinese Exclusion Act of 1882 and the internment of Japanese Americans during

World War II, illustrate the institutional racism that defined the history of Asians in America. Thus, remedial affirmative action seems as warranted for Asians as it is for other minorities. But, as Berkeley found out, such preferential treatment for Asians would effectively shut out other minorities.

Remedial affirmative action's answer to this problem is imbedded in the recognition that remedies have an end. If the aim of affirmative action is to bring the previously shackled runner up to par with his competitor, then the entitlement should stop when both are at the same starting point. In a race with many runners, each should be pushed only to the point of equality with the white runner. In response to the complaint of an Asian applicant denied admission, an official at Berkeley can plausibly say, "Look, you have already been compensated; if at one point you were hindered, you have caught up. I must now concentrate my efforts on getting the other disadvantaged runners up to the competitive level."

Of course, one may contest such a statement's validity as an empirical matter. An insidious effect of the Asian model-minority myth is that it masks the variety of the Asian community in America. That Asians make up a disproportionate percentage of America's academic and economic elite is only partly true. Not all Asians score high on the SAT, or even perform marginally well in the educational system. For the Boston school system, the dropout rate increased from 14.4 percent in 1982 to 26.5 percent in 1985, which corresponded with a surge in Southeast Asian students. Likewise, media stories touting the economic success of Asians belie the fact that half of California's Indochinese immigrants rely on welfare for subsistence, and more than 35 percent of Vietnamese families in the United States live below the poverty line.

This empirical question of when all the runners have

been adequately remedied to a point of competitive equilibrium cannot be answered here. What is important to keep in mind is that remedial affirmative action promises a definable end to race-based entitlements. Even if disagreement exists as to when the remedial goal has been accomplished, the existence of a temporal limit serves to minimize objections to using race as the basis for distributing societal benefits.

Such a temporal limit, however, is missing in the merit-based model of affirmative action. Almost by definition, the race-as-merit theory promises perpetual race consciousness; race, as a component of merit, will always be a part of any evaluation process that purports to be meritocratic. Indeed, the perpetual nature of the merit-based conception is part of its appeal to its beneficiaries. It avoids the difficult problem of how much affirmative action is enough. The merit-based answer to the question, "When will race consciousness not be needed anymore?" is: "Never!" The new conception thus promises a permanent division of society (or at least the meritocracy) along racial lines. To use the analogy of the multicompetitor race, the participants will be running on different tracks—each person competing with others of his race to get the position allotted to them.

Proponents of the merit conception may argue that the tracks need not be separated perpetually. One can imagine a time when differences in racial perspectives will not exist, and the racial meritocracy will no longer be needed. Unfortunately, such a world will never materialize if one adopts the notion that race is merit. Accepting the merit-based conception of affirmative action institutionalizes division among the races and rejects the possibility of racial understanding and convergence. In a society where many races compete against each other, the permanence of racial entitlements transforms affirmative action into its antithesis, racial exclusion. Because it presumes that members of each race cannot understand the experience and perspective of another, the merit-based conception institutionalizes the interethnic tension that characterizes a multiracial society. The permanence of such segregation and tension yields little hope of racial coexistence, and makes ethnic conflict an inevitable part of life in our society.

It may be countered that such a gloomy vision of racial coexistence is an anachronistic view of interracial relations in America and that what actually results from a merit-based affirmative action regime is pluralism, because affirmative action facilitates the advancement of racial minorities, not their subjugation. This argument, however, denies the simple truth that in our multiracial society, what benefits one race hurts another. Lowering standards to admit more African Americans and Hispanics into Berkeley, for example, requires raising standards to exclude more whites and Asians. If temporary, such reallocation mechanisms engender resentment; when permanent, they foster division and conflict.

IV

At some level, any argument about race implicates one's racial vision of our society. An optimist may hope for a societal melting pot where the color of one's skin is as irrelevant as that of her eyes or hair. At the other extreme is Aurorae Khoo, a young writer who substitutes for the melting pot metaphor that of a Laundromat, where whites and colors fare best when separate. Neither describes my vision of multiracial coexistence in America. Color blindness denies the brilliant color palette of our society and suppresses my ethnic pride and cultural heritage. But separatism goes too far, allowing racial loyalty to threaten peaceful coexistence. I don't want to deny my race, but I also do not want to hate others because of theirs. It is one thing to recognize that one's race is an integral, constitutive component of his existence in a multiracial society; it is quite another to say that our polity should be structured permanently along racial lines.

Earlier in my life as a hyphenated American, I was a racial optimist. Faced with boundless opportunity promised by the American dream, I believed that the only barriers that divided society were based on education, values, and effort—not race. But from the start, race was an artificial criterion for access and opportunity everywhere I looked. When I entered seventh grade after two years in America, I was automatically placed in a remedial English class. When I complained to the teacher that I was misplaced, she reluctantly agreed to test my proficiency, by asking me to follow her commands. In front of the class, I skipped, jumped, smiled, lay down, and sat up at her direction. Tears welled in my eyes as the class wondered if such humiliation was the price of achievement. Even when such artificial racial classification works to my benefit, I recoil in the realization that the line between racial entitlement and racial exclusion is indeed a very fine one.

The original conception of affirmative action safeguarded against the danger of crossing over that line by holding out the hope that racial entitlements are temporary. The new race-as-merit rhetoric, however, permanently embraces racial divisions, balkanizing American society into warring ethnic fiefdoms. While the quick gains from such Hobbesian competition may appear attractive, the threat of permanent racial antagonism is too high a price to pay. Because race consciousness necessarily works both ways, to favor *and* to retard, the eradication of racism in our society starts with the recognition that persons, not groups, matter, and that individual merit, not racial background, determines worth.

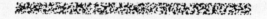

THE CHOICE

Theda Skocpol

Theda Skocpol is professor of sociology at Harvard University. Her books include *States and Social Revolution, Vision and Method in Historical Sociology,* and *Protecting Soldiers and Mothers: The Political Origins of Social Policy in the United States.* "The Choice" first appeared in *The American Prospect,* Summer 1992.

Future analysts of American politics will look back at the early 1990s as a watershed for progressives. Toward the end of the 1988–92 Bush administration, the historians will say, new openings to change the nation's political course appeared. The end of the Cold War coincided with a persistent economic recession, revealing the limits of Reaganomics. After a decade of receptivity to arguments for downgrading government, many Americans cautiously entertained thoughts of constructive public initiatives: promotion of economic growth and international competitiveness; improved education and job training; comprehensive reform of health care; and new support for families struggling to combine work and parenting.

These trends tended to favor progressives, even as conservatives found it more difficult than in 1988 to use symbols of racial divisiveness for electoral gain. The strong showing of former Nazi David Duke in the 1991 gubernatorial election in Louisiana chastened mainstream Republicans just enough to encourage President Bush to sign the Civil Rights Act of 1991.

What will the historians say happened next? I fear they will chronicle the inability of American progressives in the 1990s to overcome mutual recriminations. It is not hard to imagine how this scenario could unfold, because it is already under way. And there is historical precedent for it.

In the United States, the fragmentation of political power among different levels and branches of government and the weakness of political parties have always made it difficult for progressives to enact inclusive social policies and to assemble and sustain broad political coalitions. Consider the fate of reformers during the 1910s and 1920s who advocated health insurance, unemployment insurance, and protective labor laws limiting hours of work and setting a floor under wages. They were unable to build political coalitions uniting middle- and working-class groups and were drawn into an ever-narrowing politics of regulatory protection dictated by the vagaries of judicial decisions.

Around 1900, progressive reformers hoped that they could get state legislatures to enact, and courts to accept, limits on working hours for all wage-earners. But in 1905 the Supreme Court ruled out such limits for most male workers, while it endorsed them in 1908 for women workers alone. Much energy was expended trying to persuade state legislatures to enact laws that, in practice, subdivided wage-earners, encouraging the male-dominated trade unions to rely on "market wages," while women workers and their middle-class allies increasingly looked toward governmental support.

Then, in 1923, the Supreme Court partially reversed

itself and ruled minimum-wage laws for women unconstitutional. This left advocates of protection out on a limb, unable to deliver decent wages to low-income female workers. The 1923 reversal reinforced arguments by egalitarian feminists that surviving protective regulations served mainly to exclude and subordinate women wage-earners. But the supporters of protection dug in their heels. Their victories from 1908 to 1922 had been so hard-won that they could not bring themselves to switch strategies—even though the surviving laws were demonstrably doing harm as well as good for women, and even though those laws were hardly furthering the original goal of broad social provision for all wage-earners.

During the 1970s, reformers advocating initiatives for the disadvantaged were again enticed into heavy reliance on regulations backed up by temporarily favorable Supreme Court decisions. This happened not only among inheritors of the civil rights struggle, who ended up relying more heavily on affirmative action than many would have preferred, but also among proponents of abortion reform, who cut short state-by-state legislative struggles when the Supreme Court in 1974 suddenly legalized early abortions as a constitutional right.

The story in the civil rights area is not only more pertinent here, but also more poignant, because the aspirations of that movement as it moved North in the 1960s were potentially broad and inclusionary. The early civil rights movement achieved victories over southern segregation by appealing to the ideals and rights of all American citizens. As Margaret Weir shows in her book *Politics and Jobs*, prominent civil rights leaders such as A. Philip Randolph, Bayard Rustin, and Martin Luther King, Jr., realized that antipoverty programs focused primarily on blacks could backfire. Hoping to reorient policy toward full employment and public investments furthering the common economic interests of white as well as black workers, Rustin prepared a "Freedom Budget," which was presented at a 1966 White House conference and subsequently introduced into Congress.

By the late 1960s, however, the backlash against the War on Poverty plus the mounting costs of the Vietnam War made Congress unwilling to boost social spending. Furthermore, the decentralized structure of U.S. political parties and coalitions made it difficult to realize Rustin's longer-term hope that the Freedom Budget would "connect local demands to national economic issues," according to Weir. She writes, "Without nationally organized parties or government resources, there was no mechanism for bending local activities toward the national goals and broader alliances that Rustin envisioned."

Heavy reliance on regulatory and legal struggles to achieve employment equality for blacks did not come until the 1970s, after liberalism was in retreat politically. I do not argue that progressives were "mistaken" to urge presidents, federal agencies, and the courts to put teeth into the promises of the 1964 Civil Rights Act. Appeals to "search out" minority candidates for schooling and work were turned into actual (or more often de facto) requirements that minority students be admitted, hired, and promoted. Alternative ways to use governmental authority to promote racial equality were not readily available, and for many years the federal courts, led by the Supreme Court, gave crucial backing to strong affirmative action measures. So why shouldn't civil rights lawyers and other advocates of black opportunity have taken advantage of this opening?

Strong forms of affirmative action worked, bringing educated blacks into formerly all-white institutions. Admissions targets buttressed by generous scholarships have allowed minority students to enroll in colleges and universities where few had been seen before. Black professionals have been recruited (and to a lesser degree promoted) by corporations, law firms, universities, hospitals, and governmental agencies, which surely would not have done as much as quickly had they not feared government sanctions or lawsuits. While conservatives, including conservative blacks, plausibly point to negative side effects of these gains, we need to keep in mind that efficacious medicines often have side effects. If the medicine works for a while, it is worth it. After the moral high tide of the civil rights movement, America needed to accelerate black integration into the national elite. Strong affirmative action speeded such integration. Today many American institutions take it for granted that a substantial minority presence is natural and desirable.

Even as governmental oversight of affirmative action has weakened, many universities and corporations have kept their programs of preferential recruitment in place. The Supreme Court may soon reverse itself altogether on the legality of strong forms of affirmative action in public and private employment. But unless the Court actively encourages a steady flow of "reverse discrimination" suits by frustrated white, male job applicants—and unless an increasingly racist atmosphere in the larger society encourages a multitude of such suits—it is hard to see that most American institutions will abandon active recruitment of educated blacks and other minorities. Not only affirmative action as outreach but also affirmative action as tacit targets will persist.

Yet what will happen in the political arena? As federal agencies and courts led by a right-wing Supreme Court turn against affirmative action, will supporters of civil rights turn desperately to state legislatures and the Congress, pressuring again and again for laws, even constitutional amendments, to rewrite or "correct" adverse court rulings? If so, they will fall into one of the worst political traps.

Determined judges can never really be trumped by legislatures (as the fate of the 1991 Civil Rights Act will probably show once the Supreme Court starts interpreting it). Any legislative measure, especially on such a controversial topic as affirmative action, is bound to contain vague phrases and cross-cutting provisions that can be interpreted (and, over time, reinterpreted) by the courts. Judges can resort to constitutional language to overturn even clear legislative intent. The courts can have the last say—and they can take their time doing it, distorting the priorities of political activists for years, decades, even entire lifetimes.

Sometimes a protracted dance between legislatures and courts makes political sense. Arguably, it will be worth it after the Supreme Court eviscerates *Roe v. Wade* and throws the regulation of abortion back to the states (I do not believe that the Court will simply rule all abortions illegal). In my view, struggles over abortion rights are a distraction from the more important task of creating cross-class political coalitions to support public policies to aid children and working parents. But since majorities in most states support some version of adult women's "right to choose," advocacy of this right need not, in most places, directly undercut the formation of democratic political majorities also devoted to other progressive policies. Indeed, advocates of abortion rights can turn the antipathy of Americans toward "governmental intrusion" against those hard-line right-to-lifers who would have the government empowered to tell women that they have to carry all pregnancies to term.

With strong forms of affirmative action, it is another story. The idea that places should be, explicitly or implicitly, "set aside" for minority (or female) applicants has never been accepted by a majority of Americans, and certainly not by a majority of less privileged white Americans. And here the onus of governmental intrusion works against progressives. Conservative Republicans would like nothing better than for liberals during the 1990s to become committed to fighting repeated legislative battles to defend affirmative action quotas against court reversals. Such a situation would allow hard-line conservatives to feature themselves as the champions of "meritocratic competition" and "equality of opportunity" in America.

In response, many advocates of racial (and gender) equality would ever-more-loudly argue that competitive individualism is too limited a social framework and declare that equality of opportunity has never existed in practice. Such sophisticated arguments might well carry the day in academia, but in the political arena they would further the fortunes of conservatives. Divisions among liberals would deepen, because many can never accept the abandonment of equal individual opportunity as an ideal. Worse, progressives would put themselves at a permanent rhetorical disadvantage in majoritarian politics because most Americans remain wedded to longstanding values. As the 1990s proceeded, progressives would find themselves locked into protracted zero-sum struggles over the allocation of a shrinking pool of opportunities in American society. Meanwhile, conservatives would complete a right-wing sweep of national offices. Or else political stalemate would persist, and more Americans then ever would turn away from participation in national political life.

This is what I am afraid the historians of the future will say. But these scenarios do not have to unfold—provided that progressives can pull back from the defense (at all costs) of previously hard-won regulatory gains that are now judicially threatened. Progressives must look afresh at what they can do to further the basic goal of racial equality in

America, given the social and political realities of the 1990s.

Even if affirmative action were not threatened, it would make sense now to shift toward concerted attempts to expand socioeconomic opportunity in American society. Since the late 1960s, opportunities have been opened to blacks from middle-class families and to those who have been able to achieve good educational credentials. While efforts must continue to open doors for better-off blacks, further advances in black employment and education will surely depend on helping impoverished parents, including many single mothers, to rear their children in safe neighborhoods while supporting themselves through jobs that provide a decent income and access to health and child care.

Quite simply, most of the minority children who will provide the future pool of applicants for middle-class jobs are now being raised in impoverished circumstances. Unless such children and their parents become more secure, healthy, and well educated than they are now, the most rigorous forms of affirmative action will not pull them into universities and middle-class jobs.

To help less privileged minorities through government programs, the first step is to establish a baseline of broad benefits and services that span classes and races (and that can be supplemented by targeted services for the elderly, children, and other vulnerable people). In an earlier article ("Sustainable Social Policy: Fighting Poverty Without Poverty Programs," *The American Prospect,* Summer 1990) I argued on behalf of universal social policies. Some critics have suggested that *universal* in America always connotes policies focused on the needs of white males who are employed full-time in the private economy. Although many social programs in the past may indeed have excluded blacks and marginalized women, the new universal policies I advocate would especially address the needs of minority families headed by single mothers. I have argued for a Family Security Program that would encompass four policies: assured child support for all single custodial parents; universal health coverage; paid maternity leaves and benefits to help all working parents afford child care; and employment training and assistance in obtaining employment at a living wage.

If such universal programs were in place, minorities would be the biggest winners, though not the only ones. African-American men and women would find it easier to upgrade skills and obtain jobs. Single mothers, whether or not they chose to marry, would find it much easier to combine child care with part-time work. Low-income Americans, including blacks, could live decently without the hassle and indignity of welfare. They would be more fully included in American society through work and entitlement to the same social benefits as everyone else.

A majority of Americans will never support legislation to create and sustain such a Family Security Program if it is restricted to the poor alone. But given economic realities and family arrangements in the 1990s, there are many potential white and middle-class beneficiaries—and hence just as many potential political supporters—for every part of the Family Security Program I have outlined. Today millions of Americans need secure health coverage, and large numbers of divorced middle-class women need assured child support and job training. Dual-parent working- and middle-class families would benefit from maternity leaves and from tax credits for child care (even if the credits were structured to benefit primarily lower-income families). And as the U.S. economy undergoes fundamental restructuring to adjust to international competition and the end of the Cold War, more American workers at all occupational levels stand to benefit from effective job training and employment assistance.

Advocated by articulate and persistent political leaders, universal, race-neutral social programs have the potential both to promote equality and to revitalize democratic cross-racial political coalitions in the 1990s. These policies will also make the national economy more flexible and efficient. Progressives will be foolish indeed not to see the opening that universal policies present. We should turn away from an emphasis on zero-sum regulatory approaches to racial equality, refusing to tilt at the windmills of a Supreme Court likely to remain in doctrinaire conservative hands for decades. Instead, let those of us who care about racial equality in America work for a progressive majority politics, based on a revitalized public sector that includes everyone in an efficient economy and a full-opportunity society.

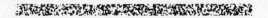

AFFIRMATIVE ACTION AND IMMIGRATION

Mark Krikorian

Mark Krikorian was press secretary for the Federation of American Immigration Reform (FAIR). He is currently the editor of a daily newspaper in Virginia. An earlier version of "Affirmative Action and Immigration" first appeared in *The Christian Science Monitor,* September 13, 1989.

Although affirmative action and immigration have been widely discussed in Congress and the media, they have always been considered separately, as though they had no effect on one another. Each year, however, our country admits hundreds of thousands of immigrants eligible for affirmative action benefits. A brief look at the interplay of affirmative action and large-scale immigration, as they exist in the United States today, shows that they are incompatible and their combination explosive.

More than twenty years ago the executive branch and the courts began mandating preferential treatment for certain ethnic groups—blacks, Hispanics, Asians, and American Indians. These special privileges in employment, government contracts, lending, and education were intended to compensate for historical discrimination: as President Lyndon Johnson said in 1965, "You do not take a person who, for years, has been hobbled by chains and liberate him, bring him up to the starting line of a race and then say, 'You are free to compete with all others' and still justly believe that you have been completely fair."

Apparently, it was assumed that the beneficiaries of affirmative action would all be Americans, since there was relatively little immigration, and little prospect of immigration, of additional blacks, Hispanics, or Asians from overseas.

Over the past twenty-five years, however, there has been a huge change in the sources of immigration to the United States. While in 1965, the U.S. admitted about 115,000 persons from what we now call the Third World, representing just under half of the total number of immigrants, by 1991 the number of such immigrants, including legalized illegal aliens, had increased more than 14 times, to 1.68 million, making up more than 90 percent of all immigrants. Over the past twenty years, more than 13 million people from Asia and the Pacific Islands, Latin America, and Africa have become permanent residents of the United States.

These newcomers have come to America to make a better life for themselves and their families, to enjoy the fruits of their labor, or to escape tyranny—all without the slightest notion that they deserved special privileges. And yet, they are eligible for affirmative action benefits immediately upon their arrival, despite the fact that they have no conceivable claim upon our nation's conscience. It is hardly nativist or xenophobic to observe that such a situation is unjust—as most immigrants themselves would agree.

The injustice of granting special treatment to foreign nationals at the expense of American citizens has created bizarre distortions and conflicts in our society. For example, our current system would allow a wealthy, well-educated Peruvian doctor to immigrate to the U.S. and claim affirmative action benefits at the expense of the son of a coal miner from Appalachia, based merely on their respective ethnic origins.

Many white Americans are prepared to endure certain difficulties for the betterment of their fellow citizens who belong to ethnic minorities. Despite a certain unavoidable amount of ignorance and prejudice, our nation's remarkable history testifies to an openness to people of diverse origins unparalleled in history. But is it not too much to expect Americans to tolerate reverse discrimination for the benefit of *foreign* citizens voluntarily come to America in search of liberty and opportunity?

White Americans are certainly not the only ones hurt by affirmative action for immigrants. Black Americans, who were billed as the primary beneficiaries of affirmative action, have also lost out to better-educated and wealthier immigrants claiming the same privileges. The hundreds of thousands of Cuban refugees who fled to Miami after the rise of Castro, for instance, were largely middle class and so were better able to take advantage of newly enacted affirmative action benefits than black Americans. Sociologist Marvin Dunn, in *Anatomy of a Riot,* has shown that resentment caused by special treatment afforded Cubans was at least partly responsible for the Liberty City riots of 1980. And as far as black Americans are concerned, the continuing influx of Nicaraguans and other Latin Americans in South Florida is merely more of the same.

Nor do black Americans lose out merely to Hispanic and Asian immigrants. Our country is now experiencing a substantial influx of black immigrants—West Indians from Haiti, Jamaica, and other islands, and Africans from Ethiopia, Nigeria, Ghana, and elsewhere. From 1981 to 1991, the U.S. admitted over 700,000 black immigrants, more than any other period in our history, more even than during the entire slave trade. Furthermore, the trend is upward—over the past several years, black immigration has increased an average of more than 15 percent per year.

Of course, it has long been true that West Indian immigrants and their offspring have held leadership positions among black Americans. Marcus Garvey, Shirley Chisolm, Roy Innes, Malcolm X, Stokely Carmichael, and General Colin Powell are just a few of the notable blacks of West Indian birth or heritage.

It is increasingly evident, however, that black immigrants, at least partly aided by affirmative action, are now actually displacing black Americans less able to compete. A study several years ago, for instance, showed that while the overall number of black students in Miami-area colleges and universities stayed about the same from 1978 to 1987, the percentage of black *Americans* fell drastically. At Miami-Dade Community College, the area's largest institution of higher education, American-born students fell from 85 percent to 55 percent of total black enrollment in just ten years. Similar displacement of black Americans may very well be occurring in Boston, New York, Washington, and other cities with substantial numbers of black immigrants.

Our country has a long and venerable tradition of welcoming immigrants. But this tradition surely does not require us to *subsidize* immigrants at the expense of American citizens. In the United States today, large-scale immigration and affirmative action have shown themselves to be incompatible, and simple decency suggests something be done. If we continue to accept large numbers of Asian, Latin American, and African immigrants, it is unjust to maintain affirmative action as it is. If we continue to use race-based affirmative action as a means to right historical wrongs, it is immoral to allow large-scale immigration of covered ethnic groups. We must choose one way or the other.

"SELF-HELP" JUST WON'T DO IT ALL

Benjamin L. Hooks

Benjamin L. Hooks was formerly the executive director of the National Association for the Advancement of Colored People (NAACP). "Self-Help Just Won't Do It All" first appeared in the *Los Angeles Times*, July 10, 1990.

Weary of colonial rule, the angry activists stood on the banks of Boston Harbor on a cold December evening, lugged about 340 crates to the river's edge, and pitched more than $10,000 worth of tea into the brisk, bustling waters.

The action of American patriots at the Boston Tea Party—which helped launch the American Revolution—was, incredibly, a pitch for affirmative action.

America's eighteenth-century revolutionaries were affirming their right to self-determination and equal opportunity. Surely, we have not forgotten their rallying call, "No taxation without representation." Or Patrick Henry's impassioned, noble cry, "Give me liberty or give me death."

This is why we bristle at the current "controversy" over the value and benefits of modern-day affirmative action.

Affirmative-action critics suggest that such policies

have not benefited poor blacks, have impeded the development of coalitions for social programs, and have inhibited black Americans through a deep sense of inferiority.

These notions would be comical if they weren't so dangerous.

The irony is that these well-trained—if misguided—academicians have the opportunity to espouse such nonsense is itself due to affirmative action.

Would they have been trained at some of the nation's leading colleges without it? Would they be professors at predominantly white universities? Would they not feel the racist sting of Jim Crow's piercing whip? Would they be published in some of America's most influential periodicals?

They fail to realize that affirmative action is simply any action taken to ensure, or affirm, equal opportunity for oppressed or previously disadvantaged groups.

What's wrong with that? If a society discriminates against a people for centuries—enslaves them, lynches them, oppresses them, denies them access to jobs, homes, a good education, the political process, etc.—the just way to offer remedy is to give that people an equal opportunity.

The affirmative-action debate often gets mired in the issue of numerical goals and timetables, which are often disparagingly called quotas by critics and opponents.

The NAACP has never promoted the concept of so-called quotas. In fact, goals and timetables would never have been necessary if corporate and municipal leaders had been willing to follow the letter and spirit of the law.

Goals and timetables came about because of the failure of parties to be sincere in their efforts to provide equal opportunity. They were built in by judges who tired of the stances of interposition and nullification. The "we can't find any" argument was most often an attempt by corporate and municipal leaders to skirt the law. So judges had to construct goals and timetables to keep parties from making a mockery of the federal court. Critics who negate or ignore white America's duty to help solve black America's problems misrepresent the issue, mislead the public, and subvert the struggle.

While we recognize that heightened "self-help" efforts among blacks will lessen our plight—and we at the NAACP promote such efforts—we believe what the Kerner Commission said more than twenty years ago still rings true:

"What white Americans have never fully understood—but what the Negro can never forget—is that white society is deeply implicated in the ghetto. White institutions created it, white institutions maintain it, and white society condones it."

In the near-exclusive focus on what blacks should do, critics largely overlook the responsibility of government, big business, and the courts in what is purported to be a fair and democratic society.

When blacks have done all they can to save themselves, white society must still do the right thing. If racism, discrimination, and unequal opportunity pervade, lone efforts by blacks will remain virtually ineffective.

Certainly, critics who suggest that black Americans need to develop their individual skills and must not eternally regard themselves as victims are not totally wrong. Neither are they wrong when they urge young blacks to study, be disciplined and conscientious, and to reject the notion that achievement somehow diminishes blackness.

But they are totally wrong when they suggest, implicitly or otherwise, that acknowledged black leaders are not pushing these concepts as well. We are. So, at best, these critics are doing no more than parroting our views.

I make hundreds of speeches a year in which I preach the gospel of hard work, discipline, and achievement. Other leaders do the same. To suggest otherwise is a gross distortion and disservice.

While self-responsibility and self-determination must play heightened roles in our communities, we believe government cannot shirk its role.

I hasten to add that I am curious as to how this issue evolved as a controversy in the first place. Goals and timetables are as American as apple pie.

You must pay your taxes by April 15. You must not drive more than the posted speed limit. You must register to vote or apply for a passport by certain dates. Car manufacturers must ensure their cars meet certain emissions standards by certain times.

America operates by goals and timetables—and we all acknowledge and accept that. It is only when it comes to human resources that we bristle at this concept.

Naturally, we at the NAACP promote the concept of self-help. And the fact is that blacks have committed to self-help since the slave ships first docked on America's shores.

In 1990 America, we see the benefits of that self-help concept and affirmative action efforts. We have black mayors, elected officials, police officers, firefighters, journalists, judges, doctors, lawyers, captains of industry, and thousands of other professionals.

More importantly, we have office clerks, secretaries, laborers, court employees, and literally millions of everyday working people whose jobs are indirectly and directly linked to affirmative action and self-help.

These would have been the people mired inextricably in poverty and despair were it not for coalition-building and affirmative action.

The critics who benefited from but oppose affirmative action obscure the legacy of exclusion and discrimination that prompted such remedial efforts. They should be ashamed.

As the U.S. Commission on Civil Rights once noted, just as medical treatment is based on the diagnosis of an illness, affirmative action stems from diagnosis of a social sickness.

The remedy cannot be divorced from the illness. Critics write much about some "corrosive effect" of affirmative action but very little about the racism, oppression, and discrimination that necessitates it—and which is much more corrosive and destructive.

We shall at the NAACP always promote self-help, but we will never waver in our push to insist that government play its role and do its part. For how long? For as long as necessary.

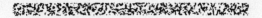

AFFIRMATIVE ACTION'S OUTER LIMITS

Jim Sleeper

Jim Sleeper is a columnist for the New York *Daily News* and author of *The Closest of Strangers: Liberalism and the Politics of Race in New York*. "Affirmative Action's Outer Limits" was written for *Debating Affirmative Action*.

Early in 1989, the music world was rocked by a controversy at the outer limits of affirmative action—the sort of collective learning experience, I remember hoping as I followed it in the press, that would firm up the national consensus about what racial preferences should and should not entail. Two powerful black Michigan state legislators, professing impatience with the fact that the Detroit Symphony had only one black member in a city 60 percent black, demanded that the orchestra hire Richard Robinson, a black bass player, or forfeit its state funding.

The logistical problem confronting this demand was that, some years earlier, the orchestra, in order to remove even the suspicion that its inevitably subjective judgments about musicians' interpretive flair were tainted by racism, had begun placing all candidates behind opaque screens at auditions. In the true spirit of affirmative action, quali-

fied black players of classical music were energetically
recruited for auditions, and, once in the pool, were assured
they'd be judged strictly on their musical merits. The blind
auditions, which became the standard practice at all American orchestras in the early 1970s, were acclaimed by black
musicians as a victory over discrimination.

But, as James Blanton explained in a comprehensive
account in *Commentary,* competition for jobs with symphony orchestras is stiff. Credible candidates usually begin
their classical-music training in childhood, and, for reasons
ranging from economic to cultural, only a minuscule number of blacks are drawn to classical music early enough to
become credible candidates. Of the five thousand classical
musicians studying in the country's top twenty-five con-
servatories in 1989, fewer than one hundred were blacks.
"If you apply the standard bell curve to their probable
talent, that means that twenty of them are qualified to play
in a major American orchestra," said Daniel Windham,
who runs the New York Philharmonic's Musical Assistance
Fund, which supports minority classical musicians. The
DSO was lucky to have one black among thirty applicants
at any audition.

Since candidates of all colors are often turned down
several times before being accepted, there was something
hollow, if not cynical, about one Michigan lawmaker's
query: "Are you telling me we can't find qualified black
musicians . . . in this nation of two hundred million
people?" Joseph Striplin, the DSO's only black member,
responded that the audition issue "is an area in which
people in the black community are wrong. . . . I know that
there isn't discrimination in auditions."

Nevertheless—and here one could observe the meta-
morphosis of affirmative action into a push for proportional
racial representation that ruins both standards and morale—the legislators demanded that the screen come down.

The DSO acceded—on a "one-time-only" basis, it said—and hired Robinson. Its state appropriation was released the next day.

No one understood the tragedy of what had happened better than Robinson himself, a well-qualified musician who had in fact performed as a substitute with the DSO. "I would have rather auditioned like everybody else," he told *The New York Times*. "Somehow this devalues the audition and worth of every other player." Yet at least one of the powerful Michigan legislators was not satisfied, and pressure has continued on the DSO to relax the blind-audition procedure for minority candidates. Affirmative action has been turned on its head: Instead of a way to help blacks participate in the best of what society has to offer, it risks becoming, in this area, a way of leveling that "best" for the sake of blacks who are no longer expected to excel. "Music is music," the legislator said. "Do-re-me-fa-so-la-ti-do. I learned that in school."

The DSO controversy did not spark the national self-examination some of us hoped it would. (*The New York Times* reported the dispute, but, remarkably, did not editorialize about it.) Something more like a serious debate was prompted a year later, when Dinesh D'Souza published equally embarrassing revelations, in his *Illiberal Education,* of parallel developments in affirmative action in college admissions. There, he found, Robinson's worst fears of stigma have been realized.

The syndrome is all too painfully familiar: College X, pressured to achieve "diversity," whether by politicians, accrediting agencies, or its own campus zealots, accepts disproportionate numbers of blacks who don't meet its usual standards. As those students do poorly, even their qualified black classmates experience white stereotyping and resentment, and, being only human, they become defensive and withdrawn. Into that chasm of mistrust flies the occasional antiblack (and, in response, anti-Semitic or antiwhite) epithet, "proving" the existence of a virulent racism which only more "diversity," discipline, and consciousness-raising can cure. Ironically, the iron logic of "diversity" and "affirmative action" suppresses other views of what may have gone wrong. Dissent—and, indeed, standards themselves—are denounced as "racist." The pursuit of diversity becomes more divisive than whatever racism the students may have brought with them to college.

D'Souza's larger conservative political agenda notwithstanding, the incontrovertible truths in his campus reportage persuaded such academics as Eugene Genovese, writing in *The New Republic*, and C. Vann Woodward, writing in the *New York Review of Books*, to take his side. If there can be said to have been a full-dress debate about the outer limits of affirmative action, here it was. Finally, it seemed, sensible liberals, black as well as white, were ready to draw some long-overdue distinctions.

Yet that is not what has happened. The debate has had little effect on college accreditors and administrators, who, for reasons we ought to explore, continue to follow the iron logic of racial representation. I saw this clearly when I covered the Middle States Association of Schools and Colleges' stunning deferral of Bernard M. Baruch College's accreditation in 1990 on the grounds that the school wasn't doing enough to retain minority students and hire and promote minority faculty and administrators. The action was startling because Baruch, a branch of the City University of New York, has one of the most gloriously diverse student bodies in the country, as well as one of the nation's best business schools. Yet disproportionate numbers of the black and Hispanic students accepted under CUNY's "open enrollment" system do drop out, and the faculty, while 18 percent minority—more diverse than Harvard's or Yale's—has more Asians than blacks or Hispanics.

Baruch's president argued strenuously that if the college committed any more of its terribly strained resources to additional student advisement and retention, it would be turning itself into a remediation center, not a college. Noting, too, that only a handful of blacks nationwide get Ph.D.'s in business disciplines each year, he argued that Baruch could "diversify" its faculty only by fudging standards, undermining the reputation of a business school that is now a launching pad for successful minority students because it attracts the nation's top corporate recruiters.

To be sure, improvements were needed in Baruch's underfunded, bureaucratic student-retention and faculty-recruitment efforts. But Middle States, driven by its missionary director, Howard Simmons, made demands reminiscent of the Michigan legislators'. This time, the stick was accreditation, upon which federal student aid is conditioned. And this time, too, Baruch caved: Money was quickly found to elevate a black dean to a vice-presidency; affirmative action plans were expanded; the college president resigned; a black acting-president was chosen to replace him; and Baruch's accreditation was renewed.

This was too much for Secretary of Education Lamar Alexander, who challenged Middle States' own "accreditation" as an arbiter of federal aid. As the federal review of the agency dragged on, it revised its diversity guidelines to reflect the reality that there is only so much a college can do to unclog a "pipeline" that delivers too few qualified minorities to its gates.

The root cause of the clogging isn't diversity itself, as D'Souza insists, but the bad public schools, poverty, and family breakdown that set minority youths back. D'Souza is right to argue, though, that a university that thinks it can solve such social problems through its admissions and hiring offices, rather than its research, doesn't understand its mission. The same is true of a great symphony orchestra, a great newspaper, or any other corporate entity whose first priority must always be the excellence of its "product."

That this lesson remains unlearned was evident in 1993, when CUNY's Board of Trustees announced the selection of Yolanda Moses as the next president of City College. In a number of essays written in the three years before her appointment, Moses, the provost of an obscure California State University campus at Dominguez Hills, had outlined clearly the principles she would use to restructure a university to promote diversity. Too few minority faculty are hired and promoted, she wrote, because "service on committees, student advising, and university community activities (especially those that promote cultural diversity)" are not "ranked as highly as research. . . . That will have to change if cultural pluralism is to flourish." Changing the reward structure in this way is appropriate, she added, because American universities "are products of Western society in which masculine values like an orientation toward achievement and objectivity are valued over cooperation, connectedness, and subjectivity."

This seems hopelessly inadequate for a City College where Professor Leonard Jeffries exploits the values of "connectedness and subjectivity" to advance a mystical and divisive black separatism. But Moses's ideas seem equally wrong for the City College whose engineering and science programs draw top students of color from all over the world—people who, like CCNY graduates Felix Frankfurter and Colin Powell before them, want their minority status to count for less, not more, in their academic and public lives. Yet when I broke the story of Moses's impending appointment and made such arguments in my column in the New York *Daily News,* much of New York's liberal establishment directed its outrage not at Moses or CUNY, but at critics such as Herman Badillo, a politician who, as an orphan from Puerto Rico, had worked his way through City College and graduated, cum laude, in 1951.

When Badillo, a CUNY trustee, urged his colleagues to put Moses's appointment on hold until they had studied her writings, CUNY Chancellor Ann Reynolds went into overdrive. She got the trustees to outvote Badillo by putting her own credibility on the line, promising that Moses would pursue diversity without compromising standards in any way. One intrepid columnist who backed Reynolds was Sheryl McCarthy, a black woman whose identification with Moses was instant and intense. "Both Badillo and the *Daily News* have tried to equate the hiring of Moses to the college's retention of Jeffries," she wrote. (In fact, we'd argued that a Jeffries can't exist without enablers, often well intentioned.)

Reynolds sent Moses to *The New York Times* editorial board, which, instead of asking any of the hard questions CUNY should have posed about Moses's vision of university restructuring, moved swiftly to her defense. The criticisms of Moses, an editorial declared, were "wildly overstated, an irresponsible invitation to bigotry. They will make a tough job even tougher."

The suggestion that criticisms of a woman of color encourage, if they do not in fact reflect, bigotry, has become a standard trope in diversity debates, effective in shutting off questions about Moses's beliefs which the editorial in fact declined to pursue. It is worth noting that *The Times* itself has embarked on an ambitious diversity initiative; an *Esquire* profile of the paper by Robert Sam Anson, appearing three months before the Moses controversy, tiptoed up to the possibility that some overreaching in that area—in staffing and the tenor of reportage—had contributed to a sense of drift and malaise among reporters of all colors.

American institutions must diversify as a practical and

moral imperative, but everything is in the details. Culture is messy; it's not easy to disentangle what's stodgy and parochial in a tradition from the shared understandings and loyalties that nurture character, morale, and, yes, "excellence." But, as the examples I have cited suggest, such subtleties are lost on the cutting edge of the affirmative action movement, which brooks no dissent.

Why? I think the answer has something to do with the morphology of the liberal mind and with the needs of liberal elites more than the needs of society. Like the parlor left's fellow-traveling in the 1930s, the diversity movement as it has emerged in universities, newspapers, and other important institutions is expiatory because it is, unconsciously, elitist: redemption is achieved through a fictive yet passionate embrace of the oppressed—the "proletariat" then, "people of color" now—that has more to do with the satisfaction of its champions than of its intended beneficiaries. The latter, like Richard Robinson, are summarily boxed and labeled by skin color or surname, often to their own chagrin.

It is because this sort of liberal missionary zeal is irrational, at least at its outer limits, that it cannot tolerate dissent: just as fellow-travelers cast critics of communism as tools of fascism, promoters of diversity cast critics of even its worst excesses as the handmaidens of bigots. Ironically, the implication that Yolanda Moses was attacked because of her race and sex, not her ideas, reflected a willful denial of a far deeper truth: Her champions selected and defended her for precisely that reason. Certainly, no white need have applied for CCNY's presidency.

As in the 1930s, too, a leveling impulse increasingly drives the affirmative action movement. In a 1990 *New York Times* essay, Julian Bond argued, with tart irony, that whites should love "affirmative action" because of all the lazy and incompetent whites it had sheltered for centuries.

While true as far as it goes, this argument is too often used as an excuse to relax standards, as when the Michigan legislator observed, "Music is music."

If the charge of bigotry is unfair to affirmative action's responsible critics, the argument for leveling is just plain sad. Throughout American history, insurgent groups have broken down doors by proving that they're better, not that everyone else is as bad. They've deluged the gatekeepers with talent; if rebuffed, they've started their own colleges, law firms, and banks, making brilliant end runs around a stodgy establishment in their drive to enrich America.

This, of course, is precisely what blacks have done, from W.E.B. Du Bois and the founders of black colleges through historian John Hope Franklin, Harvard Law Professor Randall Kennedy (who edits the iconoclastic black magazine *Reconstruction*), and, on a different plane, the partners of the black corporate law firm of Arnelle & Hastie, profiled early in 1993 by Nicholas Von Hoffman in *The New Yorker*. That is also what City College has stood for.

It is against that heroic legacy that one reads, with overwhelming sadness, Sheryl McCarthy's "defense" of Moses: "Why is it that the only time anybody talks about standards is when women or people of color are trying to advance or be heard? Mediocrity is a common characteristic of white male academics. . . . Let's hire women and people of color who are as ordinary as the white males who already dominate academia, and there will be no trouble in keeping up current standards. No trouble at all."